Testament of
Lost Youth

Testament of Lost Youth

The Early Life and Loves of Vera Brittain

Kathryn Ecclestone

First published in Great Britain in 2024 by
Pen & Sword History
An imprint of Pen & Sword Books Limited
Yorkshire – Philadelphia

Copyright © Kathryn Ecclestone 2024

ISBN 978 1 39903 665 8

The right of Kathryn Ecclestone to be identified as
Author of this Work has been asserted by her in accordance
with the Copyright, Designs and Patents Act 1988.

A CIP catalogue record for this book is
available from the British Library

All rights reserved. No part of this book may be reproduced or
transmitted in any form or by any means, electronic or mechanical
including photocopying, recording or by any information storage and
retrieval system, without permission from the Publisher in writing.

Typeset by Mac Style
Printed in the UK by CPI Group (UK) Ltd, Croydon, CR0 4YY.

Pen & Sword Books Limited incorporates the imprints of After the Battle, Atlas, Archaeology, Aviation, Discovery, Family History, Fiction, History, Maritime, Military, Military Classics, Politics, Select, Transport, True Crime, Air World, Frontline Publishing, Leo Cooper, Remember When, Seaforth Publishing, The Praetorian Press, Wharncliffe Local History, Wharncliffe Transport, Wharncliffe True Crime and White Owl.

For a complete list of Pen & Sword titles please contact

PEN & SWORD BOOKS LIMITED
47 Church Street, Barnsley, South Yorkshire, S70 2AS, England
E-mail: enquiries@pen-and-sword.co.uk
Website: www.pen-and-sword.co.uk
or
PEN AND SWORD BOOKS
1950 Lawrence Rd, Havertown, PA 19083, USA
E-mail: uspen-and-sword@casematepublishers.com
Website: www.penandswordbooks.com

In memory of my lovely, much missed sister Julie.
1960–2019

Contents

Acknowledgements		ix
Abbreviations		x
Introduction		xii
Chapter 1	'We Went to Buxton in the Motor'	1
Chapter 2	'A Mentally Voracious Young Woman'	18
Chapter 3	'That Other Side of Myself, The Frivolity I Hold So Dear'	32
Chapter 4	'Oxford! What It Doesn't Call Up To Mind!'	50
Chapter 5	'This House of Many Comforts'	65
Chapter 6	'A Good Strong Splendid Man, Full of Force & Enthusiasm … There Must *Be* Such!'	85
Chapter 7	'More Influence Upon Me for Good and Strength than Anyone'	103
Chapter 8	'A Terrible Moment When the Great Movements of the World Enter Like an Earthquake'	122
Chapter 9	'A Nature Restless With Search And Strife'	135
Chapter 10	'Oxford I Trust Will Lead to Something, But Buxton Never Will'	153
Chapter 11	'The Day Will Come When We Shall Live Our Roseate Poem Through as We Have Dreamt It'	169
Chapter 12	'I Found a Lot of Old Dance Programmes Which I Tied Up And Put Away'	182

Chapter 13	'I Say Goodbye to All I Care For'	201
Chapter 14	'A Provincial of the Provincials, In Heart Though Not In Mind'	209
Chapter 15	'Where the Tawny Crested Plover Cries'	225

Vera Brittain's Life – A Brief Chronology   237
Notes   241
Selected Bibliography   251
Index   255

Acknowledgements

I am indebted to archivists, especially Renu Barrett at McMaster University Ontario, and Kate O'Donnell at Somerville College, for their extensive knowledge about, and interest in, Vera's life and work, and their help in providing access to sources. I am grateful to Amy Jordan, commissioning editor at Pen & Sword, for her enthusiasm and support.

Mark Bostridge, co-author of the superb authorised 1995 biography of Vera Brittain, and literary executor for the Vera Brittain Estate, has provided advice, unpublished material and photographs and answered many small and large questions. Thanks also to Sophie Leighton, Roland Leighton's great-niece for permission to use two poems and extracts from his letters.

I am grateful to those who have kindly commented on draft chapters, provided information and listened to my obsessive ruminations about Buxton's most significant resident: my Buxton Civic Association colleagues Alan Roberts, Debbie Fox, Julian Cohen, Alyson and Steve Phillips; my Melrose neighbours Chrissie Vanyo and Rachel Child; Diane Davies, Sandra Orme, and Alex Lakowski. Thanks also to David Roberts, John Kingsland, Alan Atkinson and Christine Mullen, Gwen Hobson and Pam Roberts (Manchester High School for Girls), Hannah Brown (Withington High School for Girls), Rachel Roberts (Cheltenham Ladies' College), and Vicky Dawson, Books Director for the Buxton International Festival.

Special thanks to my dear friends Sally and Simon Cocksedge, Janet and John Phillips, Lynne Rybacki and Karen Willis, my goddaughter Ella Rybacki, my nephew Luie Glover, for their feedback, and especially to Christine Skelton for her inexhaustible patience and wise advice.

But this book would never have been finished without John Leigh's remarkable, seemingly infinite interest in the lives of Vera, Edward, Roland, and Winifred, his many, many helpful suggestions and unceasing encouragement.

Abbreviations

Vera Brittain **VB**
Edith Brittain **EB**
Arthur Brittain **AB**
Edward Brittain **EdB**
Roland Leighton **RL**
Winifred Holtby **WH**
Gordon Catlin **GC**
Paul Berry **PB**
Clare Leighton **CL**

Vera Brittain Archive, William Ready Library, McMaster University, Hamilton, Ontario. **McM**.
Derbyshire Libraries photographs, Picture the Past, **PTP**
National Portrait Gallery, **NPG**
Paul Berry Collection, Somerville College, Oxford. **PBC**.
Shirley Williams Collection, Somerville College, Oxford. **SWC**.
Somerville College, **SC**.
Devonshire Estate Archive, Chatsworth House. **DE**.
Mike Langham Archive, Derbyshire Record Office. **MLA**.
Buxton Advertiser. **BA**.
Imperial War Museum, **IWM**.

Permissions

Quotations from Vera Brittain's published and unpublished works are included by permission of Mark Bostridge and T.J. Brittain-Catlin, Literary Executors for the Estate of Vera Brittain 1970. Photographs are included by permission from the Principal and Fellows of Somerville College (SC), the William Ready Library at McMaster University (McM, Hamilton, Ontario, Mark Bostridge and Picture the Past (PtP). Source of permission noted under each image.

Other

Anecdotes at beginning of chapters are based on information from VB's diary and other sources. Diary quotes in text use Vera's date format and writing style; references to diary in endnotes use day/month/year. Extracts of correspondence between VB and RL are quoted from Bishop and Bostridge 1998/Berry and Bostridge 1995. Other letters are quoted from original sources. Bibliographic references to place of book publishers are London unless otherwise stated.

Introduction

On 26 July 1935, the morning bus from Leek to Buxton ground its way slowly up the steep hill onto Blackshaw Moor and past the brooding red boulders of Ramshaw Rocks. Vera Brittain gazed out of the window. Sitting beside her was her husband, the political scientist Gordon Catlin: a month earlier, they had celebrated their tenth wedding anniversary. On Vera's lap was a notebook with ideas for her third autobiographical novel, *Honourable Estate*, a feminist, anti-war, inter-generational saga. As part of Vera's research for it, the couple had spent a few days delving into the history of her father Arthur Brittain's Staffordshire family, visiting her birthplace in Newcastle-under-Lyme and the ruins of the home where Arthur grew up and staying at Ash Hall, the imposing mock-Elizabethan mansion built by her father's great-great-grandfather which became a popular golf hotel in 1924.[1] Vera and Gordon's two children, 4-year-old Shirley and 7-year-old John, were at home in London and the following day was Shirley's 5th birthday, making this detour to Buxton the most fleeting of visits.

The bleak moors between the Leek and Congleton/Macclesfield roads reminded Vera of her father's daily round trip of 30 miles between Buxton and Brittains' paper mill at Cheddleton near Leek. In the early 1900s, Arthur Brittain had been one of a small but fast-growing number of wealthy businessmen to own a motorcar, and unusual in preferring to drive himself rather than have a chauffeur. Vera mused that his journey, in all weathers, on what were then rough crushed limestone roads, must have been exhausting. Dangerous too, especially in Buxton's harsh winters, although the steep winding roads surrounding the

Vera Brittain, 1936. (*NPG*)

town could be hazardous at any time; she remembered a driving lesson with Arthur in September 1915 when she had crashed his beloved Wolseley into a wall on the road to Leek, smashing the windscreen into hundreds of pieces. It was surprising they were not badly injured. With a pang of acute nostalgia, Vera recalled a final bicycle ride across those moors with her adored brother Edward in August 1915, and their 'splendid tea in an isolated cottage'.

Alighting at Buxton marketplace, Vera and Gordon walked past the imposing town hall, pausing briefly while she pointed out the meeting room above the grand entrance door where, in 1913, she and her mother

Edward Brittain aged 20, Buxton, July 1915. (*McM*)

Edith attended social history lectures run by the University of Oxford as part of its nationwide 'extension' programme. This experience had spurred Vera to apply to study English at Somerville College, her passport out of a dreary provincial future. The door brought back another memory, of being in a crowd surrounding the mobilisation notice pinned to it on 4 August 1914. Its large black letters ordered all army recruits to 'take up the colours & all Territorials to go to their headquarters'. Today, twenty-one years later, she was about to see the name of her dead brother on the war memorial.

As the couple walked down The Slopes to the obelisk, Vera steeled herself before looking for Edward's name amongst those of local boys and men killed in the First World War; of over 880,000 men killed, 1600 enlisted from Buxton. 368 are listed on the memorial.[2] She was shocked to see the inscription had omitted his Military Cross, awarded for conspicuous gallantry and leadership on the first day of the Battle of the Somme in July 1916. In the face of horrendous casualties pouring back into the trenches from the first wave of attack, Edward had induced his terrified platoon to go over the top. Seriously wounded and in great pain, he crawled back through dead bodies to secure help for men left injured in no man's land, before being evacuated to hospital in London. Two years later he was killed in action on the Italian Asiago Plateau.

Resolving to remedy his missing honour as soon as she returned to London, Vera looked down the list.[3] Amongst the names of boys she knew was Jerry

Buxton First World War Memorial, with Town Hall in background, c.1920.

Knowles Garnett, Edward's friend from their Buxton preparatory school. When he died of enteric disease in the Dardanelles on 6 November 1915, Vera had written to her mother 'it is so difficult to believe that person you once met almost daily & danced & played tennis with is dead. His parents commissioned a memorial plaque in Buxton's St John's Church.

The war memorial had been unveiled in 1920, five years after 21-year-old Vera left Buxton to serve as a Voluntary Aid Detachment nurse in London. In the year of her return, she was 41 and basking in the international acclaim that followed the publication in 1933 of her ground-breaking feminist First World War memoir, *Testament of Youth*. After a decade of wondering if she would ever achieve her lifelong ambition to be a famous writer, Vera was enjoying life as a literary celebrity, travelling to America in the staterooms of luxury cruise liners, her rooms filled with flowers and telegrams. On a successful but extremely gruelling promotional American tour in 1934, she was 'treated more like a prophetess than a human being', noting 'twenty years ago it would have seemed like a wild fantasy. I pictured myself writing, but never at the centre of cheering, exalted, wildly excited crowds.'[4] At the University of Minnesota, her enthralled audience of students and members of the public was 5,000 strong. By the time of her 1935 Buxton visit, Vera had given 170 speeches and lectures around Britain and the United States.

For over ninety years, readers have been moved and inspired by *Testament of Youth*, an autobiographical study of the years 1900–1925. Vera's biographer Mark Bostridge observes, 'there is nothing in the prose literature of the First World War that so eloquently and movingly conveys the suffering and bereavement inflicted on the generation of 1914'.[5] The cover notice, written by Vera's great friend Winifred Holtby, described it as 'like no other book yet published' and praised the setting of personal experience against a 'heroically-sustained panorama' in which 'the individual stories illuminate with their fortuitous symbolism the great march of European tragedy'.[6]

Testament of Youth charts Vera's descent from stifling 'provincial young ladyhood' and escape to university into the horrors of a brutal war in which she nursed wounded soldiers, and lost her brother, fiancé and two close friends. It is also a story of resurrection and recovery, in which a broken, traumatised Vera resumed her studies at Oxford, met Winifred Holtby who became her greatest friend, forged a career as a feminist, pacifist writer and campaigner and married Gordon Catlin. In an era when memoirs were about the achievements of famous men, Vera's skilful interweaving of personal narrative with political analysis and history redefined the genre of autobiography.

Of the memoir's 600 pages, just 60 narrate Vera's provincial young ladyhood in Buxton, a fashionable, prosperous spa resort, between 1905 when she was 11, and 1915 when she was almost 22. She did not have a good word to say about it:

> I felt trammelled and trapped....I hated Buxton, in spite of the austere beauty of its peaks and dales and the health-giving air ... with a detestation that I have never felt since for any set of circumstances ...[7]
>
> [Buxton] stood, and stands for ...the estimation of people for what they have, or pretend to have, and not for what they are. Artificial classifications, rigid lines of demarcation that bear no relation whatsoever to intrinsic merit... while contempt for intelligence, suspicion and fear of independent thought, appear to be necessary passports to provincial popularity.[8]

Vera's language is relentlessly hyperbolic: 'my furious Buxton resentments', 'hatred', 'detestation', 'indignation', 'resentment', 'imprisonment', 'being trapped', the town's 'mean censorious spirit', 'dull, mentally restricted residents', 'the utter futility' of her existence, and 'my warfare against Buxton'. In a publicity interview for *Testament of Youth*, Vera said her portrayal was 'not in the least exaggerated; if anything Buxton was more snobbish, more obscurantist, than I have shown it'.[9] In 1947, she remembered that 'the uncongenial obligations of provincial adulthood' froze her into 'resentful silence' where, unable to write anything worthwhile, war and falling in love drove her to pour her literary ambitions into letters and a diary.[10]

Testament of Youth was not Vera's first or most critical account of her early life. Her diary for 18 October 1913 first mentions collecting material for 'my Buxton story'. This became her second novel, *Not Without Honour*, published in 1924. Using many verbatim extracts from Vera's diary, the first half of this high-blown melodramatic story mirrors her portrayal of Edwardian middle-class provincial life in *Testament of Youth*. Christine Merrivale (Vera) is a spirited, very attractive, intellectually accomplished young woman from a wealthy family in Torborough, a fashionable health resort. Returning to live there after an inspiring education in the south of England, Christine rails against a claustrophobic home life, censorious society matrons and dull, pompous young men whose single ambition is to follow their fathers into business, and a pointless existence of dances, promenades, tennis and tea parties, activities whose sole purpose was to display her as a marriage prospect.

Vera said in *Testament of Youth* that she had never enjoyed anything more than decanting her hatred of Buxton into *Not Without Honour*. She never softened her anti-provincialism and her dislike of Buxton in particular, continuing in her letters and journalism to criticise the reactionary, narrow-minded thinking in 'prosperous and complacent towns like Buxton', and the vacuous lives of their middle-class female inhabitants.

Biographers have accepted Vera's condemnations of provincial young ladyhood without challenge. According to Hilary Bailey, Vera 'hated Buxton and despised her own rather stuffy provincial background', had a 'stultifying empty existence for an energetic girl' and, with 'little to do' except wait for a marriage proposal, was 'reduced to helping her mother at home'.[11] A study of Vera's writing tells readers that 'growing up in Buxton was a form of imprisonment.'[12] The preface to the 1980 edition of *Testament of Youth* informs us that 'Vera carried on a running battle with her parents to be allowed to go to university and chafed against the claustrophobia of her middle-class existence, the pointlessness of hunt balls', while the 2004 preface describes Vera's Buxton years as 'a living death'.

* * *

When Vera completed her manuscript of *Testament of Youth* in 1933, she observed to Winifred that it would make people in Buxton angry but 'I don't really mind about that'.[13] Decades later, Vera's derision of the town and its inhabitants still rankles in Buxton. In 2020 I came to live at Melrose, her home between 1907 and 1915, and soon became accustomed to hearing that 'Vera Brittain hated Buxton'; indeed, it is usually the first response to any mention of her. Occasionally someone embellishes this with something along the lines of 'Buxton doesn't much like *her* either!' Tellingly, the town has no public commemoration of its most significant resident, and many Buxtonians and visitors have never heard of her.

Yet Vera's portrayal is rather one-sided. Living in Melrose, the home she described in 1913 as 'this house of many comforts', I became fascinated with her early life. Could her gilded existence during Buxton's vibrant Edwardian heyday, with three live-in servants, affectionate parents and an adoring and adored brother, really have been as dull and restrictive as she claimed? What made Buxton so attractive to the Brittains and many other wealthy families who flocked to live there during the late nineteenth and early twentieth century? If her upbringing was so stifling and her social circle as 'mentally restricted', boring and censorious as she said, how did she develop her impressive intellectual ambition and idealism? How did Vera's provincial upbringing shape her character and interests? And why did she choose to present it in such a remorselessly critical way?

This is the first biography of Vera Brittain to focus on her 'provincial young ladyhood'. Its unique sense of place comes from living in her former home, with access to photographs of Edwardian Buxton and the Brittains at Melrose, a complete copy of her handwritten diary notebooks from 1911, 1913–1917 and my knowledge of all the Buxton places Vera frequented. Framed by a backdrop of great social change, her engaging, lively voice is at the heart of a narrative which brings Buxton characters into her story for the first time: her neighbours and acquaintances, teachers, dressmaker, a hapless would-be lover, and two people who fascinated and influenced Vera: the wife of a hotel proprietor and a radical young curate in a nearby working-class village.

A richer, more nuanced account of Vera's early life in a fashionable Edwardian town goes beyond the rather one-sided version she offers in *Testament of Youth* and her other writing. It highlights just how much this extraordinary and intriguing young woman lost in the First World War and explains how 'provincial young ladyhood' enabled Vera Brittain to become one of the twentieth century's most important literary and political figures.

Chapter One

'We Went to Buxton in the Motor'

Vera's Provincial Young Ladyhood Begins

'Through the misty moorland ... and over the precipice'

In early March 1905, Edith Brittain made a final tour of Glen Bank, the harmonious home she had created for her husband Arthur and their two children, 11-year-old Vera, and 9-year-old Edward. Four months earlier, Arthur had seen a notice in the *Buxton Advertiser*'s 'To Let' column for High Leigh, a detached, seven-bedroomed house on Manchester Road, available, furnished, or unfurnished to a 'good family', for £90 a year (about £7,000 today). Demand for residential and holiday homes in the booming spa resort was high and Arthur had to act quickly. Two weeks later, he signed a short-term lease on the Buxton property.

After ten years at Glen Bank, the move was a big upheaval. The Brittains would miss the tranquil elegance of their home, with its orchard, paddock,

The Brittains and Koko the pug dog outside Glen Bank, 1904. Vera is in the front with Arthur, Edward, a friend and Towie in the back. (*McM*)

gardener's cottage and coach house, set in over an acre overlooking fields and a river on the outskirts of Macclesfield, a thriving silk town in Cheshire.[1] The family's new Buxton home was quite different, being austere grey gritstone with an unprepossessing front and back garden and surrounded by neighbouring houses. And with their loyal housekeeper, Mrs Townsend (Towie) and much-loved governess, Miss A.M. Newby, staying in Macclesfield, there would new servants to get used to. Still, once the children were settled in new schools, Edith and Arthur could take their time to find a better house.[2]

The removal men finished loading one of the motorised vans that, in the early 1900s, wealthy families like the Brittains were beginning to use in place of a horse and cart. Edith ushered Vera, Edward and Koko into the back seats of Arthur's beloved 8-horsepower Wolseley Eight and climbed into the front. It was a beautiful, blue-skied day; with blankets and the roof rolled down, the Brittains could enjoy the spectacular views on the ten-mile drive to Buxton.

Leaving the lush green Cheshire plain in which Macclesfield sits, Arthur navigated the steep, sharply winding road out of the town onto the open moorland. To the left were the distant blue hills of the Goyt Valley, with the smoke of Manchester factories on the horizon. To the right were the rolling hills and dramatic peaks of Wildboar Clough stretching into the Manifold Valley, dotted with drystone walls, farmhouses, sheep and little wooded valleys. The stunning views compensated a little for the uncomfortable bumpy ride

The Brittains c.1898. (*McM*)

over the dusty crushed limestone road. A few months later, the roads would be, as Vera described, 'blindingly white', and the 'rhododendron bushes… as if they had been dipped in flour because of the dust flung on them by the motor charabancs pounding along the dry white roads'.[3]

From a young age, Vera loved beautiful scenery and motorcar journeys. When Edith was away a few months earlier, Vera had written excitedly to her about a trip to Buxton with Arthur, Edward and Towie:

> …it was all mist as soon as we began to mount the hills and soon it got so misty that we could scarcely see three yards in front of us … it was nice going through the misty moorland to Buxton, and over the precipice. We had a sugary bun in Buxton, and it was the nicest ride we ever had. Coming back the mist had quite cleared away, except on the horizon, and we tore down those hills in one place as though we were in fifth speed instead of the third so you'll be glad to hear we are all alive and kicking.[4]

But while Vera had enjoyed that misty trip in 1904, this journey felt very different. She would eventually come to love Buxton's distinctive scenery but always missed the warm red brick of Cheshire buildings and the 'smooth pretty lanes with their benign hedges and wildflowers'. It is very unlikely any of the Brittains were looking forward to Buxton's notoriously cold, wet climate, despite the best efforts of the town's official guide to promote its health benefits:

The road towards the Cat and Fiddle from Buxton, c.1905. (*PtP*)

4 Testament of Lost Youth

> Buxton as a mountain Spa … enjoys an atmosphere largely free of pathogenic microbes … the death-rate owing to these and other favouring causes is only about half the mortality of the great towns of England … being 9.572 per 1000 and … no case of epidemic cholera has occurred in Buxton during any visitations of this fearful disease …The most experienced civil and sanitary engineers of the day have created unusual facilities for drainage… The altitude provides exceptional velocity in the winds …The abundant rainfall averages 50 inches a year … so that the atmosphere is well-washed and made bright and pure, any possible impurities being swept away to the earth.[5]

At the summit of the steep twisting road, the green of Wildboar Clough gives way to peat moorland stretching brown and treeless into the distance. Arthur slowed to allow horse-drawn chaises to draw up at the Cat and Fiddle, a busy coaching inn, thronged as usual with day-trippers admiring the view and having refreshments while carriage drivers, and the unfortunate men paid to drag wealthy clients in bath chairs up the steep hill from Buxton, took a well-earned rest.

The car swept down into Buxton, passing the unsightly lime slips of the vast quarry at Grin Low and the village of Burbage, home to quarry workers, lead and coal miners, and women who supplemented the men's meagre wages by taking in washing. Ahead were the wide tree-lined roads of Buxton's wealthiest areas, framed by views of the extensive plantations of larches, beech, sycamore, mountain ash, birch and chestnut, paid for by the Devonshire Estate to soften

Day-trippers at the Cat and Fiddle on Buxton–Macclesfield road, early 1900s. (*PtP*)

St John's Road towards centre of Buxton, Pavilion on the right, early 1900s. (*PtP*)

Buxton's once rather desolate moorland surroundings. The Brittains' entrance to Buxton was along St John's Road, with the stunning Gardens and Winter Pavilion to their right.

'The most important day Buxton has ever had'

A couple of months before the Brittains moved to Buxton, its first official royal visit on Saturday, 7 January 1905 signalled just how fashionable the resort had become. An exuberant editorial in the *Buxton Advertiser* hailed 'the most important day Buxton has ever had … In addition to being the highest town in England, it will today be the proudest.'[6]

The paper gave a detailed itinerary. Invited by their friend the eighth duke of Devonshire, Edward VII and Queen Alexandra went to the Devonshire Hospital and the town's beautiful Georgian centrepiece, the Crescent. They had lunch at St Ann's Hotel, attended by staff from Chatsworth House, the Devonshires' Derbyshire home, before driving 'the full length of the principal promenade' in the Pavilion Gardens for which the railings had to be removed to allow the royal entourage through. The editorial lamented that a winter visit would not enable the royal guests to see the Gardens at their best. Normally the Devonshires stayed at St Ann's but on this occasion, they joined the king and queen at the Empire, Buxton's largest, most opulent hotel which had opened in 1901. According to the *Advertiser* a week later, 'polite Manchester society turned up in droves'.

Royal motorcade by Baths, 1905.

The following week, the *Advertiser* praised the lavish hospitality provided for the royal visitors by St Ann's proprietors, John Milligan Harrison, and his wife. Eight years later, Mrs Harrison would be a focus of great fascination for Vera Brittain and an important influence on her future.

'No English town surpasses Buxton in the salubrity of its situation'

What made Arthur and Edith move their family to Buxton? They had a lovely home and loyal servants in Macclesfield, and years that were, according to *Testament of Youth*, as 'serene and uneventful as any childhood could be'. The move created new challenges for all the Brittains. Vera and Edward were sad to leave Newby behind in Macclesfield, and a little daunted by the prospect of not only going to school but also having to mix with children their own age for the first time. Being a Buxton society matron would require Edith to display the family's social status in a more prosperous, snobbish town and Arthur now faced an onerous daily round trip of 30 miles over the bleak moors to the paper mill.

According to *Testament of Youth*, the overriding reason for this upheaval was so that Vera and Edward could attend 'good' preparatory schools before going to boarding schools elsewhere. A few weeks before their move, Arthur and Edith must have been pleased with another of the *Advertiser*'s fulsome editorials, this time lauding the town's educational credentials and its rapid shift from having 'nothing but a dame's school and a very elementary town school [to] becoming known – not only for the fame of its water and air, but also for scholastic successes which form another inducement for parents to make the "Spa of the Peak" their place of residence.' Thrilled that boys and girls, including 'bright girls from the Grange', could now take 'Local Examinations connected with the University of Cambridge', the *Advertiser* was especially pleased that 'for boys especially, there is no doubt that, in these days of severe competition, the sooner [they] are taught [how to sit an exam] the better it will be for them in the strenuous fight for existence which comes when happy schooldays have passed away'.[7]

With private day and boarding establishments competing to attract wealthy parents, Buxton certainly offered its growing number of middle-class families much better schools than Macclesfield. There were four for girls: the Grange ('a high-class school for girls'); Craigholm ('a school for the daughters of gentlemen'), Kempsford Ladies' School ('pupils are prepared for university and other examinations') and Marlborough College ('provides a thorough education on the most approved Modern principles … with professors of high standing and who are well-known as successful teachers'). There were three boys' schools, including Holm Leigh ('Nowhere is the air purer or more bracing: water supply good and soft. Health is the first consideration. The standard of work ensures entry into Public Schools. Games are systematically taught'.) Arthur and Edith chose the Grange and Holm Leigh, both within walking distance of their new home.

Better schools were only one factor in Arthur and Edith Brittain's social aspirations. Buxton had similar attractions to genteel Harrogate and upper-class Bath but it was no ordinary provincial backwater nor typical genteel spa town. Its unique social atmosphere came from 200 years as an 'estate resort', developed and tightly controlled by managers, architects and landscape designers for the Devonshires, one of Britain's richest aristocratic families. Until the late nineteenth century, they owned virtually all of Buxton, surrounding villages and huge swathes of the Peak District, as well as vast estates in Ireland and other parts of England, and property in London. Not far from Chatsworth House, the Devonshires (from 1869, in partnership with the newly-created Buxton Improvement Company) had turned Buxton from a small sedate Georgian resort centred around the stunning Crescent, into one of Britain's most fashionable spa towns. By 1905, it had an annual town guide, two thriving newspapers, advertisements in major provincial papers, the *Illustrated London News* and railway stations, and exhibitions of new developments at the Royal Exchange in Manchester.

In 1898, Dr Samuel Hyde, a specialist in water treatments and creator of the Peak Hydropathic Hotel, summarised the town's attractions:

> No English town surpasses Buxton in the salubrity of its situation; the beauty of its surrounding scenery; the extent, comfort, and luxury of its baths; the music and other charms of its Pavilion Gardens; its opportunities for every form of indoor and outdoor recreation; its magnificent hotels and lodging houses; its cleanly roads and well-lighted streets; its ample supply of the purest water; its complete and efficient system of drainage and sewage disposal; its easy accessibility and splendid railway services from all parts of the kingdom. These and many other advantages, the origin and result of steady development, have won for Buxton a foremost position amongst the health resorts of Europe.[8]

The year of the Brittains' move was, according to the *Advertiser*, Buxton's most successful yet. Since the 1850s, the resident population had expanded to 12,000, with a 400 per cent increase in staying guests and day-trippers to over 4,000 a week during the high season. Expansion had been extremely rapid: the population of Buxton grew by 149 per cent between 1859 and 1879 – much faster than other spa towns. In 1901, 40 per cent of weekly visitors were staying at Buxton's most upmarket hotels and 'hydropathics' which offered the latest water treatments and entertainments in opulent surroundings. By 1891, one in seven of Buxton's population served in private homes, hotels and lodging houses, and one in ten were in the building trades supporting the housing boom to accommodate thousands of wealthy families. With money made in trade, manufacturing, and business, most of the families wanting to live or have a second home in Buxton were from the north-west and midlands. Regular train services to London and Manchester were another attraction.

This influx created a preponderance of extremely grand houses. Bought by businessmen and industrialists, wealthy spinsters, widows, and wives of prosperous men, these were either a main residence or second home, or rented to families like the Brittains. Buxton offered a great deal of freedom. Wealthy clients commissioned acclaimed architects to design impressive houses, including some Arts and Crafts gems. The most distinctive designs featured in architectural magazines. The resort also had elegant amenities designed by renowned landscape designers, including Edward Milner's acclaimed Gardens and Winter Pavilion and Joseph Paxton's Serpentine Walks, Corbar Woods and The Park, with its cricket ground and carriage drive.

'A dedicated paper maker'

While by no means the richest in their Buxton social circle, the Brittains were typical middle-class incomers. When Thomas Arthur Brittain moved his family there, he was 41 years old and running his Staffordshire family's highly successful paper making business. In 1890, Arthur's grandfather bought the company from the Foundrines, a Huguenot family whose invention of a highly innovative machine of that name revolutionised the paper industry. When he died, his fortune was £131,000, making him a millionaire several times over in today's terms.

One of eleven siblings, Arthur started work at the paper mill at the age of 18. At 26 he became one of four founding directors of Brittains Ltd based at Hanley, Stoke-on-Trent. Under Arthur's direction, Brittains' innovation of duplex transfer paper in 1896 was the basis for the great bulk of pottery decoration throughout the world. Brittains also manufactured a highly successful range of exquisite fine papers, including the thin, tough, opaque paper for prayer books and bibles produced by the Oxford University Press at its mill in Wolvercote near Oxford, and carbonised typewriting paper. Brittains' 'Oxford India Paper' won many awards and added significantly to the company's prestige.

Arthur Brittain, c.1913. (*SC*)

In 1905, Brittains acquired a second mill at Cheddleton, near Leek. According to a former employee, Arthur was a meticulous, thorough employer, and a 'dedicated paper maker'. On a typical day he would arrive at Cheddleton in time for lunch, eat his sandwiches in the car and then do his work:

> I don't think he ever missed anything…while he walked around the mill, Percy Grovesnor would clean his car for him. Then about four o'clock, he set off for home again… He had a very considerable say in what went on. If Arthur Brittain didn't like something, it had to be changed.[9]

In 1906, Arthur's annual income was about £1,300 (about £190,000 today) and, like many Edwardian businessmen, he also had investments in railway contracts. A staunch free trader, Arthur was politically and socially conservative. Boasting 'never a trade union near the place', he prided himself on good relations with his workforce and was generally solicitous of their welfare. When workers at the

Oxford paper mill began to agitate for a union, his business partner Frederick Haigh reflected the company's paternalistic standpoint:

> Trades Unionism …brings no real help or healing to the workers themselves…the real remedy is the hearty and active effort of the Employers, with the willing and loyal cooperation of the workers, to bring about better and happier conditions both with regard to work and wages.[10]

Arthur's interests did not extend beyond his family, business, and motorcar. The car was his pride and joy. After moving to Buxton, he was to trade in the Wolseley for a highly fashionable de Dion Bouton.[11] A few years later, he was to replace this after visiting the 'Wolseley people in Birmingham' and returning to enthuse 'eloquently over dinner over the beauty of the new car', with its navy-blue paintwork and silver trim. Vera noted in her diary that it 'sounded most attractive'. A favourite pastime was taking neighbours and family on tours around the surrounding countryside.

He was a somewhat reckless driver, boasting that his journey to work took just 20 minutes. This is unlikely: even if Arthur broke the national speed limit of 20 mph, the journey, on rough roads, with frequent fog, would have taken an hour each way, and longer in winter. On one occasion, he was seriously injured when he swerved to avoid an old woman driving a horse and cart and turned

Arthur and his car, c.1907. (*McM*)

the car over into a ditch. Arthur spent several weeks in a critical condition in a 'tiny moorland inn on the Staffordshire side of the county boundary' and the woman who ran it reported 'he must have been completely mad to drive like he did!'[12]

Vera's mother came from a very different background. The third of six children, Edith Bervon was born in Aberystwyth, and was living in Hanley when Arthur took singing lessons from her father, Inglis Bervon, an organist, composer of church music and teacher who advertised himself as a 'Professor of Music'. 'Charming, feckless and generous-hearted', Inglis had to move his wife and six children numerous times in search of better circumstances.[13] When he died suddenly at the age of 53, his estate was just £250 (about £20,000 today).

Edith Brittain, c.1912. (*SC*)

Like most Victorian women from genteel but poor families, Edith was expected to seize upon the first possibility of a good marriage, although Vera commended how Edith's sisters 'made their way in the world long before independence was a typical aspiration for women'.[14] After being a lady's companion, Edith's oldest sister Florence ran St Monica's boarding school near Reigate, which Vera would attend in 1907, the youngest, Lillie, taught Art at St Monica's until she married, and Isabel ('Belle') was a governess to an English family in India; she was to return just before war broke out and, when it ended, to run a tea shop in Kent.

When wealthy Arthur Brittain proposed marriage, Edith, with no pedigree or money, and 'nothing but her shy and wistful prettiness to recommend her', had little choice but to accept.[15] Edith

Vera and Edith, 1893. (*McM*)

would later confide in Vera that she married for a 'life of steadily increasing comforts'. His family thought he had married beneath him. In 1892, their first child was stillborn. Vera Mary was born a year later, at a 'small decorous villa' in Sidmouth Avenue, Brampton, Newcastle-under-Lyme. Eighteen months later, the family moved to Glen Bank where Edward Harold Brittain was born in 1895.

In their plans for upward mobility, Arthur and Edith Brittain did not expect Vera to earn her own living. Instead, when she turned 18, she would, like middle-class girls across Britain, follow a tradition established in the 1780s and make her debut at a society ball. After that, Buxton's rich array of cultural and leisure activities would hone the social accomplishments necessary to make Vera a desirable marriageable prospect.

Edward, 1895. (*McM*)

While Vera would eventually rebel against her provincial life, society balls in Buxton's opulent hotels, hydropathics and private homes, and promenades through its elegant Georgian centre and Edward Milner's beautiful Gardens, fostered her lifelong enjoyment of dancing, beautiful clothes and being admired for her striking appearance. And while Vera and Edith would always favour London for clothes shopping, they could still appraise, as the *Advertiser* boasted in 1905, 'the latest Paris fashions and cream of the fashion world' in Buxton's elegant, colonnaded shops and perhaps attend fashion shows in a grand villa on the Broad Walk.

Arthur and Edith Brittain, early 1900s, date unknown. (*SC*)

'We Went to Buxton in the Motor'   13

Buxton Gardens promenade, early 1900s. (*PtP*)

The pinnacle of Buxton's attractions was Frank Matcham's acclaimed Opera House. Opened in 1903, this exquisite little theatre, with its elaborate gilt décor, stained glass and plush seating, would be the setting for Vera's successful foray into amateur dramatics in 1913. All the Brittains would enjoy performances by national and provincial touring opera and drama companies, orchestras, well-known actors, musical and comedy performers.

Buxton also offered impressive all-year round sports facilities which had been created from the 1870s onwards to combat cartoons in London newspapers showing a resort filled with sick people in bath chairs. Every August, Vera and Edward would join thousands of spectators from all parts of Britain for the All-England national tennis tournament in the Gardens. Established in 1884, this renowned event was soon attracting top players. As well as tennis, Vera and Edward would enjoy golf and bowling, watch international and county cricket teams at the picturesque cricket ground on The Park, created in 1854, and Edward would become a member of the Buxton cricket team. And of the many winter sports that had extended Buxton's social season, they would venture onto the long toboggan slope down Manchester Road.

Two weekly newspapers, the *Buxton Advertiser and Weekly List of Visitors* and the *Buxton Herald and Gazette*, promoted the resort's lively social season and attractions with great enthusiasm. Established in 1852, the *Advertiser* was the largest. Under its dynamic editor John Cumming Bates, it devoted two full pages listing weekly visitors, reported London society gossip, the royal family's schedule,

Sledging down the Manchester Road, Buxton, early 1900s.

the results of Wimbledon and other major sporting events, national and local news. Lively editorials opined on diverse topics, including the importance of royal visits, the town's rapid rise as a tourist destination for the wealthy, the pros and cons of an increase in motorcars, problems with Irish union, the tragedy of Scott's expedition to the Antarctic, and women's suffrage. Much space was devoted to enthusiastic reviews of Buxton's society balls, musicals, concerts by one of the town's four orchestras, and daily music programmes in the Gardens.

'An unparalleled age of tranquil comfort and rich materialism'

Edwardian Buxton offered aspirational families like the Brittains a higher level of genteel exclusivity, in more salubrious surroundings, with grander homes, public amenities, social and cultural activities, than other provincial towns. Fashionable enough for a royal visit, it was a resort created by a duke to see and be seen in, from where residents could watch a show in London and catch the last train home, where opera, top performers and Paris fashions in the shops were in walking distance from splendid residences, hotels and lodging houses. Buxton encouraged the rising middle classes to display the fruits of their hard work and signal their intentions for a better life.

This exclusivity came from an unusual degree of social segregation, engineered by the Devonshires through land ownership, chief rents, restrictive covenants and tight control over the value and quality of amenities. Before debts and death duties led the Devonshire Estate to start relinquishing some of its control and patronage from the 1890s onwards, Buxton was a net earner for the Devonshires. Up to that point, although there were other 'estate' towns, such as Eastbourne,

Taking the waters at the Pump Room, 1912.

none were dominated by one family as Buxton was. For over 200 years, the Estate had overseen every facet of the resort: provision of utilities, public health standards, hotels and street layout, the size and design of buildings and, not least, the class of resident and visitor it wanted to attract.[16]

Carefully engineered physical segregations obscured poverty from Buxton's wealthy residents and visitors. The Gardens were enclosed by railings and had seven formal entrances, with admission charges. Servants could only enter if their employer added them to the family ticket for an annual fee of 5 shillings (about £40 today). Quarrymen, miners, and washer women lived in villages outside the town, while terraced houses for artisans and tradesmen were built well away from grander residential areas. Miners and cotton operatives treated at the Devonshire Hospital had separate entrances to the Baths and their own gardens in the hospital grounds.[17]

In return for all their privileges, middle class residents were expected to help run Buxton, invest in amenities such as the Gardens, and take on civic duties. In the 1860s, the Estate offered shares in new developments, such as the Palace Hotel whose investors included the director of London North-West Railways, an Oldham cotton spinner, a local quarry owner and the editor of the *Buxton Advertiser*. In 1869, the Estate set up the Buxton Improvement Company to enhance the town's cultural and social amenities, increase prosperity and encourage residents and external investors to own shares in the Gardens, hospitals, and Free Library.

With no welfare state, national health service or council tax for local services, wealthy residents were expected to raise money, do charity work and serve on all manner of committees: Technical Education, Guardians of the Poor, the Mechanics and Literary Institute (which ran lectures on philosophical and scientific topics), and University of Oxford 'extension' lectures. Middle-class women like Edith Brittain raised money for overseas missions, local churches, the Mothers' Union, and Girls' Friendly Society, visited and made clothes for poor families. As members of hospital Ladies' Committees, they organised volunteers and fund-raising events for hospital Ladies' Committees.

For Buxton's prosperous families and wealthy visitors, the short-lived Edwardian era, from 1901 to 1914, was, as Vera later described, an 'unparalleled age of tranquil comfort and rich materialism that, to those of us born at its close, appeared to have gone on from time immemorial, and to be securely destined forever'.[18] To Buxton's wealthy middle-class, the growing social unrest, industrial conflict, and increasingly militant campaigns for women's suffrage and Irish Home Rule during the early 1900s seemed remote and irrelevant. In this sheltered society, the outbreak of war in August 1914 seemed to erupt without warning.

Over the next ten years, the Brittains would make the most of the cultural, social and sporting facilities, subscribe to the Devonshire Hospital and sponsor a fundraising ball at the Palace Hotel. After finishing her education, Vera would make her Buxton debut in 1912 and enjoy provincial life before finding her escape to university in Oxford. And whatever Edith's misgivings about Buxton's demanding social etiquette, she would fulfil her civic duties, and create

Devonshire Hospital, c.1905. (*PtP*)

another harmonious, well-run home and a social life that reflected her family's aspirational status.

'A tall grey house'

All that was still to come. On the day of the move in March 1905, Arthur drove his family past the grand residential villas and hotels that line St John's Road. With the dome of the Devonshire Hospital, one of Buxton's most stunning landmarks, in front of them, he turned left onto Manchester Road. Halfway up the hill towards the edge of town was High Leigh, the 'tall grey house' Vera mentions in *Testament of Youth*. Drawing up at the front door, with its pretty carved stone lintel, and stained-glass windows above, the Brittains clambered down from the car. The new servants had lit fires, the removal men were waiting outside and, perhaps, the kettle was on for a welcoming cup of tea. While the children explored their new home, Edith and the servants began the task of sorting out where to put furniture, and men from Saunders Garage came to take Arthur's precious car to a lock-up store with wood block floors and heated pipes, from where it would be delivered each morning and collected each evening.[19]

Over the next week, Vera and Edward enjoyed their last days of freedom before starting school, Edith embarked on life as a Buxton society matron and Arthur began his daily 30-mile return drive over the bleak moors to Cheddleton. The ten years Vera would refer to in *Testament of Youth* as 'provincial young ladyhood' had begun.

View of early twentieth century Buxton from the Slopes. Crescent in centre, Palace Hotel behind. High Leigh is towards the top of white Manchester Road on left hand side of photo, the Devonshire Dome on the right.

Chapter Two

'A Mentally Voracious Young Woman'

Vera at School

'A school for the daughters of gentlemen'

A few days after the move, Vera and Edith walked up the hill from High Leigh and turned left onto The Park. Pausing in front of the ostentatious Empire hotel, they waited while taxis taking wealthy guests to the train station trundled past, then walked a few yards further to the Grange, Buxton's largest, most highly regarded girls' school.

Vera joined the Grange halfway through the Easter term. With no experience of mixing with other children, leaving her 'devoted', 'intelligent', 'adored' governess, was a huge wrench. Miss Newby was in her thirties when she worked for the Brittains and under her competent charge, Vera and Edward had gained a good grounding in French, history, geography, drawing and painting. Newby had also indulged Vera's literary aspirations by using offcuts from the paper mill to make notebooks. Vera and Edward were to stay in regular contact with Newby until she died in 1933, just weeks before *Testament of Youth* was published.

Lacking friends in Macclesfield, Vera developed a passionate interest in five 'pretty daughters' of a family who lived nearby, and 'around the imaginary lives of these young women, I wove my dreams and built my stories'.[1] By the time Vera was ten, she had put Newby's notebooks to good use by writing five novels: *The Five Schoolgirls*, *Edith's Trial*, *The Feud of the Cousins*, *A Mistaken Identity* and *The Breaking in of Dorothy*. In their precociously fluent style, accompanied by Vera's rather good pencil illustrations,

Vera aged 5. (*McM*)

The Grange c.1905.

the stories were full of 'misunderstanding and catastrophes, early deaths, agonised soliloquies, deathbed scenes and repentances'.[2]

Whatever Vera's misgivings about starting school, she had become a confident and avid learner. Letters to Edith when her mother was away reveal an inquisitive, enthusiastic child who enjoyed all her subjects at the Grange, especially cricket, science, gymnastics, and painting. Vera's first report described her as a 'very intelligent pupil' and at the end of her first term, she passed the University of Cambridge's Preliminary Local Examination in Dictation, English Grammar and Composition, Arithmetic, History, Geography, French, Freehand Drawing and Religious Knowledge. Her proud parents hung a framed certificate on the wall of their dining room.[3]

After Vera's first year at the Grange there was a new headmistress, Lena Dodd, who ran the school with her younger sister 24-year-old Eirenne. They lived with their 72-year-old mother in a large house opposite the school. Vera noted dismissively in *Testament of Youth* that Lena Dodd's 'unimpeachable degree' was a rare attribute for a Buxton headmistress. Yet, in 1906, Lena's qualifications and experience were unusual for a headmistress in any but the most prestigious girls' schools. With a teaching qualification from the University of London, Lena was a pupil at Cheltenham Ladies College (CLC) under its pioneering headmistress Dorothea Beale who led the College to rival Roedean as the country's foremost girls' public school, offering an academic education on a par with a boys' public school.[4] Lena taught at CLC before spending five years as a teacher at Preston High School for Girls (PHSG) which catered for 100 pupils, before being appointed as its fourth headmistress in 1890. In Preston, Miss Dodd also organised Oxford University 'extension lectures', part of a pioneering movement that provided adult education in provincial towns.

Between 1906 and 1912, Lena increased the number of pupils at the Grange from 15 to 29 and raised its sights. In 1904 it was advertised as a 'high class school for girls'. In 1912, another advertisement boasted of teachers who were 'graduates of the Universities of the United Kingdom, trained for teaching; a foreign Mistress for languages, and teachers holding diplomas of the Royal Academy of Music', while another proclaimed the Grange as 'a school for the daughters of gentlemen'.[5] The 1912 prospectus advertised a 'thoroughly good general education' that enabled older pupils to specialise in Art, Music, Literature or Languages 'according to their special tastes and the future career for which they may be preparing'. Lena was a fan of 'Sjojd' education, a progressive Swedish approach to the systematic manual development of children; the Grange offered three hours of daily exercise, either outdoors or on Swedish apparatus in the new gymnasium, and medical drill for 'delicate girls'.[6]

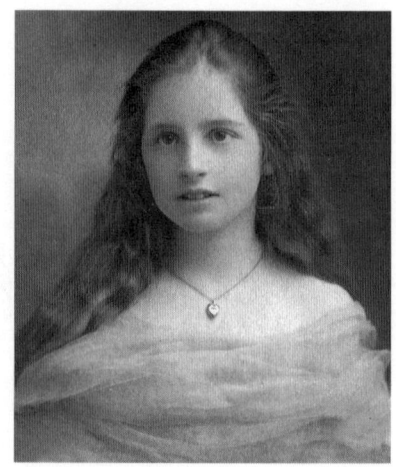

Vera aged 12. (*SC*)

Making her mark in a competitive schools' market and needing to support her mother seems to have made Lena feel she should conceal her real age; she was actually 48 in 1906, not the 37 she claimed. Born in 1858, census records show that Lena reduced her real age for decades. She ran the Grange until 1927 when she was sixty-nine. It is also possible that when Lena came to Buxton, she concealed the financial difficulties she had run into during her final year at PHSG where she had been bailed out by a grant from the Council, on condition three members from its education committee sat on the school board.[7]

'A refreshingly broadminded and enlightened education'

The Grange turned out to be more than an adequate preparation for Vera's next school. When she turned thirteen, Vera could, like other middle-class Buxton girls, become a day pupil or boarder at one of two highly regarded schools within travelling distance by train or motorcar. Founded in 1874, Manchester High School for Girls (MHSG) was one of the first to teach Chemistry, Physics and Biology and to prepare pupils for university in those subjects. This groundbreaking spirit caught the attention of political reformer Emmeline Pankhurst who sent her three daughters there between 1893 and 1902. Withington HSG was similarly progressive. Established by eminent Manchester families who 'wanted the same educational opportunities for their daughters as already existed for their sons', one of its founders, Charles Prestwich Scott, became editor of the *Manchester Guardian* when he was 25 and endowed an entrance scholarship to the University of Manchester.[8]

Arthur and Edith did not consider these possibilities. In 1907, Vera went to St Monica's, a boarding school set in impressive grounds in Kingswood a couple of miles from Reigate in Surrey. Founded in 1902 by Louise Heath-Jones when she was 33, one of its two principals was Florence Bervon, Edith's 'oldest and ablest' sister. The school had an impressive list of patrons, including the Bishop of Gibraltar and Canon Scott-Holland of St Paul's Cathedral, and aimed to prepare girls for a changing world and for public service:

> To us women comes the cry for larger opportunities for wider freedom, but it is foolish to demand these good things if we have not educated them in character and brain to use them.[9]

For Vera, it would prove to be a wholly positive alternative to a public schools such as Roedean or Cheltenham. Arthur paid fees of £42 a year (about £3,800 today). In 1907, this was about the same as a year's wages for a semi-skilled industrial worker.

Vera loved St Monica's immediately. Set in six acres of grounds and formal gardens, its imposing red-brick mansion overlooked the rolling Chipstead Valley

Louise Heath Jones, date unknown. (*Daniel Catlin*)

Florence Bervon, date unknown. (*McM*)

from a south-facing terrace.[10] She appreciated the school's stylish, comfortable interiors, of 'rich heavy curtains with a Jacobean pattern hung about the big bay windows, and slender blue vases filled with saffron tea-roses stood gracefully isolated upon dark oak tables', comparing them unfavourably with the homes of her Buxton neighbours.[11]

It was a world away from Buxton's austere gritstone buildings and wild, remote countryside. Just as the Buxton Town Guide and Edward's Buxton school proclaimed the health benefits of the local climate, so did St Monica's, informing parents that 'as [it] is bracing, sunny and dry, the neighbourhood is strongly recommended by medical men for growing and delicate girls'. During school holidays and after leaving St Monica's, Vera missed Surrey's much warmer climate and the green rolling countryside.

Its social make-up was very different from her Buxton social circle. Cora Stoop, one of Vera's two school friends, came from a large Dutch/Scottish family. They lived in West Hall, an enormous house with extensive grounds and a large retinue of servants near Byfleet in Surrey. Described by Vera as 'rolling in wealth', Cora's father had made his fortune in Shell oil. Her other friend, Stella Sharp, was also from a wealthy family; after leaving St Monica's, she went on to a finishing school in Brussels before being presented at court.

Despite sometimes feeling socially inferior to girls with 'more imposing connections', Vera was dismissive of their aspirations. *Not Without Honour* presented her fellow pupils as 'singularly narrow-minded and stupid…they didn't know what they wanted to do… most didn't want to do anything except go to dances and get engaged.'[12] In *Testament of Youth*:

> Many of them were fashionable young women to whom universities represented a quite unnecessary prolongation of useless and distasteful studies… I was quite without standing among those wealthy girls …with their town addresses in Mayfair or Belgravia, and their country homes of which the name 'Hall' or 'Park' was frequently a part. My parents could not afford the numerous theatres and concerts to which may of them were taken by request of their families…In those days… …almost every girl left school with only two ambitions…to impress her school-fellows with the glory of a grown-up toilette, and to get engaged before everyone else.[13]

Whatever her reservations, Vera threw herself enthusiastically into school life. Praising St Monica's as 'refreshingly broad minded and enlightened' compared to other girls' schools at the time, it had a profound and lasting influence on her. Florence Bervon and Louise Heath-Jones had created a curriculum in which pupils studied scripture, arithmetic, geometry, geography, nature study, English literature, history, French, German, Italian, Classics, singing, drawing, handiwork, cooking, gymnastics, dancing, and games. Heath-Jones was a stimulating and inspiring teacher:

> [her] mental vision leapt far ahead of contemporary teaching standards… the barriers, then rigidly divided history, literature, politics, economics, and religion into watertight compartments, tumbled down before me for ever.[14]

All her life, Vera eulogised the 'remarkable' relationship, both a business partnership and intimate friendship, that her aunt and Heath-Jones had created.[15] She described Louise Heath-Jones as a 'brilliant dynamic woman', religiously idealistic and an 'ardent but discreet feminist'. The teacher took a particular interest in her clever, motivated pupil. Florence Bervon oversaw the school's administration and welfare. She had no qualifications, but Heath-Jones' father, a

Vera aged 14. (*SC*)

manufacturer in Wolverhampton, had sent his daughter to Cheltenham Ladies' College and Newnham College, Cambridge.

St Monica's encouraged pupils to engage with ideas and current affairs. Vera took part in debates on topics such as 'life in the colonies is better than life in Great Britain' and 'art has declined since the invention of machinery'.[16] She read a carefully curated selection from *The Times* or *The Observer* 'unmodified by contrary political opinion':

> the fact we had [the newspaper articles] at all testified to a recognition of the importance of current events far from customary at a time when politics and economics were still thought by most headmistresses to be no part of the education of marriageable young females.[17]

A visiting teacher, Edith Fry, introduced Vera to more challenging and radical ideas through the work of John Ruskin, Thomas Carlyle and Robert Browning, William Morris and H.G. Wells.

Brought up in a home with few books, Vera developed an insatiable appetite for literature. She loved Shelley, a writer whose rebelliousness and romantic outlook appealed to her own. His poem *Adonias*

> …taught me in the most startling and impressive fashion of my childhood's experience to perceive beauty embodied in literature, and made me finally determine to become the writer I had dreamed of being since I was seven years old.[18]

St Monica's cricket team. Vera is in the centre of the middle row. (*SC*)

School also influenced Vera's ideas about religion. Interested in religious questions from an early age, she was very taken with *Robert Elsmere* (1888), Mrs Humphry Ward's bestselling, highly controversial novel about the Victorian 'crisis of faith' in the Anglican church. A bold choice for a girls' private school, it converted Vera from 'an unquestioning if somewhat indifferent churchgoer into an anxiously interrogative agnostic'.[19] Vera could not know, of course, that two years after leaving St Monica's, she would befriend a real-life Robert Elsmere in Buxton.

'A world in which women would no longer be the second-rate, unimportant creatures they were now.'

Edwardian girls' schools had to navigate the competing expectations of the various dignitaries, patrons and subscribers who established them as profit-making companies, and parents. Some wanted schools to turn girls into, as *Testament of Youth* described, 'an ornamental young lady', others to prepare them to earn their own living because they might not be married off easily and would need to support themselves.[20] A smaller but growing group believed in a woman's right to have a career. In 1880, a decade before Lena Dodd became headmistress of PHSG, Major General Fielden was the principal speaker at its annual speech day. Elected that year as Conservative Member of Parliament for Middleton in Lancashire, and with the women's suffrage movement beginning to gain prominence, he cautioned the pupils and teachers on reading material. Admonishing that 'those papers and books published with regard to what was called women's rights' were often mistaken and 'injurious publications', Fielden warned that wives already had sufficient influence over their husbands. The extension of 'women's rights' would do them no good; they should know their position and be glad to remain in it.[21]

By the time Vera went to the Grange in 1905, Fielden's sentiments were fast becoming out-of-date. From the 1890s, activists in the women's suffrage movement had succeeded in pushing some schools to do more than simply equip girls with feminine attributes to attract a husband and run a home. While the quality of middle-class girls' education was still much more variable than it was for boys, schools were starting to include elements of a masculine curriculum and extra-curricular activities, alongside traditional feminine subjects. Beyond prestigious schools such as CLC and Roedean, others offered an empowering, more progressive curriculum, while universities, including Manchester, were admitting more women.

Books on the women's movement, talks about leading figures in the Women's Social and Political Union and a trip with other senior pupils to a suffrage meeting in a neighbouring village, introduced Vera to feminism. Reading *Woman and Labour* by South African feminist Olive Schreiner was an epiphany:

> I first visualised in rapt childish ecstasy a world in which women would no longer be the second-rate, unimportant creature that they were now considered, but the equal and respected companions of men.[22]

A crucial inspiration for Vera's early feminism were the new models of womanhood offered by the independence of Edith Fry, who was in her twenties, the self-sufficiency and successful partnership of Florence Bervon and Louise Heath-Jones. A stream of consciousness that sprawls passionately across several pages of her diary conveys Vera's almost overwhelming admiration for Edith Fry and her own growing idealism:

Vera aged 17. (*SC*)

> I never met anyone who so attracted me, both intellectually and otherwise. She is not good looking really, but has one of the most fascinating, clever and sympathetic faces that I ever saw… whether due really to her, or whether due to some development that growing out of childhood must bring, I cannot say – I only know that the strange, irresistible, yet beautiful shadows of greater things, which had puzzled yet fascinated me for so long shaped themselves into a world, not of this one, but in it, since I am in it, in which visions and imaginations and ideas became sometimes more real than the everyday world.[23]

Vera's feelings reflected an ethos in many girls' schools, especially boarding schools, that a 'romantic friendship', such as the admiration of a younger girl for a prefect or teacher, encouraged loyalty to the school, and self-control. Emotions could run high and 'G.P.s' (Grand Passions) were regarded as a natural rite of passage. Vera's highly charged admiration for Fry reflected what would become a propensity for intense, passionate attachments to the few people she admired.

'As yet there is nothing equivalent to public schools for boys.'

By the age of 17, Vera realised the limitations of her parents' aspirations for her. Neither Arthur nor Edith had gained much benefit from education: after a term at Malvern, a minor public school, Arthur rebelled against its discipline and his father moved him to Newcastle-Under-Lyme High School for Boys. Since his father did not regard a university education as necessary for running the family business, Arthur had gone straight to work after school. As the daughter of a genteel but poor family, Edith's education was, as Vera described in *Testament of Youth*, 'spasmodic and unorthodox'.

Both parents wanted better for their children. Edward's education would reflect the family's raised social standing in an aspirational, prosperous town. With other middle-class boys, a local preparatory school would enable him to prepare for admission to a renowned public school, followed by university in Oxford or Cambridge. After that, he might enter the Indian Civil Service or, as Arthur hoped, the family business. As for their attractive daughter, not needing to work reflected the family's social status. At that time, about a third of the workforce were women, of whom over half were under 25, almost 80 per cent single and 14 per cent married. Half of female school-leavers went into domestic service, 25 per cent to mills and textile factories, about 12 per cent became teachers and governesses, 6 per cent worked in shops, 3 per cent in clerical and administrative work and about 1 per cent (including Lena Dodd, Louise Heath-Jones and Florence Bervon) were self-employed. Only a tiny number were scientists, doctors, artists and actors. Even if Arthur and Edith had been more open-minded about the possibility of a career for Vera, there were few jobs for women from her background: most became a private governess, lady's companion or teacher, occupations they had to give up when they married.[24] Back in Buxton, Vera's desire to become a professional writer fell on deaf ears.

Teachers and headmistresses with feminist sympathies were caught up in conflicting aspirations. They wanted intelligent, ambitious girls to have more opportunities, and to be exposed to feminist ideas. Louise Heath-Jones was not interested in raising girls to be 'ornaments' and supported the advancement of women alongside older values associated with Victorian femininity. Nonetheless, although she and Edith Fry sympathised with Vera's literary aspirations, St Monica's did not prepare her for university entrance examinations nor enable her to consider other possibilities for her future. Instead, like Vera's parents, her teachers assumed she would marry rather than go to university and have a career.

A few years after leaving, Vera would criticise her school for 'paying too much attention these days to elegance & good manners & not enough to intelligence', adding that 'Miss Heath-Jones always says she does not turn out fashionable girls, but it seems to be just what she is doing'.[25] In *Testament of Youth* she said St Monica's was dedicated to turning out women 'to be men's decorative inferiors'.

As her own education progressed, Vera became increasingly envious of Edward's. His Buxton preparatory school, Holm Leigh, was run by thirty-year-old Stephen Pettit, who Vera described in her diary as a 'vigorous Buxton man' with whom she enjoyed dancing and talking. Pettit had been a pupil at the school when it was run by his mother. Before returning to Buxton to take over as headmaster in 1900, he taught at a school in the south which prepared boys for Eton. This had given Pettit a clear idea of what was required for boys from a small provincial town to progress to well-regarded public schools. By the time Edward Brittain went to Holm Leigh in 1905, Pettit had had some notable successes in getting pupils scholarships or bursaries to such schools. In 1908, Edward went to Uppingham in Rutland, accompanied by Buxton friends Maurice Ellinger and Jack Whitehead. Another Holm Leigh friend, Jerry Garnett, went to Charterhouse.

Edward aged 12 in 1908, the year he went to Uppingham school. (*SC*)

Uppingham's appeal to the families of prosperous industrialists and merchants meant it did not have the upper class and upper middle-class atmosphere of Eton and Harrow. The school was committed to a notion of 'manliness' that valued physical courage, loyalty to superiors and followers, a love of Empire and, through its large and enthusiastic Officer Training Corps (OTC), a pervasive atmosphere of patriotic militarism. In 1912, the headteacher claimed 'we don't go in for making scholars, we go in for making men'. Boys were not allowed to take part in athletics or sporting contests or win a school prize without first passing a shooting test.

Uppingham also wanted every boy to learn to do something well, supplementing a traditional curriculum with opportunities to develop talents in music and languages. Although Edward did not shine academically, he enjoyed school. His inspiring music teacher, Sterndale Bennett, encouraged him to take up the viola and organ to complement his existing interest in the violin and piano, and to compose songs and short concertos.[26] According to *Testament of Youth*, Edward 'visualised himself in his dreams as a conductor, a junior Henry Wood'. After applying unsuccessfully for one of 30 University of Oxford scholarships, he gained a place at New College in 1914.

Three years after leaving St Monica's, Vera lamented '…as yet there is nothing equivalent to public schools for boys – these fine traditions & unwritten laws

'A Mentally Voracious Young Woman'

Fairfield Board School, early 1900s.

that turn out so many splendid characters have been withheld from [girls], much to their detriment'.[27] Yet while Edward did have more freedom than Vera, his options for the future were constrained; his musical aspirations would be overlooked if, as Arthur hoped, Edward followed him into the family business because, as Vera noted, 'there is so much money & promise in [the works] that we may someday be really rich & Daddy naturally wants his only son to have a part in it'.[28] She thought the other option, going into the Indian Civil Service, would give Edward more time for his beloved music and books.

Whatever the drawbacks of Vera's education, and despite her resentment about not having the same opportunities as middle-class boys, it hardly needs saying that educational prospects for her and Edward's working-class counterparts were bleak. With six out of seven children having to leave school at 14 to work, the most that servants at Edward and Vera's schools and at home could expect was a rudimentary schooling provided by local boards set up under the 1870 Education Act. Vera and Edward's education was a world away from the amenities and expectations of Buxton's three board schools.

'The stuffiness of complacent bourgeoisdom'

After failing to persuade her parents to let her go with Stella to finishing school in Brussels, Vera spent an extra term at St Monica's. Just before leaving, Vera played the part of the Madonna in 'Eager Heart', a Christmas mystery play which gave a 'peculiarly memorable and emotional quality' to her final weeks at school.[29] She returned to live in Buxton at the end of 1911, just before her 18th birthday.

How did Vera's education shape her character and aspirations? St Monica's reinforced her desire to pursue a literary career, challenged her Anglican beliefs and began her lifelong feminism. Exposure to different possibilities of

Vera as Madonna in 'Eager Heart', 1911. (*SC*)

womanhood and the aspirations of moderate Edwardian feminism led Vera to begin identifying her dissatisfaction with the limited role offered to most women of her social class and to recognise the opportunities denied to women like her mother.

St Monica's also turned Vera into, as she described in her memoir, a 'mentally voracious young woman'. Idealistic and intellectually ambitious all her life, school inspired Vera's belief that a necessary desire to think deeply 'must be induced before the power [of education] is developed' and that 'most people, whether men or women, wish above all else to be comfortable, and thought is a pre-eminently uncomfortable process'.[30]

But spending four years away from Buxton during term time alienated Vera from her family and social acquaintances who she now regarded as philistine.

Her sense of alienation was not helped by an air of intellectual superiority and a voice cultivated through elocution lessons to remove any trace of the regional accent Arthur and some of her Buxton acquaintances had. Vera saw herself as exceptionally gifted and ambitious, a perception reinforced by being constantly held up as an example by her teachers.

Years later, Vera would present the Grange in *Not Without Honour* as second-rate, uninspiring and snobbish. She was equally unflattering in *Testament of Youth*, reporting she did not make friends and was bullied by older girls who regaled her with graphic details of sex. She dismissed her Buxton peers:

> ...most were local; in consequence the class-room competition was practically non-existent...:at the age of twelve, I was already preening the gay feathers of my youthful conceit in one of the top forms, where the dull, coltish girls of sixteen and seventeen so persistently treated me as a prodigy that I soon lost such small ability as I had possessed to estimate my modest achievements at their true and limited worth.[31]

Vera's dismissal of 'dull and coltish' local girls was off the mark. Other young middle-class women in Buxton also had an enlightened education at a prestigious school, including pupils from the Grange who went to MHSG and WHSG.[32] Nor was Vera the only young middle-class woman in Buxton wanting more than a provincial future. For example, Carrie Morrison, who lived near the Brittains, was educated in Germany, followed by MHSG in 1904 and then Cambridge University, before becoming England's first woman solicitor in 1922. Vera's apparent ignorance that such women even existed in Buxton had the unfortunate effect of reinforcing her alienation.

Testament of Youth portrays Vera's determination to escape as soon as she could:

> Once I went away to school, and learnt... what far countries of loveliness, and learning, and discovery...lay beyond those solid provincial walls which enclosed the stuffiness of complacent bourgeoisdom... my discontent kindled until I determined somehow to break through them to the paradise of sweetness and light which I firmly believed awaited me in the south.[33]

This determination, and her assertion that 'desire for a less restricted existence and future had become an obsession', were far from as immediate or clearcut as this suggests. She had a vague desire to be a writer but her diary does not mention university until spring 1913. In the meantime, Vera would enjoy life as a provincial debutante, make the most of Buxton's fashionable amenities and develop interests she was to enjoy all her life.

Chapter Three

'That Other Side of Myself, The Frivolity I Hold So Dear'

Life As A Provincial Debutante

'Miss Brittain wore a lovely gown of canary satin charmeuse'

Seven years after Mrs Harrison and her husband hosted the royal lunch at St Ann's Hotel, she sat at the side of the ballroom of the luxurious Buxton Hydro, waiting for the season's most prestigious event, the High Peak Hunt New Year ball, to begin. With its ornate decorated ceilings, gigantic chandeliers, exquisite stained-glass scenes from Shakespeare and, unusually, a

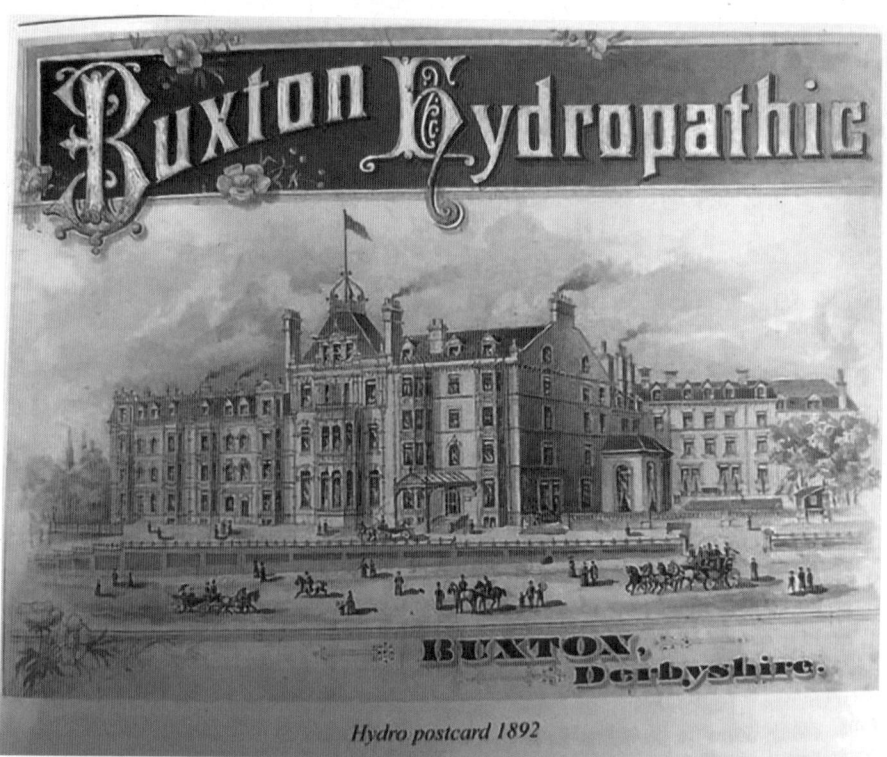

Buxton Hydro, early 1900s.

fully sprung dance floor, the ballroom was just one attraction which enabled the 260-bedroom Hydro to rival the Empire hotel for lavish opulence and the most modern facilities. Occupying a huge site overlooking the Gardens, it hosted celebrities such as D.H. Lawrence, W.S. Gilbert (of Gilbert and Sullivan operetta fame), the suffragette Emeline Pankhurst, society hostess Ottoline Morrell, and over 60 very wealthy permanent guests.[1] And, unlike Buxton's other luxury establishments, the Hydro boasted the most up to date water treatments, sporting facilities, its own orchestra and one of the most imaginative entertainment programmes in Buxton.

Mrs Harrison admired the Hydro's inordinately expensive London furniture and stylish decor, its electric lighting and the latest American elevators, hot-water radiators, and bathroom flushing systems. It was a far cry from the elegant but crumbling Georgian facilities of St Ann's which she and John Harrison had leased from the Devonshire Estate since the death of its previous proprietor, John's father. Although Buxton was commercially buoyant enough to support many upmarket hotels, having to compete with the privately owned Hydro and Empire involved John Harrison in endless wrangling with the Estate about repairs and updating facilities. In 1912, the drains and windows would require attention, and the Devonshires' Buxton manager was asking for £5 a year to be added to the rent. Even getting the Estate to sweep the ceiling of the Colonnade was a battle.[2]

Mabel Ellinger leant over to Mrs Harrison and pointed out her young neighbour. On the other side of the vast ballroom, a petite, dark-haired, strikingly

St Ann's Hotel, early 1900s. (*PtP*)

attractive young woman with beautiful hazel eyes was surrounded by men asking her to add their names to her dance card. For some imperceptible reason, Mrs Harrison felt an immediate affinity with this interesting-looking girl and looked forward to meeting her.³

Unaware of the woman regarding her, Vera had already decided that none of her dance partners looked especially interesting but certainly did not like the idea of having to sit out a dance or be reduced to dancing with another girl.⁴ She was beginning to realise men found her attractive and was pleased with her flattering debutante photograph portraits from one of Buxton's most fashionable studios.

One of Vera's formal debutante portraits, 1912. (*McM*)

She was less enamoured with the standard debutante costume of white and blue satin with pearls. Still, with her father's eighteenth birthday present of £30 (about £3,800 today) and the news she would now receive this amount as an annual dress allowance, Vera would soon be able to hold her own amongst the glittering fashionable gowns on display.

A young woman's 'coming out' ball was a girl's social baptism into a life as a debutante, the main route to securing a marriage proposal: as E.M.Delafield observed, 'if a girl was neither married or engaged by the end of her third season, it was usually said, discreetly, amongst her mother's acquaintances, that no-one had asked her'.⁵ The middle-class marriage business was very competitive: there was a surplus of women in 1911, and of every 1,000, 579 were married, 119 widowed and 302 unmarried.⁶

The oppressiveness of being an Edwardian provincial debutante was a popular theme in a burgeoning market for autobiographical feminist fiction in the 1920s and 1930s. *The Crowded Street* by Winifred Holtby, published in 1923, portrays the humiliation of Muriel Hammond who fails to secure dances, let alone a marriage proposal. Typical of the genre was the cynical stance Vera took in her Buxton novel, *Not without Honour*:

> It was for this, and for endless repetitions of this, that she was compelled to give up her dreams of freedom and independence for the ocean-like expanse of the smooth floor reflecting the garish yellowness of the immense chandeliers.⁷

Buxton Hydro ballroom.

In a similar vein, *Testament of Youth* singled out Buxton's society balls for criticism. Dance partners were 'physically boisterous and conversationally inept' and the occasions themselves were:

> ...by no means the mere gay function that they seemed: they were supposed to test out the marriageable qualities of the young women on the basis of their popularity as dancing partners, and were therefore attended by numerous competitive chaperones who watched the proceedings with ...apprehension and anxiety. Judging from the inferiority-complex permanently implanted in one or two of my contemporaries ...I am inclined to believe that provincial dances are responsible for more misery than any other commonplace experience.[8]

In this telling, such events were just one aspect of an 'utterly futile' existence:

> I went to more dances, paid calls, skated and tobogganed, played a good deal of Bridge and a great deal of tennis and golf, had music lessons and acted in amateur theatricals ....I passed my days in all those conventional pursuits with which the leisured young woman of every generation has endeavoured to fill the time that she is not qualified to use. Even my persevering attempts to follow...the intricacies of Home Rule and the Welsh Disestablishment through the columns of The Times gradually slackened and ceased for lack of external encouragement.[9]

Written many years after Vera had left Buxton, these jaded narratives erased all the youthful exuberance and palpable enjoyment that run through her diary. Dancing was one of young Vera Brittain's favourite pastimes, a pleasure embellished by poring with her mother over the gushing reviews of society balls in the local newspapers. The 1913 New Year Hunt Ball at the Hydro, for example, garnered three columns by 'our lady correspondent' on the front page of the *Advertiser*. As well as listing the 230 guests and detailing every festoon, flower arrangement and plant, the supper menu and 'charming music' programme, our lady correspondent enthused at length about the dresses. Sometimes she went overboard with flattery. On this occasion, 'the beaded fabrics, so much the rage in Paris, were in great evidence'… 'Miss Lowe was a fairy-tale vision in crystal embroidered white tulle over white satin…while her pretty flaxen hair was encircled by a filet of silver'. Vera would have been disappointed with her cursory mention ('Miss Brittain's dance frock was of pale blue ninon over satin') but happier three days later with the *Herald*'s report of another ball where 'Miss Brittain wore a lovely gown of canary satin chameuse with gold and jewelled embroidery over which was most gracefully draped sky-blue ninon'. A year later, Vera was again thrilled to see herself mentioned:

> Tuesday January 13th, 1914
> We bought a Herald this afternoon in which both our dresses for the Cottage Hospital Ball were described. Mother's was called 'a superb toilet' & mine 'ultra-fashionable'!

New Year 1913 began with a ball at Cold Springs, the home of Vera's wealthy friends the Garnetts. As usual, women outnumbered men and Vera relished being in demand:

> Wednesday January 1st, 1913
> Strictly speaking I did not begin the New Year Day when I got up this morning, but before I went to bed…I don't know why I enjoyed it so much, except that I suppose that it is gratifying when there are too many girls at a dance, never to have to dance with girls or sit out.

Two days later, Vera enjoyed herself again, at the Cottage Hospital Ball at the Peak Hydro:

> …9 till 2 – but it was till 3.0 for me! I am really beginning to love dancing for dancing's sake. I danced every one, including three extras & could have gone on for hours.

'That Other Side of Myself, The Frivolity I Hold So Dear'   37

Palace Hotel, Buxton, early 1900s. (*PtP*)

Depending on the size of the host's residence, 'At Home' dances would typically have between 20 and 40 guests, while balls at the Hydro often had over 200 guests. At those, Vera sometimes enjoyed watching a conjuror or play cards between dances, while Edward and his friend Maurice Ellinger made a bee line for the billiards table.

Such events were not merely opportunities for young people to meet, for women to show off their latest gowns or, as Vera rhapsodised, to enjoy dancing for its own exhilarating sake. Sponsored by wealthy residents or organisations like the Hunt, dances also raised funds for charities and hospitals. The Brittains' own dance was at the Palace Hotel on Tuesday, 7 January 1913.[10]

Vera reported that 'a most jolly party of seven', including Edith's sister Lillie and her husband, left Melrose in two taxis:

Although I was in the not-altogether-enviable position of hostess – one-dance-to-each sort of thing – I managed to get 4 dances & supper with Ernest & and all my other partners were very nice. I did enjoy it – & got quite a reputation for finding sitting-out places; I also tried Turkey Trots and things much to the amusement of some of the company. Douglas Spafford & I got out on to the balcony on the top landing & had a good view of Buxton lighted up; if I don't catch something I ought to!

Mother looked lovely …There was not a dress to touch it in the whole room; it was mauve and white lace with electric blue draperies and a tinsel ninon draped sash…Mrs E had on a dress much too young for her but looked nice all the same…Mine I believe was quite pretty, rather a deep sky blue statin with a bit of silver on the bodice, & white panniers filled with lace….

But here I am writing at a quarter to 4.00 and ought to be in bed. I can only say that if all enjoyed the dance as much as I did – & I believe most of them did – it was a great success.

At the Garnetts' sponsored ball at the Hydro on 21 December 1913, Vera wore 'a primrose coloured gown with a deep blue waistband …& a circlet of bright blue beads over my forehead. I don't know when I have appeared to look so nice to myself. I danced every dance including the Boston, an Americanised waltz…Daisy Whitehead disapproved; I'm sure she thinks I am dreadfully fast! The whole affair was a great success'.

Girls were chaperoned to ensure propriety, and to help organise the filling of dance cards. When Edith or her brother Edward did not accompany Vera, her neighbour Mabel Ellinger stood in:

Friday 10th January 1914
I joined Mrs. Ellinger's party [of eight girls and five men]. I went over to dinner …and found Mrs. Ellinger and Dorothy in various stages of undress. Mrs Bagnell and Beryl Arrowsmith came soon after into the bedroom which seemed to be a sort of reception room for the occasion. Mrs Ellinger's dress was simply lovely, a nicer one than I have ever seen, pink & blue charmeuse with a great deal of shadow lace and silver gauze; quite impossible to describe…..Mrs E worked like a Trojan & got all our programmes filled. I danced with very few people I knew. Mr Maxwell is a good dancer and Mr Johnson danced beautifully. He also complimented me on mine, which was…quite a shock. I enjoyed myself immensely; doubtless because I didn't know many of my partners; for all the abominable chancers & stupid talkers, the Buxton men take the bun…Some of the dresses were beautiful, but I liked none so well as Mrs Ellinger's…We got home at 5.0 and Mr Maxwell came up the drive with me. I felt most fresh and not at all sleepy.

The next morning, Vera got up at the usual time and then slept all afternoon. A few days later, 'quite the nicest [ball] of the season' was in Corbar Hall, one of Buxton's grandest houses:

Thursday January 15th, 1914
[The Bowens] have just bought the place & done it all up on a very costly scale, & the dance in elegance & ornateness certainly matched the house.

Corbar Hall, early 1900s. (*PtP*)

> Everything was beautifully done; the supper was arranged by Parkers of Manchester... we danced in two rooms which were opened to the hall by folding doors, and the hall itself. There was a big smoke room & refreshments were placed in the drawing room. The chief sitting out place was the conservatory where there were all sorts of tall plants hiding the seats, & which was quite cool... There were about 44 people there... a much more interesting set of people came than usual... Even Edward liked it.[11]

'I looked quite a dream!'

The popular Edwardian ritual of promenades was another target for 1920s and 1930s feminist fiction, and Vera capitalised on her Buxton experience:

> she knew that her father and mother were looking Derrick [Edward] and herself up and down with complacent appreciation, occasionally turning aside to bow with satisfied smiles to an acquaintance, as if crying out, 'See what we've accomplished!' to all beholders...[S]he objected intensely to her position as a family exhibit... Above all, she objected to her white coat and skirt, and the ingenuous hat of white muslin with wired bows that made her feel like a dressed up doll.[12]

Again, Vera's diary tells a rather different story:

> I put on my new white serge and the Paris hat with the white tulle bows, white shoes & stockings & low necked blouse and looked quite a dream. The people in the Gardens after Church stared like billy-oh.

Genteel elegant Buxton offered many locations for Vera to be admired for her striking appearance, and her diary has many references to her enjoyment of it:

> I sat in the Gardens all morning. The day was most lovely & I was amused to see everyone doing their best to look fascinating in their best Sunday clothes. I had on my little ecru hand-embroidered lawn dress, & black hat with the pink roses & aeroplane-like tulle wings. Mother said I looked most smart.

Vera dressed for promenade, 1913. (*McM*)

On another occasion:

> Sunday, June 1st 1913
> In my black pedal hat with veiled pink rows of big tulle bows at the back, [I] sallied off to St John's [church]… I think my rather extraordinary hat encouraged a few glances.

Sartorial standards in middle-class Edwardian Buxton were high, and women were expected to shine for 'At Home' bridge parties and musical evenings, sitting or strolling in the Gardens, receiving and visiting neighbours, at the theatre and balls, even for a trip down to the shops. Different activities required different costumes; Vera refers, for example, to putting on 'my calling attire'. She thought Buxton too conservative, recording that 'it needs a little courage to be really chic here' but this did not stop her making a lot of effort, an interest she shared with her elegant mother.

Like her fictional alter ego, Christine Merrivale, Vera regarded herself as pretty. She adored clothes, reporting often, at length and with great relish, her enjoyment of being admired for the fabrics, styles and accessories of her many outfits. She especially liked hats ('all headgear seems to suit me without difficulty')

Broad Walk, early 1900s. (*PtP*)

and had strong opinions on what was eye-catching yet also 'appropriate', using her diary to disapprove of women who looked 'dowdy', 'vulgar' or 'fast'.

Vera seems to have had an enormous wardrobe. With an evening dress costing about £3, Vera described her annual dress allowance of £30 (about £3,800 today, a sum equivalent in 1913 to a cook's yearly wage and significantly more than a housemaid's £20) as 'tiny', lamenting 'how fast it seems to disappear'. Edith supplemented this with a quarterly allowance for 'ribbons etc' of 15/- (75p, about £60 today). Arthur added numerous gifts, including £50 for her 21st birthday, a semi-skilled worker's annual income in 1913 (about £5,000 today). A few months later:

> Sunday March 22nd, 1913
> Quite an uneventful & harmless day except that Daddy has given me another £50 as an Easter present, just because I said I could not afford as good a quality material for a new coat as he wanted me to have.

Both Vera and Edith enjoyed replenishing their extensive wardrobes in London shops. Travelling from Buxton by train, they stayed at the Ladies' Constitutional Club in Kensington and divided their time between shops, afternoon tea and the theatre. From five enthusiastic pages in Vera's diary:

March 31st/April 1st, 1913
After lunch …we sallied forth to begin our shopping…we had our grey coats and skirts fitted (mother's…a Donegal – mine a pretty grey) at Dunn's. Next we bought my brown jersey – a sort of golden dead-leaf colour and after some little trouble we managed to match it with a frieze for the skirt …. [next day] After a hasty lunch…we were fitted at Josephine's. Mother's silk costume & purple & blue summer dress seem to be beginning very well. After some bargaining …I persuaded [the dressmaker] to do me up a pink evening dress for £3–3 – to be draped with pink ninon [a lightweight sheer fabric] under some purply-pink flowers, a little shadow lace and a sash of deep purple velvet with an embroidered end…Mother wasn't very keen on my white whipcord material … I think it will turn out quite well & the little pleats at the top of the skirt will suit my thin person!

A visit to an expensive milliners produced numerous hats, followed by the theatre for 'Open Windows' by A.S. Mason which Vera described as '….a serious society story in which, after many dramatic moments I felt sad…but not the bitter sadness that spoils life, more the kind that sanctifies it'. The next day produced five pairs of shoes…. 'a very good patent pair with ribbon laces, patent indoor-outdoor shoes, lovely white suede two-button shoes, white tennis shoes & some pink evening shoes to go with my new dress'.

A Buxton dressmaker, Mrs Fowler, the wife of a quarryman in the working-class village of Fairfield, just over a mile from Buxton, supplemented Vera's extensive wardrobe:

May 4th, 1913
We went to see how Mrs Fowler was getting on with the last few of my summer garments… she sent up my linen shirts after dinner; she really is clever, they are beautifully cut & made.

A vain young woman like Vera sometimes felt vulnerable about her appearance. In the 1911 school holidays she had a lot of dentistry, travelling to 'our dear old dentist, Mr Elmitt' in her birthplace Newcastle-under-Lyme. The journey took all day, first to Leek with her father in the motor, and then by train. Two years later, Vera had more extensive dental work; one visit left her face badly bruised and she was unable to do anything all day for two days ('a dreary life', she wrote in her diary). A few months later, Mr Elmitt gave Vera some bad news:

'That Other Side of Myself, The Frivolity I Hold So Dear'   43

> Friday 13th June 1913
> …oh how I dread a dentistry excursion. And not without reason! He was honest enough not to say glowing things about my teeth & in all probability I can be prepared to have them all out before many years are over… now I have simply dozens to be stopped [filled], fortunately with porcelain, so it is to be hoped my appearance won't be spoiled for the present. Of course several more visits have to be paid…I am most distressed; it seems such a shame when all my teeth to all appearances look so strong & nice, but evidently they are too good to be true.

With each filling costing fifteen shillings (75p) in 1911, and a full set of dentures £7 (about £550 today), only the wealthiest could afford dentists. Far more concerned with the effects on her appearance than the cost, Vera reflected 'I suppose it is better than having to wear glasses, or to be deaf or have a bad complexion, but it is very annoying – this treasured beauty, only skin deep!' She was pleased to report a few weeks later that the first 'stoppings' had not hurt as much as she feared, and the porcelain looked better than her own teeth.

'From the moment I came on everything simply *romped*'

Buxton's lively social season enabled Vera to indulge an interest in amateur dramatics that began at St Monica's. In March 1913, Mrs Ellinger recommended her for a part in 'Amazons' at the Opera House: 'they want someone small, slight & good-looking & the pleasure of a small singing voice'. Vera agreed she did indeed have those qualities but worried she was 'really not much good'.

Joining a cast from Buxton and Manchester, she described the Victorian romantic farce, written in 1893 by Arthur Wing Pinero, as 'screamingly funny'. She loved its defiant story of three daughters of an aristocratic family brought up in private as male heirs and in public as girls turned traditional ideas of womanhood on their head. In 1913 it was revived in London and became popular in the provinces.

After her father's birthday on 6 April, followed by church at Burbage, Vera went to the Ellingers' to practise songs:

> Coming up their drive I thought Mr and Mrs Ellinger must be having words but it turned out they were loudly rehearsing 'The Twelve Pound Look' [this play by J.M. Barrie was the curtain raiser]. After dinner, rehearsing, rehearsing, rehearsing! In the evening, we three Amazons agreed to act in our boys' clothes so as to get used to them, I had an awful performance getting them on at home, both Nora and Margaret [the house

and parlourmaids] helped me… we ransacked Edward's bedroom for a soft shirt, golf stockings and braces; finally…I was rigged out. I walked along Spring Gardens with my long coat over the top, looking like a bolster and keeping in all the dark corners lest anything of my male attire should be visible. The things fit very well & look awfully nice but I was horribly conscious of my legs all the time, especially in Edward's thick golf stockings! It is certainly lucky I am so thin![13]

Vera recorded scornfully that her school friend Stella disapproved strongly of this enjoyable foray into boys' clothes. The next day, she enjoyed rehearsing her songs:

Miss Sharp accompanied my songs on the guitar which Mr Spafford lent. Instead of 'When maiden loves' she has found me a darling little song in quite a low key; an unpublished fragment by Beethoven which is much easier to sing…the guitar is a beautiful tone & sounds very well.

There is an infectious energy in Vera's long reports, especially of rehearsals in Manchester to which she travelled by train with the rest of the Buxton cast. As well as a seemingly insatiable desire for praise, Vera was obsessed with trying to learn from everything she did, and to throw herself enthusiastically into new experiences. She also had an impressive determination to conquer feelings of

Opera House, early 1900s. (*PtP*)

being daunted or inadequate, trying not to think about opening night, afraid of 'shivering with stage fright' and overcoming fear by immersing herself in rehearsals ('I am unable to think of anything else'). Vera noted her first time in a 'real theatre', with 'real dressing rooms', with 'a tremendous lot of changing to do' and only one and a half minutes to get into her evening dress at the end. She enjoyed the novelty of showing a 'lot of leg', noting approvingly 'my legs are nice ones!' Despite a difficult dress rehearsal ('as they are supposed to be') and despite her own terrible stage fright, the first night went down a storm:

> *The* first night & my first appearance on any stage. Mr Pelter said 'Splendid, Miss Brittain, excellent' but I don't think I believed him, even though Mr & Mrs Ellinger & Maurice & others repeated it… I drove back with the family who called for me at the stage door; they seemed very bucked up with the whole performance & pleased with me; Daddy said he had laughed till he cried. The audience, which started being only mildly amused, were quite hysterical by the end.[14]

The 'house went wild' on the following night, especially over the 'simply ripping' and 'gorgeous' third act:

> Saturday April 13th, 1913
> Late as it is (3 o clock) I must before I go to bed, write about our second, our best, our splendid night! Once more I was free from nervousness, trusting implicitly in my lucky year, my lucky year. From the moment I came on everything simply *romped*. I enjoyed every moment (except the 1st song) from beginning to end… Mr Pelter asked me if I would come to supper following the play, at the Hydro. I didn't know what sort of thing it would be, this being my first appearance, but instead of possessing Mother's shrinking from the unusual, I possess a love to find out the unknown & accepted purely for the experience. I went to the Hydro … & while I was tidying in the cloakroom Mrs Ellinger simply raved about my frock, to my great satisfaction. Well, as for enjoying the supper – I simply *loved* it & haven't laughed so much for ages.

An extremely long, exuberant diary entry describes the after-dinner speeches from 'our joyous assembly' ('extremely witty and left me in fits the whole time'). Although Vera and some other young women did not speak, and despite wanting to, she 'judged it best to be low throughout my first appearance'. In one of many diary references to her high spirits, Vera got up the next day for breakfast 'feeling as fresh as a daisy; excitement for me is a wonderful tonic'.

In socially segregated Buxton, it seems that amateur drama was sometimes organised on class lines: Vera reports that 'the tradespeople set' in the company put on a performance of 'Liberty Hall', and 'some found the difficulty of pretending they had no accent rather too much for them'.[15]

A month later, Vera took part in another form of theatre, this time a religious tableau at the local Board school. Known colloquially as a 'pictures-in-dumb' show, these popular entertainments often depicted religious or mythological scenes:

> Saturday May 31st, 1913
> I was not too delighted but I could not very well get out of it as I promised Miss Mothersill to act next time she wanted anyone. The first scene represented a little missionary child convert inducing several of her companions to come & look at a sacred picture-book. Meanwhile, 'The Sower went forth sowing' went on at the back. Next tableau showed me, the only white person…at the dispensary. First I bind up an arm, then I rub a rheumatic knee, then I bandage someone's eyes & and then rush off to an urgent call…The Rev. Mr Dicker, who came in towards the end, remarked 'Yes, there's something very touching about that picture, very touching'. *I* was touched with inward hysterics.

Criticising the dubious missionary message and its sentimental depiction and feeling 'quite a hypocrite for taking part', Vera was thrilled that children in the show seemed to find her fascinating:

> Wednesday June 11th, 1913
> The amusing-serious entertainment came off – & for this first time, actually without mishap! As the missionary lady I felt inordinately good – & consequently quite incongruous… Giving our dispensary things, tending the sick, comforting the widows (& inspecting their sewing!) & helping the neglected did not move me, I know, because they are mission things …I remain of the same opinion – i.e. that most missions do more harm than good. No, it is simply that the fundamental springs of love & pity & gentleness towards all the world are stirred by these almost humorous representations… the compliments showered on me were simply over-whelming.

Proclaiming 'I love acting so much', Vera took a small part in 'Raffles' a year later, performed over two nights in aid of the Devonshire Hospital. There were hopes the duke of Devonshire would attend. It was 'very thrilling; people fling themselves about & try to commit suicide indiscriminately'. Following her successful first night, a Sunday promenade was an opportunity to bask in praise:

> Sunday June 21st June 1914
> The service at St John's was dull & the place crowded. I had my new pale blue coat & skirt on so I escaped... into the Gardens, where I had the time of my life...crowds of people came up & congratulated me on the performance, my appearance, my clothes etc. I being the centre of the circle only had to smile sweetly & say "I'm so glad you liked it" – whatever "it" might be.

Buxton offered residents and visitors many opportunities to see opera, music, musical comedies and popular plays by amateur groups and professional companies. Train services to London and Manchester widened the choice of cultural events. These included a 'great day to-day, impossible to describe adequately', going with Edith to Manchester for lunch at the Midland Hotel with neighbours from Macclesfield days, before being enchanted with portraits by Reynolds, Leighton and the pre-Raphaelites at the art gallery. Later they went to the 'simply packed' Free Trade Hall (Vera offers an extremely unflattering account of the ugly, badly dressed 'Lancashire men & women') for a 'simply glorious' concert conducted by Sir Henry Wood. Vera's diary describes every piece of music and the deep emotions it stirred.

'The energetic twitching of my athletic limbs drove me... out of doors for an afternoon of golf or tennis'

Frequent, extremely detailed diary entries indicate that Vera played and watched a phenomenal amount of tennis. In 1911, she and Edward went every day to Buxton's now-famous annual tournament in the Gardens, in which Edward competed in the Gentlemen's Singles Handicap. As well as tennis parties on the courts of her wealthier Buxton acquaintances, Vera was a member of a private club. She was 'simply longing' to get into the club team; 'I have played so much & I think not badly, & yet never had the good fortune to actually win anything'.

Vera and friends at tennis, c.1913. (*SC*)

Vera also enjoyed a great deal of golf with her mother, Edward and friends at the Burbage Club which had a popular women's section, and where the duke of Devonshire sometimes played. Although Vera was, by her own account, not very good at golf, it showed her persistence in trying to mask things she found difficult and making strenuous efforts to improve.

In the long winter months, the closing of Manchester Road to make a fast, often raucous run sometimes tempted Vera onto a sledge:

Monday January 13th, 1913
Too cold for words! There was about a foot of snow on the ground and of course grand tobogganing & some ski-ing. There was a mist all over the lower part of the town this morning & I thought it would be a horrible day but walking up to the toboggan-runs I walked out of the mist & and there were all the hill peaks bright & glittering. It was glorious on the track & though I am not a wildly keen tobogganer like the natives, I enjoyed it. The hills all round were beautiful as Purity, but also as cold as Purity without the warmth of Love!

Vera and Edward dressed for tennis c.1912/1913. (*SC*)

'That Other Side of Myself, The Frivolity I Hold So Dear' 49

Vera tobogganing with the Garnetts c1912 (lefthand sledge with Jerry Garnett at the front, and his sister Nancy on the other). Vera was pleased to see this photograph published in the *Manchester Evening News*. (*MCM*)

As for the civic and philanthropic duties expected of middle-class women, Vera did not mind enjoyable fund-raising activities like amateur dramatics, concerts, sponsored balls and playing piano to entertain patients at the Devonshire hospital. She was much less keen on accompanying Edith on charity visits to poor residents in Burbage, sewing babies' frocks for her mother and Mrs Ellingers' overseas missions (Edith's was in Guinea), and helping at fetes in the Gardens to raise money for Burbage church.

But for all Vera's evident enjoyment of debutante life, it was never going to be enough. In 1913, Mrs Harrison secured one of Oxford's most senior academics for the university 'extension' lecture programme she organised in Buxton and encouraged Vera and Edith to attend. This was a turning point in Vera's fortunes, sparking her ambition to study at Oxford. Over the next year, the idealism which she said formed one half of her 'divided spirit' would take precedence over 'the other side of myself, the frivolity I hold so dear'.[16]

Chapter Four

'Oxford! What It Doesn't Call Up To Mind!'
Escape to Somerville College

'Unintellectual Buxton all over!'

On 19 February 1913, Vera sat by the fire in the morning room going over the notes about the history of trades unionism she made that morning in Buxton's Free Library. Having listened for years to Arthur's trenchant opposition to unions, she was keen to hear what John Marriott, the University of Oxford lecturer teaching a six-week course in social history at Buxton town hall, might have to say on the subject that evening.

Vera and her mother had chosen a dance over Marriott's first lecture. At the second, she lambasted the poor attendance:

> Wednesday January 22nd, 1913
> I went with Mother this evening to...'The Problems of Wealth and Poverty'... It was extremely interesting, & I was very glad of the lessons I had on the subject in my last term at St. Monica's. It was dreadfully badly attended – unintellectual Buxton all over... Most of the questions asked were stupid; no women asked any or else I would soon have followed suit, with a large risk of being squashed. The lecturer is a big fair man, somewhat like the Duke of Devonshire.

Students had the option of writing essays and having them assessed. Marriott's feedback on Vera's first essay re-ignited her enthusiasm for learning:

> Wednesday February 5th, 1913
> I asked for my essay back, somewhat in fear & trembling as I knew how sarcastic he could be...To my surprise he said 'Is that *yours*? It's a *very* good essay indeed' ...he had given me 'A-' at the end & had written... 'This is an *excellent* piece of work. You have made your points very clearly & your criticism is sober & to the point. I hope you will write regularly.' I seemed as indifferent as I could manage though the inward elation was at bursting point!... The smallest intellectual success always brings back

to me the longing for the harder, less comfortable but more idealistic life that I would choose – that I *do* choose, though circumstances seem to withhold it. The smartest clothes I know I possess – the prettiness which people say is mine – what satisfaction can they give…compared with the slightest of intellectual achievements?

Two weeks later, while Vera sat by the fire, John Ransome Marriott was travelling by train from Oxford for his third Buxton lecture. As a dyed-in-the-wool Conservative, Marriott was no fan of organised labour; in fact, he had written several inflammatory articles in opposition to them which he knew had antagonised colleagues at Oxford. Nonetheless, as an experienced historian, he found it a fascinating subject. While he did not always manage to rein in his own strong views, being provocative could sometimes spark a reaction from unresponsive students. As the train powered over the spectacular viaduct at Monsal Head and through the dramatic Chee Gorge, Marriott pondered how to liven up his Buxton class. At his second lecture two weeks earlier, he had informed them, rather irritably, that 'Buxton did not seem particularly inquisitive'. The poor acoustics of the large first floor meeting room at the town hall did not help. Marriott wondered if it was his teaching style: at the age of 53 he was hardly a novice but had come to realise his working-class students found him 'obscurantist and reactionary'. Marriott tried to avoid the Liberal strongholds of northern industrial towns and did better with middle-class audiences. He had, as he put it, become 'fairly familiar with most of the cathedral class of Southern England'.[1]

John Ransome Marriott, 1917. (*NPG*)

When Vera met John Marriott in 1913, he had been 'Secretary of the Oxford Delegacy for the Extension of Teaching Beyond the Limits of the University' for eighteen years, and an 'extension' lecturer since the movement was founded in in 1878.[2] He had become its most prolific lecturer, doing hundreds all round Britain whilst also teaching students at Oxford. Sometimes Marriott taught abroad: in Dresden, 400 attended one of his lectures, 'including the Crown Prince and many eminent men'.³ In 1913, the schedule that included Buxton also took him by train from Oxford to Alderley Edge, Preston, Wrexham, Bradford, and Denbigh.⁴

Marriott's frustration with Buxton had been ameliorated by a small, elegantly dressed young woman with shining eyes who attended his lectures with her mother. Returning her excellent first essay, Marriott had praised the quality of Vera's writing and ability to construct an argument. Seeing her barely concealed delight and surprise, Marriott was reminded, yet again, how rewarding adult education could be; you just needed one lively, bright student to compensate for the less-than-enthusiastic rest!

After waiting a few minutes at Millers' Dale for the branch line connection, Marriott's train pulled into Buxton's London-Midland station. Following his lecture, he would stay the night with Mrs Harrison and her husband; one of the perks of being an extension lecturer was the hospitality of enthusiastic organisers and students. Over the next few weeks, John Marriott would not only get to know Vera and her family; he would also be pivotal in her decision to apply to study at Oxford.

'To make all who come within its influence fuller and better and nobler.'

Buxton's extension lectures were part of a nationwide project to create a more 'open' Oxford in which the university adjusted 'arrangements to the various needs of the different classes of the community…without losing any part of their present dignity and usefulness'.⁵ It was a radical proposition for an elite university to champion liberal education for adults in provincial towns with little or no formal intellectual training but was not the first such initiative. In the 1860s, some towns had 'Ladies' Educational Associations' which arranged 'Lectures for Ladies' and, if numbers warranted it, engaged a peripatetic lecturer from universities such as Leeds, Durham and Manchester.⁶

In 1878, Oxford joined the universities of London and Cambridge in the 'University Extension Movement' and soon became the main provider. It was a product of the train age: by 1885, 6,000 students around Britain were being taught by train-travelling Oxford academics. Just four years later, 20,000 were attending 192 courses which, depending on local interest, might be in history, political economy, literature, arts and natural science. By the early 1900s, there were 140 centres from Devon to Cumbria, Buxton to Bath, Carlisle to Chester, in Rotherham and other northern industrial towns, from Carlisle to Chester. There were many more provincial students than those in residence at Oxford. In 1913, Vera's former hometown Macclesfield was also running lectures.

'Oxford! What It Doesn't Call Up To Mind!' 53

After years of coaching the sons of the gentry and aristocracy in history, John Marriott shared the almost missionary-like enthusiasm of his dynamic, forward-thinking predecessor, M.E. Sadler, who founded Oxford's extension movement and ran the Delegacy for seventeen years before becoming vice-chancellor at Leeds. Sadler encouraged Marriott to take it over in 1895 and he was to run it for 25 years. Oxford's Extension Board for 1912–1913 reported its aim:

> …not merely to instruct, merely to add to the sum of human knowledge, but through the enlargement of the mind to reach on to the enrichment of the character, to make all who come within its influence fuller and better and nobler than they might have been otherwise…within the limits of each community there should be a centre round which the intellectual and higher life of that locality can flourish.[7]

Each town had an organising committee to raise enough from fees and subscriptions to cover the cost of each six-week course which had to cover the lecturer's train fares and the cost of transporting wooden crates of books by train from Oxford for students to use in their essays.[8] Success required an enthusiastic local organiser and committee who understood the complexities of teaching adults with diverse motivations and abilities, were willing to ask prospective students about topics of interest, could raise money from donations, whole-course subscriptions and on-the-day tickets, send out pre-lecture reading lists and preparation tasks, and arrange overnight accommodation for lecturers in the homes of committee members and students. In Buxton, Mrs Harrison's committee included two shopkeepers, Vera's neighbour Mabel Ellinger, and Dr Cox (one of the directors of the Devonshire Hospital), whose wife and daughter Eugenie attended the lectures. The *Buxton Advertiser* played its part in promoting their broader civic relevance by publishing a summary of each lecture on the front page.

Testament of Youth complains that 'neither the local Free library nor the little collection of schoolbooks on my bedroom shelves contained any relevant works'. Her diary is rather different, reporting enjoyable mornings researching and writing in the Free Library which was then housed in the town hall. Local libraries would obtain relevant books on request and Vera could also use Oxford's system for transporting books to the provinces.

The Oxford lectures were not Buxton's first attempt to offer educational and cultural opportunities to adults. Fifty years earlier, prominent trades and businessmen in Buxton had, like other towns, set up a Literary Society, followed a few months later by a Mechanics' Institute. These provided lectures and debates on philosophical, literary and scientific topics.[9] In 1856, the two societies were amalgamated as the Buxton, Fairfield and Burbage Mechanics and Literary Institute with its own library and reading room. It lasted only ten years. Forty years after its demise, Buxton ran its first extension lectures, taught by one of Oxford's most popular lecturers, Reverend Hudson Shaw, who could attract hundreds of students in northern towns like Manchester and Rochdale. His Buxton topic in 1904/1905 was 'John Ruskin'.

There is no record of who organised those first lectures, but it is possible it was Mrs Harrison. The long gap before she started them up again in January 1913 was not unusual; some centres ran for years, while others came and went. Nationally, two-thirds of attendees were women and, apart from a few successes where lectures in northern towns attracted some female millworkers, students tended to be middle-class. A few towns did attract working-class students and, for some, the lectures were transforming: in one town, a miner walked five miles to and from lectures before beginning his work underground. Workers tended to be from the skilled, unionised upper reaches of their class. A single lecture was 6d (3p, and about £2 today). In industrial towns, co-operative societies and trades unions often subsidised or paid the fees of working men (in one year, Rotherham had 400 students from the Artisans' Cooperative) but there was no such support for Buxton's un-unionised quarry workers and miners.

Vera's claim to be the 'sole essayist out of the whole town' reflected the difficulty of attracting people who attended out of general interest, those prevailed upon

Buxton Town Hall, early 1900s. The large first floor lecture room was used for debates on various topics, as well as for the Oxford lectures.

by their parents, and more serious students who wanted to do the essays and, in some centres, a final examination: schoolteachers, for example, often used extension lectures to upgrade their qualifications. By 1912, the Extension Committee at Oxford was concerned that compared to 20 years earlier, the 'ordinary' extension audience was more apathetic and fewer wanted to take examinations. Nonetheless, the committee reiterated the university's founding aim to include a whole community, where 'the enthusiasm of the tutorial group mingled with the general elements', continued.[10]

Vera loved the lectures, especially 'Mr Marriott's dramatic, intellectual & lyrical & style – I should never find anyone quite to touch it'.[11] After attending 'Chartism and Social Movements' with Arthur, she submitted another well-received essay:

Wednesday March 5th
After the lecture I was paid quite a big compliment by Mr Marriott. On returning my essay on Chartism he said 'This is really excellent. I like your work immensely…' & ended up with 'You know how to *write*; that's the secret of it,' & looked at me so kindly & quite deferentially…

'Oh! to have such a thing to dream about & look forward to. Oxford!'

The lectures were a turning point in Vera's aspirations. Following her first attendance, she was restless and irritated:

Thursday January 23rd
Edward went back to Uppingham to-day. Now the boring time begins – but I shan't let it be so this year if I can help it! Mrs Deakin called and also Gwen Spafford, who talked about nothing but her neighbours' affairs and club squabbles. Unhappy, shut up little Buxton, laying at the bottom of a basin! It seems to have the effect of making its inhabitants' minds as closed as its natural formations & it is indeed a little box of social strife. The people seem so short of something to do that the only way of making the time pass is by prattling about each other. Oh! to escape from it!

Two days later, Vera hoped fervently that her parents were serious when they announced their intention to leave Buxton:

Saturday January 25th, 1913
Mother & Daddy started talking again about moving south, & Daddy said he had practically decided we were going to!! … Daddy said he could

easily arrange to go up to the works for two days every week & be with us all the rest of the time; it is absurd to think it hardly takes any longer to get to Stoke from London than from here. I sat dreaming of a home – no matter if it be small – with a garden & a smiling warm country instead of a grey one, & as I looked out of the window I saw the sunset all red – the first colour that has broken the greyness for days, glowing like an emblem of hope in the sky!

…I took my 'Iliad' into the dining room to read but …[cried] with relief at the thought of leaving this hateful artificial place, & these cold, emotionless, unimaginative people for a softer climate, warm bright country & people who love and understand! It seems so heavenly to see an end to the dreary monotony of our existence here – strangers in a strange & cliquey land! Even as a child when I heard we were coming here I shrank from the thought & knew we should never like Buxton with its cold austerity & provincial narrow inhabitants. But I don't think we will ever realise it until we leave how dull, wearisome and unendurable has been our lives here. Perhaps to me, having just left school & my beloved south & more beloved friends … it has seemed [illegible]… but how narrow and unsatisfying it has been for all of us.

The Brittains did not leave Buxton until 1915 and if they did discuss the idea again, Vera's diary makes no mention of it. A couple of weeks later, she was back to her exuberant self after Marriott's feedback on her first essay rekindled her intellectual ambition. Mrs Harrison asked Edith if Marriott could stay at Melrose after his final lecture on 19 March and Vera had an unexpected opportunity to attend one of Oxford's 'summer meetings':

Monday March 10th
The most exciting thing has happened…I was only beginning to-day to feel that things were becoming a little monotonous when a letter came from Miss Heath Jones telling me that she & Miss Bervon had arranged to go to the great Summer Meeting …at Oxford from Aug.1st-13th & asking me to go with them! There jolly well wasn't a moment of indecision in my mind. Mother & Daddy were not only quite willing, but even seemed pleased about my getting this glorious & unique opportunity… I will go – oh! so gladly….oh! to have such a thing to dream about & look forward to. Oxford! What doesn't it call up to the mind. The greatest romance of England…the mellowed beauty of time & association – the finest lectures the world can produce – wonderful libraries and fascinating old bookshops (no small attraction to me). Oh! God have pity on my fierce excitement

and grant that it may come to pass & be even better than I dream. I feel as if I shall never sleep from excitement!

Before John Marriott and Vera walked home after his final lecture, he and Mrs Harrison discussed a different lecture topic, such as Ruskin which 'people would not be so afraid of' (the theme of Buxton's Oxford lectures in 1904/1905) and suggested a speaker Vera had heard at St Monica's. On their walk back to Melrose, Marriott told Vera he was 'disgusted with the attendance here and the badness of the room for sound'. That evening, she told him she was going to the Summer Meeting, and he suggested she try for one of the prize essays.[12] *Testament of Youth* claims that the turning point in softening Arthur Britttain's resistance to Vera going to Oxford was Marriott's support for the idea. Her detailed diary entry tells a rather different story, omitting any mention of her interest or discussion with Marriott about it: instead, the only topic of conversation was Edward's plans for Oxford and which college he should apply to.[13]

After Marriott's stay, Vera followed his advice and submitted an essay:

It's quite one thing to write the best paper in a little town like this & quite another entering for a competition open to the whole United Kingdom.... My essay comes to 23 foolscap pages in spite of care!

On 7 May Vera had 'a postcard from Oxford saying my essay had arrived & was "receiving attention" – as though it was an order for curtains or provisions!' Three weeks later, she heard she had won one of ten prize scholarships:

Oh! I didn't know I could feel so glad. The honour & glory is the great thing, the actual prize does not matter much...I often dreamed of what I should feel like if I actually got a prize...My first really public effort & success!

Arthur and Edith were thrilled. Vera was indebted to Mrs Harrison who had encouraged her to attend the lectures, obtained the necessary information from Oxford about the essays and put Vera's name forward, 'without which I could not have managed'.

'The magic spell of Oxford's beauty'

The theme for the 1913 Summer Meeting was 'The historical evolution of France and its contribution to literature, fine art, science and thought'. Students were told some classes might be delivered in French. Attended by 1,200, Michael Sadler, who was now vice-chancellor of Leeds university, gave the inaugural address to an audience of 1,200. A month earlier, he had been the main speaker at Buxton College's annual speech day. The 1913 Extension Board report praised an 'extraordinarily high level of excellence of lectures …the whole temper and tone …was happy and harmonious… and the spell which Oxford wove around them is not broken even yet'.[14]

Oxford's Summer Meetings were based on the American idea of an 'education vacation' where people from all walks of life and place came together for a couple of weeks in an inspiring location, away from the pressures of home and work, to learn about subjects quite outside their experience. In most years, over a thousand attended; for many it was their only holiday. Lecturers enjoyed the events too, and over the years, some esteemed politicians delivered the keynote address, including H.H. Asquith, Lloyd George and William Beveridge. John Marriott eulogised about the transformative effects of Summer Schools:

> What it meant for an elementary teacher from a country school, or to a Lancashire mill-hand or a collier from South Wales, to come even for a month, under the magic spell of Oxford's beauty to listen to some of the great authorities in history, science, or art, come into daily contact with men and women inspired by a similar zeal for higher education, and to exchange ideas with them, can be understood only by those, who like myself, were privileged to be their confidant, and to see the leaven briefly working.[15]

While in Oxford, Vera went to see her father's business associate, the director of Oxford University Press, and accompanied Florence Bervon and Louise Heath-Jones to dinner with John Marriott and his wife in their grand North Oxford villa. It was then that she decided to apply to study at Oxford and asked Marriott's advice about which college she should try. Ignoring his suggestion for Lady Margaret Hall, Vera decided to apply for Somerville College which was harder to get into. A preliminary interview with its principal, Emily Penrose, did not seem to be an auspicious start to Vera's plans. There is no diary report, but *Testament of Youth* paints a vivid picture of their meeting in Somerville's beautiful gardens:

> Being quite ignorant of the plain-Jane-and-no-nonsense conventions of Oxford women dons, I had carefully changed, in accordance with the sartorial habits of Buxton, into evening dress, and was wearing a flimsy lace frock under a pale blue and grey reversible satin cloak, and an unsubstantial little pair of high-heeled white suede shoes.[16]

Perhaps Vera's inappropriate dress and lack of knowledge about the 'barbed wire fence of qualifications that must be scaled for entry' led Miss Penrose to assume she was not really a serious candidate. She advised Vera to read English and not to apply for a Scholarship. But back in Buxton, Edward praised Vera's exceptional intelligence and said she should aim for a Scholarship. There were two examinations to pass. Arthur agreed to pay for a tutor in the Latin and mathematics Vera required for the Somerville entrance examination in March 1914. If successful, she would take the Oxford Senior Local examination for admission to the university in July.

Edith found the necessary tutors, and from October 1913 Vera prepared for the two examinations at Mr Lace's local 'crammer' in a large, detached villa opposite Melrose. Lace coached local boys for Sandhurst and was, according to Vera, benevolent and patient but not very imaginative. Another tutor for Latin 'repulsed' her and made her feel uncomfortable:

> How I do dislike that man. He is so indolent although he teaches well & anyhow I cannot endure people with beards, especially when they can't pronounce 'th'. Daddy calls him 'The Cheese' and his poor meek-looking wife 'The Maggott'.[17]

'Thank goodness for one more person who is not horrorstruck.'

For over ninety years, readers of *Testament of Youth*, especially women, have been inspired by what Vera called 'my battle royal' to be allowed to apply to university against her parents' wishes, and by her claim that 'I never ceased to pester [them] to send me to college'. With spirited vigour, Vera's memoir portrays her single-handed feminist revolt and determination to escape, her solitary preparation in a chilly north-west facing back room, with freezing hands and feet because her mother would not bother the maids with preparing a fire, foregoing her social life and having to spend her 'tiny' dress allowance on books. She was also:

> constantly bombarded with infuriating requests to do jumble sales, amateur dramatics and replace individuals at bridge... how strenuously each uninterrupted hour had to be fought for in the petty, busy-busy atmosphere of a pre-war provincial town.[18]

It is certainly an uplifting story, but Vera's diary suggests it is greatly exaggerated. Once Arthur and Edith got used to the idea, they supported her wholeheartedly, finding and paying for a tutor. And, given Edith's domestic assiduousness, it is very unlikely Vera suffered such physical privations. Nor did she forego her social life. But what **is** impressive is that, with no real knowledge of the standard she was aiming for, Vera combined a disciplined schedule of intensive morning study with her customary enjoyment of dances, tennis and amateur dramatics. It was an onerous undertaking. Yet, despite fluctuating confidence about her ability to master mathematics, even with her friend Maurice Ellinger's help, Vera's diary is full of optimism and fierce determination.

According to *Testament of Youth*, Edith had 'quite a bad time' at charity meetings where 'stalwart middle-class mothers' and 'censorious Buxton ladies' criticised Vera's plans. Again, the diary offers an intriguingly different account, one of curiosity rather than criticism:

> Tuesday October 21st
> Mother had a Mothers' Union meeting at Mrs Cox's today… At the end …Mrs Cox [wife of the director of the Devonshire Hospital] …'it is all over the town that Vera is shortly going to begin lecturing!' Mother, with some dignity, drew herself up & replied to the effect that 'Vera is at present working for two exams, one in March and another in July, after so which she be so fortunate as to pass them, she *may* go to Oxford the following October'. 'Oh! so it's a *very* long time ahead,' says Mrs Cox, somewhat taken aback no doubt at having got the rumour so wrong. 'There is of course a chance,' continues Mother, 'that if she *should* manage to go to Oxford, she may become a lecturer in time, but the whole thing is very much of a supposition at present.' 'And what if she goes & gets married before it is all finished?' exclaims Mrs Spafford. 'In that case,' replies Mother, still with the dignity which she is able to exercise on other people's behalf but never on her own, 'not a moment of what she has done will be wasted, as what she has learnt will be of inestimable benefit to her'.

According to the memoir, Vera struggled constantly against provincial prejudice:

> …writers and lecturers and university women were all equally unnatural to the censorious Buxton ladies, and equally obnoxious. Had I possessed a gift for drawing and wanted to study in Paris; had I been, like Edward, a potential musician, and contemplated a career beginning at the Royal College of Music…my parents' acquaintances would probably have thought me interesting…But so unpopular at the time was the blue stocking tradition, and so fathomless the depth of provincial self-satisfaction, that my decision to go to [Oxford] caused me to be labelled 'ridiculous', 'eccentric' and 'a strong-minded woman'.[19]

The diary never uses these pejorative labels and, intriguingly, the only 'censorious Buxton lady' appears to have been Lena Dodd, Vera's former headmistress at the Grange. After learning that Lena had told Edith her daughter should 'stay at home & help mother', Vera was scathing:

> ...(she needs so <u>much</u> help!) and [Miss Dodd's] great idea is that girls should marry as soon as possible after leaving the school room, before they have any ideas...evidently no side of the women's movement has taken hold of her. Disapproval from such a person is almost equivalent to encouragement...the impracticability of it too – as though marriage is just there for the asking & as though every chance of it was suitable to be taken! I am thankful that my reasons for doing as I am are good enough for me & that I am quite independent of any outside person's discouragement or approval.[20]

In the light of Lena's organisation of Oxford extension lectures whilst headmistress at Preston and her success in raising the sights of the Grange, her standpoint is very surprising. A couple of months before her comments to Edith, Lena told Vera she did not take 'her girls' to the lectures because she 'had been to too many herself to feel much enthusiasm for them!' Vera speculated in her diary that perhaps Miss Dodd resented the fact, 'though she swears she doesn't... that Mrs Harrison doesn't consult her about the lectures'. Vera added contemptuously that she couldn't 'imagine anyone who pursues knowledge pursuing it with such tempered enthusiasm.... aspiration is aspiration always!'[21]

Other 'stalwart' Buxton mothers encouraged and 'warmly commended' Vera's ambitions:

> Tuesday October 23rd, 1913
> I met Lady Vaudray [and] told her I was hoping to go to Oxford & she said she had heard it, & to my great surprise was perfectly sensible about it & said she had a niece who had just left Somerville, where she had been reading English. Thank goodness for one more person who is not horrorstruck at the idea of my working with a purpose.

Lady Vaudray was not the only woman in Vera's social circle to support her plans. Nor, as we saw earlier with the example of Carrie Morrison, was Vera the only young woman in Edwardian Buxton who went to an elite university. At a very 'pleasant little dinner party' on 24 October, Vera's Oxford ambitions had lifted her educational aspirations:

> I had a very entertaining conversation with [Mr Robinson], chiefly about college, education and the futility of girls' schools. It may be disloyal to

think such things, but I remember how little I learned at St Monica's compared to what I am capable of learning.

In October, Mrs Harrison invited Vera to join her lecture committee. Noting 'it is wonderful they will deign to have anyone as young as I', Vera hoped this would give her the opportunity to air her views and get to know Mrs Harrison better. At her first meeting, Vera helped plan the January 1914 programme on 'The Rise and Progress of the British Colonies' and offered to host the new lecturer overnight at Melrose after his first lecture.

'The beginning of something which is to be a great joy & blessing in my life'

With preparations for the Somerville entrance examination in full swing, Vera's feelings about Buxton were erratic, swinging between euphoria about another ball in one paragraph and disaffection in the next:

> Wednesday December 24th
> In the evening we went to bridge at the Ellingers'. Oh! much as I love bridge, I would not become one of those bridge-playing, cigarette-smoking, parasitic beings for any amount of money. There is an atmosphere of dissoluteness & slackness about the whole place.

Her annual end of year reflection was, as usual, despondent:

> Friday December 26th
> I am so thankful Christmas day is over; I cannot remember one that has not depressed me. Of all events that make for melancholy & mark the passage of time [the worst] are those which recur at fairly long & regular intervals & are always like each other – at least all Christmases have been alike so far to me. I was able to start working again to-day with much thankfulness.

Four days later, tobogganing made her realise how 'other people's merriment' and her ability to seem to enjoy events 'makes it all the more evident to me from how many of them I am really alien'. She was disturbed by three accidents on 'the rough run', including a youth with 'his head bashed in. A ghastly sight'. That evening, Vera was in a reflective mood:

> Tuesday December 30th
> Alas! I fear that the year I foresaw as 'lucky' is after all ending in gloom. Apart from the fact that I am (I suppose) a child of worldly fortune, it

doesn't seem to have brought me much actual luck, though many more things have happened in it than the year I first came out…it may be that in future years I shall look back upon this one & find that it marked the beginning of something which is to be a great joy & blessing in my life – the significance of which I do not recognise now, but shall realise then.

She went tobogganing again on New Year's Eve and was once again optimistic:

The bells are ringing outside & sounding very clear across the snow so I suppose it is time to close this book & 1913 with it. Well, good bye Old Year! You have brought me many good things, but the best of all is, maybe, what I do not recognise yet as such. May 1914 bring me a truer joy, a greater happiness, a higher purpose, than I have ever felt before. May I continue to strive & in striving, if it may be so, in part achieve.

1914 did indeed mark the 'beginning of something'. In January, Vera attended the next series of Oxford extension lectures, and during the lecturer's stay at Melrose, the Brittains enjoyed an interesting discussion about the situation in Ulster. In March, she spent four hectic days in Oxford, competing with eighty-two entrants in the Somerville examination for one of eighteen places. It was extremely daunting. Without real understanding of what was required, Vera had over-emphasised literary criticism and had not studied the literature itself adequately. Unable to answer some of the questions, she had to improvise. Meeting Miss Darbishire, one of Somerville's tutors, afterwards, the woman 'seemed pleased I had worked alone and against opposition'.

Vera was convinced she had failed. But her determination and intellectual ability had shone through. She received a letter on 31 May awarding her a College Exhibition – a scholarship – of £20 a year for three years (about £2000 today) – one of two awards Somerville made for English that year. Vera's annual scholarship was the equivalent to the wages of one of the Brittains' servants. She would also depend on Arthur for termly fees of £35 which included board, meals and tuition. This was a considerable sum: in 1914, the average annual wage of an adult male industrial worker was £75, that of a male professional £340. Nonetheless, Arthur and Edith were extremely proud:

I was not at all disturbed by the announcement, though Mother got quite flustered in her delight & wanted to tell everyone at once & Daddy seemed quite overjoyed – though I wish they would not make demonstrations.[22]

So Vera was over the first hurdle. When Edward gained a place at New College, they looked forward to being in Oxford together and Vera's diary recorded her huge gratitude to Mrs Harrison. Now she had to prepare for the university's entrance examination at Mr Lace's. In July, Arthur paid £1 7s. 6d (about £70 today) for Vera to sit it in the highly alien surroundings of Leek's 'dusty Board school' (the town's technical school) where she was 'surrounded by rough-looking and distinctly odoriferous sixteen-year-olds of both sexes' doing other exams.[23] Two weeks after Britain declared war against Germany on 4 August, Vera heard she had passed and was jubilant:

> The Oxford exam. is the final obstacle in my path & when removed released me to follow my own ambition as I will throw off the chains that have bound & restricted me here.

Things did not look so good for Mr Lace's crammer. Already in financial difficulties, it closed a few months after Vera finished her studies there.

Why was Oxford the only university Vera considered? By 1913, sixteen per cent of undergraduates were women and regional universities, including Manchester, not only had more female undergraduates than Oxford and Cambridge but also awarded degrees to women. It would not be until 1921 when Oxford did, followed by Cambridge in 1948.

One biographer presents Vera's choice as merely a reflection of her assumptions that only an elite university was appropriate for a woman of her 'upper middle-class status'.[24] This not only misinterprets Vera's social position (she is more accurately described as 'wealthy middle-class') but also overlooks other factors that made Oxford attractive to her. Its social and academic standing were undoubtedly appealing but, as we saw earlier, Vera had also been very moved by the novel *Robert Elsmere*, in which university in Oxford begins Elsmere's intellectual and religious transformation. And, as a feminist, Vera wanted the same opportunities as Edward. But the biggest factors spurring Vera to Oxford were the inspiration of John Marriott, the encouragement of Edith, Edward, Mrs Harrison and, as we shall see, of Reverend Joseph Ward.

Vera was to re-meet John Marriott again in 1924 when he was giving extension lectures in Reigate, and she was teaching part-time at St Monica's. Knighted that year, he had become Conservative MP for Oxford City. In 1926, Vera would repay her debt to the transforming impact of the Oxford lectures by becoming an extension lecturer herself, with a course on 'Ideals of World Unity' in Westgate-on-Sea, Kent.

In the meantime, back in 1914, Vera had her escape route from Buxton.

Chapter Five

'This House of Many Comforts'

Home Life

'We then kept three servants and a garden boy'

Following a leisurely late breakfast brought to her in bed by the 28-year-old housemaid Annie Skeet, Vera lay on the green and white patterned chaise longue in front of the fire in the morning room at Melrose, engrossed, as she so often was, in a book. She loved reading, noting joyfully about *Ramola* by George Eliot 'it is wonderful to buy so much rapture for 2/6d!' Literature often led to one of Vera's many long diary reflections about her hopes for the future, the nature of moral integrity, God, truth and love.

Despite being July, it was exceptionally cold, even for Buxton. With the distant hills of Grin Low submerged in a leaden mist, the summer lace curtains at the French windows onto the terrace were open to allow some grey light into the room. Vera thought, yet again, how much she hated Buxton's weather; in the winter, her bedroom was too cold to write her diary and it was not uncommon for snow to lie on the ground for weeks, or to fall in May and June. But today, at least, Edith had allowed a fire and while Vera read, her mother sat at a table catching up on household accounts and planning the week's menus to discuss with Mary Omeroyd, the 35-year-old cook.

When Annie Skeet rose that morning at her usual time of 5.30, her heart sank. From May to September, she usually had some respite from the daily grind of fetching coal from the cavernous cellars, cleaning, lighting, and keeping fires going in three living rooms and, in the evening, the bedrooms. If a summer day was especially cold, Mrs Brittain might ask for a fire. Annie had a feeling she would today.[1]

Fires were not Annie's only tasks before breakfast. She had to carry hot water up to the bedrooms and clean all the boots, before helping Annie Price, the 29-year-old parlourmaid, prepare breakfast.[2] After that, she opened bedroom windows, stripped or made beds, and sorted out the washstands. She had to black the kitchen range daily and keep its fire lit, do the endless daily dusting and sweeping created by many coal fires and rugs over bare floorboards. Then there would be whatever tasks were on the weekly cleaning rota. Once a week, the housemaid washed smaller items in a stone sink in one of the five cellar rooms, heating the water with a coal-fire. Ironing was done with a heavy press iron heated on the kitchen range. Larger items, such as bedsheets, were collected and returned by one of Buxton's commercial laundries before any necessary mending and then storage on labelled shelves in cupboards and bedroom chests of drawers. There were personal tasks too. A maid washed Vera and Edith's hair every Sunday, helped them dress for a special occasion, and sometimes brought breakfast to Vera in bed, especially after a late night. Occasional light relief came from bantering with one of the boys delivering provisions for the cook, or from the weekly free afternoon maids were allowed.[3]

Annual spring cleaning was an onerous upheaval, often involving re-decorating, cleaning every ornament and picture (and a typical Edwardian home had many of these), rug and kitchen utensils, removing winter curtains and drapes and replacing them with summer lace or muslin ones. In the grandest homes, spring cleaning could last a month; it was probably about two weeks at Melrose, overseen by Edith with Vera's assistance. Arthur found it so disruptive that he would take himself off for a holiday or business trip.

Vera's diary mentions the Brittains' three live-in servants very rarely and only in passing. Typically for a middle-class young woman of the time, she would have known very little, if anything, about them. Nor is there any information about what Vera's servants thought of her, or how she treated them. Margaret Powell, an Edwardian kitchen maid, hints at what a housemaid like Annie Skeet might have felt about the 'young lady of the house':

Vera on steps outside morning room at Melrose, 1912. (*McM*)

> ...what a different life hers was from mine!....she could speak French, play the piano, sing well. I was envious of her life, envious of all her accomplishments. Not all the time...but when she came down to the kitchen to ask for something and I was at the sink...immersed in bowls of greasy water, clad in a sacking apron, and there she was... dressed up to the nines, with her cultivated voice, asking for something which I would

immediately have to rush to get her, I wouldn't have been human if I hadn't felt envious.[4]

Vera was not unusual in taking for granted the relentless labour that enabled her to live, as she put it in *Testament of Youth*, 'securely sheltered in the greenhouse warmth of bourgeois comfort and provincial elegance'. After a trip to Paris with Edith and Arthur:

> May 23rd, 1913
> It is lovely to be back among all my books… with a bright fire & all the familiar objects dearer for having been left even a short time… my darling cat and the maids were all there & the house looked comfortable and fresh… coming back is always the best part of being away…I spent the afternoon till bed-time messing about with clothes etc. The new cook started quite well with dinner so I hope mother will have a little peace at last.

When servants had time off, Vera had to help with housework, such as cleaning boots and the silverware, cutting up oranges for marmalade, and dusting

Arthur and Edith outside Melrose, c.1913. (*McM*)

bedrooms ('the usual pantomime'). In the normal run of domestic life, young women like Vera were not expected to do housework:

> Tuesday September 8th, 1914
> Daddy went off for his holiday this morning. The maids also all went & Mrs Fowler [the dressmaker] came in to help look after the house with Drabble, & we began the unaccustomed & very salutary tasks of looking after ourselves a great deal more than usual.

It was not until going to university that Vera would realise just how exacting her mother's standards of cleanliness and comfort were.

In the early 1900s, four million women worked, a million and a half as domestic servants. Servants were not necessarily an indication of significant wealth; most were single-handed maids in small households. In Buxton, families like the Brittains typically had three live-in staff. Those with small children also employed a nurse or governess. In Buxton, 1 in 7 served in private homes, hotels, hydros and lodging houses (a greater proportion than in Bath where it was 1 in 9). By 1911, 50 per cent of Buxton servants were incomers: the census for Melrose shows Annie Skeet was from Burton-on-Trent, Annie Price from Oswestry and Mary Omeroyd from St Helen's.

By 1913, these servants had moved on, replaced with Norah the parlourmaid, Margaret the housemaid (Vera does not mention surnames), and Mrs Kay, 'our elderly cook' whose son Tom was chauffer for the Johnsons, friends of Edith and Arthur. Norah stayed a year and Mrs Kay worked for Vera's parents until they left Buxton in December 1915; there is no record of Margaret's departure.

We do not know why the Brittains' servants left. The fact that Edith had retained loyal servants for ten years in Macclesfield suggests she was a good employer; at Melrose the two maids shared a bedroom, and the cook had her own. Typically, domestic servants had one afternoon off a week and one Sunday a month. Perhaps, like some employers, the Brittains also gave Christmas presents (although these were generally something functional, such as a length of fabric to make new aprons).[5] Nonetheless, however benign an employer might be, domestic service was arduous, demeaning and badly paid. In Buxton, demand outstripped supply. There was also fierce competition from abroad, including Australia: a 1913 notice in the *Buxton Advertiser* offered 'good pay for good work in a land of sunshine and prosperity'. Buxton servants also experienced social segregation not found in other towns: for example, they could not walk or sit in the Gardens unless their employers paid to add them to the family ticket. We do not know if the Brittains did this or not.

Domestic servants earned very little. Vera's annual school fees of £45 and her £30 dress allowance cost Arthur more than the yearly wages for their three servants: the going rate for a housemaid was £15 (about £1,400 today), a parlourmaid £20–£23 (about £1,800–£2,000), and a cook £30 (about £3,800 today). Low wages excluded them from the Liberal government's 1911 National Insurance Act which required employers to contribute to insuring workers earning over £70 year against sickness and unemployment (a typical male industrial worker earned £75). If they became ill or were injured, they had to rely on their employers' generosity; for example, when Billy, the Ellingers' bulldog, attacked and bit Norah, Arthur paid for the family doctor to treat her.

Depending on their own upbringing and expectations, women like Edith varied in how confidently they dealt with servants and how comfortable they felt having them at all.[6] Most employers, including Edith, recruited from one of many domestic registries that had sprung up across the country. Obtaining 'good' servants, managing and keeping them were perennial preoccupations. The Brittains were no exception:

Sunday March 19th, 1913
The Forsyths came in to supper. The conversation after supper was just getting beautifully down into the usual servant question when I managed to change it adroitly & we were luckily free of it for the rest of the evening.

Sunday April 12th, 1914
An atmosphere of very inappropriate storm hovered over the house all day owing to mother's servant trouble which she seems quite incapable of keeping on her own shoulders & which put her into a temper that she communicated to everyone else.

The following day, the parlourmaid who had replaced Norah did not last long:

Monday April 13th, 1914
Various storms disturbed the household equanimity just after breakfast owing to the disgraceful insolence of the new parlourmaid, who in the end was paid her month's wages and turned out.

Edith was not the only Buxton woman with problems. Sarah Meggitt-Smith, wealthy wife of a railway contractor, lived at Gadley, not far from the Brittains, and complained to a Birmingham registry service about a cook who refused to give her age:

Don't get her a place until she does. After all these years, I never thought you would send me anyone so old…If you can't get me a cook, you must please get me a maid, not old or too experienced but one willing to do anything.[7]

'There was nothing beyond the stark obviousness of the house'

Fewer than 15 per cent of Edwardian Britain owned their home. The rest rented them, usually unfurnished. After two years at High Leigh, Arthur took out a lease on semi-detached Melrose, just round the corner on The Park. It had six bedrooms, four large reception rooms and accommodation for three servants. In 1905, Breezemount, which adjoined Melrose, was advertised for rent at £135

Melrose today.

a year (about £11,000 today). Arthur would probably have paid about the same for the new family home, £15 a year more than detached High Leigh.[8]

Drawing on details of decoration, furnishings, typical meals, and domestic routines at Melrose, *Not Without Honour* portrays a dull, conventional home:

> Before she went in past the gate she looked with a pessimist's eye at the steep drive between the stone wall and the slip of lawn, divided by a fence from the slip of the next-door neighbour, which her father always referred to as 'the grounds'. At the top of the drive stood the grey stone house, semi-detached but spacious, with square corners, square porch and big square windows. From above the shelving lawn, its bare, wide face stared down… with a blandness that was almost indecent. There was nothing behind the stark obviousness of the house – no mystery, no secret, no fierce hidden exultation to prove that things were so much more than they seemed.[9]

Built in 1884, Melrose is typical of a nationwide fashion in the second half of the nineteenth century for semi-detached villas with entrances at the sides designed to give occupants a high degree of privacy from neighbours, and visitors the impression of a home twice as big. Matching arched windows, iron balconies, lintels and stonework with adjoining Breezemount epitomise the architectural illusion of one grand house, leading twenty-first century visitors interested in Vera Brittain to ask if her home was really 'just' semi-detached.

It is not surprising people assume Vera's home to be grander than it is. One biography misinforms readers that it had 'long lawns, tennis courts and many servants'.[10] The 1979 BBC dramatization of *Testament of Youth* also exaggerated Melrose. Location shots of Cheryl Campbell (Vera) walking her bicycle up the drive and looking from upstairs windows to the hills beyond are supplemented with studio sets of an enormous drawing room with imposing fretwork, stained glass bay windows and ornate fireplace, and a huge hallway with sweeping staircase. They bear little relation to the much more modest Brittain home. The 2014 film was even more misleading, showing Melrose as an enormous stucco faced detached house surrounded by imposing formal gardens in a rural setting.

Vera at Melrose, 1912. (*SC*)

Despite over-playing its grandeur, the BBC dramatisation did style an authentic Edwardian provincial middle-class interior of dark wood skirting boards, window frames, doors, and architraves; layers of curtains (sometimes as many as four); valences, drapes and tassels; many ornaments, heavily patterned wallpapers and upholstery, and lots of heavy dark furniture. Images of Vera outside the morning room show the Edwardian fashion for replacing heavy winter drapes with lighter muslin or lace curtains for summer.[11]

Moving from a detached house to a more expensive, semi-detached reflected Arthur and Edith's aspiration to live in a more prestigious area. The Park was one of seven upmarket residential developments commissioned by the Devonshire Estate in the second half of the nineteenth century. It had the additional cachet of being designed by Joseph Paxton, the Devonshires' head gardener and an acclaimed landscape designer. He based Buxton Park on his successful designs for similar projects in Birkenhead and Liverpool, where grand villas were set around gracious parkland.[12]

'What a lambent place it was in the dusk of the evening'

Vera's home of 'many comforts' is one of only four semi-detached houses on The Park. With long front gardens framed, in those days, by ornate railings

Lee Wood Hotel. (*PtP*)

and gates rather than the tall hedges or rather dilapidated fences that obscure many of them today, The Park's villas are set around what was then a wide limestone carriage drive encircling a cricket ground, and expansive parkland for which Paxton shipped in hundreds of mature trees. Houses on the north side, including Melrose, have lovely views up to the woods and moors surrounding Buxton.[13]

Vera in front of Melrose, with Empire behind on the left. (*SC*)

In Vera's day, The Park was elegant and tranquil. The only sounds disturbing the silence would have been occasional chauffeur driven motorcars, horse drawn carriages, postmen on one of their four daily rounds, boys on bicycles delivering provisions, and a horse-drawn van from one of Buxton's commercial laundries collecting or returning laundry. With the centre of town a few minutes' stroll away, there would have been a steady stream of residents and visitors dressed in their smartest clothes and servants running errands or on their afternoon off. During the summer, the pleasant sounds emanating from the cricket and bowling clubs accompanied horse and motorized taxis ferrying wealthy guests between the railway stations and the Lee Wood and Empire hotels.

Both these establishments attracted Buxton's richest visitors. Just down the hill from Melrose, Lee Wood was the first Buxton hotel to attract long-term guests, including Manchester businessmen and 'men of science and letters'. In the late nineteenth century these included Sir Theodore and Lady Martin (a leading actress of her day) who spent months at the Lee Wood while he wrote his biography of Prince Albert. Some guests stayed permanently, including someone from the chemical industry in Manchester who died there after intending to stay for two weeks and prolonging his visit by 25 years.[14]

A few yards up from Melrose, the opulent Empire dominated its surroundings and could be seen from afar. Occupying over 80 acres, set in formal gardens and tennis courts, it was a potent symbol of Edwardian Buxton's commercial and social buoyance. Opened in 1901 and paid for by Spiers and Ponds, London owners of a chain of railway restaurants, it was only open during the summer season. A one-time guest reminisced in the *Buxton Advertiser*:

Empire hotel, early 1900s. (*PtP*)

How regal the old days, and in what a grand situation was the old Empire hotel… Set in a vast soaring landscape…it was rivalled only by the superb position of the Palace Hotel… I can still picture their house flag at the mast head proudly waving…over The Park…I think of the hotel's old opulence, its expensive furnishings, the never-ending ascent and descent of elevators, its volatile messenger boys in pillbox hat and buttons…[its] Continental air.

On the edge of Buxton, with the spectacular Goyt Valley a short walk up the hill, Melrose was ideally placed for Vera's many walks and cycle rides. A favourite place was Corbar Woods, just five minutes from the house and rumoured to be another of Paxton's projects:

Friday February 27th, 1914
A perfect morning, sun shining brightly at 8.30 & mist floating over everything… Corbar Woods… were perfectly still, wrapped in all the morning beauty; I saw not a soul except a workman walking along one of the paths. The birds were twittering in the trees, & the air was very warm, altogether it felt more like April than the end of February. When I got on to the heights the view was glorious. I felt like a being lifted up into some sublime air where calm reigned supreme, while around my

feet the turbulent world eddied, & I heard 'The restless sounds of man's uneasy life Rise muffled from below'. The hills to the west were gradually becoming clear of mist, but still their outline seemed to melt into the sky, and Burbage village seemed to sleep behind a hazy veil. The white cottages gleaming through looked like jewels on the hillside. The sky was perfectly clear except for a few rose-coloured clouds just above Axe Edge. To the east I could see Fairfield Church like a ghost in the mist. I stood in the sunshine on the edge of the rock, alone in the world.

'Mentally restricted local residents'

Many years after leaving Buxton, Vera criticised her social circle as 'typical of those who inhabit small towns'; cautious family doctors, dull, unenterprising businessmen and solicitors, and boring teachers ...I cannot remember anyone ever coming to the house of more interest to me than relatives or mentally restricted local residents and their even more limited wives ...'.[15] In *Not Without Honour* and *Testament of Youth*, she railed against Buxton's censorious snobbishness and its dull, self-satisfied men and its 'stalwart matrons'. What sort of people did Vera mix with?

By the time the Brittains moved to Buxton, the upper-class residents who once dominated the town were heavily outnumbered by families like Vera's whose 'new money' and more humble origins had transformed its social make-up and atmosphere. Nonetheless, old snobberies and class rifts persisted: for example, Vera reported indignantly that Mrs Hubbersty, a rich woman from Burbage, 'never called on Mother' and when she came to bridge parties at Melrose, was 'charmingly condescending to me as usual'.

Census records for The Park in 1891 list solicitors, manufacturers (a drysalter, flour miller, cotton spinners, cotton bleacher), merchants, architects, a chemist and engineers. Some residents came from other countries, including Germany and Mexico.[16] The Dodd sisters and their mother also lived on The Park, supported by income from running the Grange. Just round the corner on Manchester Road, the Forsyths took over High Leigh from the Brittains in 1907 after returning from India and became close friends. Also on Manchester Road were the Taylors, whose son would go on to become A.J.P. Taylor, the renowned historian. His father had made his fortune as a cotton merchant in Manchester.

Before the Brittains moved to Melrose, it was occupied for eight years by the family of George Hicks, an insurance underwriter and major investor in the Manchester Ship Canal. Just up the road were the Stephensons who moved to Buxton from Hertfordshire in 1905 and stayed seven years. Their wealth came from manufacturing cardboard boxes and their son Robert would go on

Left to right front Maurice Ellinger, Vera and Arthur on trip to Peak District, 1912. Possibly Mabel Ellinger back left, and Edith back right. (*McM*)

to become an award-winning film director.[17] Next door to the Stephensons was Arthur McDougal, a generous Buxton philanthropist, and director of his family's flour milling company in Manchester.

The Buxton families Vera mentions most often in her diary are the Garnetts, Spaffords and Ellingers, and of these, the Garnetts were the wealthiest, occupying a large, detached house on the edge of town with stables, a ballroom and tennis courts, coach house and five servants. These families all originated from the north-west, making their money in various branches of the cotton trade and moving to Buxton in the early 1900s. The Brittains also socialised with the Lawsons from Surrey who took over the failing fortunes of Buxton College, Buxton's only public school, in 1911, and the Harrisons who ran St Ann's Hotel from 1904.

The Brittains' closest friends and neighbours were Barnard and Mabel Ellinger, who rented semi-detached Ashleigh, just down the road from Melrose, and their only son Maurice who attended Uppingham with Edward. From a German family, Barnard ran his family's cotton trading company in Manchester and London. His 39-year-old wife Mabel shared a love of stylish clothes with Edith and Vera, was a garrulous host of many dinner parties and musical evenings and enjoyed society balls. Mabel and Edith were members of the Ladies Committee of the Cottage Hospital, and Mabel was a member of Mrs Harrison's Oxford lecture committee. She was outspoken and independent, reporting indignantly to Vera that a dramatic part offered to her was 'of a meek, submissive woman… whereas my very walk expresses independence'! She was also interested in politics, giving a lecture on 'Free Trade' to a meeting of Buxton Women's Liberal Club in January 1911.[18]

Vera did not approve of Mabel, referring to her as a 'social butterfly', a neglectful mother and a profligate spender; on one occasion, she told Vera she had got into debt over her clothes expenditure and Barnard gave her another £100 (about £10,000 today). Vera thought it 'disgraceful; I hope I shall never be as dependant as <u>that</u>, wasting the hard earned income of someone else'.[19]

'We had an 'at home'… for grown-up unmarrieds'

How did Vera's family and social circle spend their time? Her 1924 novel *Not Without Honour* describes dull family meals with unimaginative food, boring callers and a life of endless tedium:

> Every morning she went down with her mother to help with the shopping; every afternoon she read, listlessly, novels in the garden; every evening she sewed her laborious way through a set of cambric underclothing.[20]

Testament of Youth tells us that Vera was 'trammelled and trapped' in 'my hated Buxton prison', leading a life of 'utter futility' in which 'my desultory reading of George Eliot offered an occasional respite' and where, with 'nothing to do and no one to talk to', there was the ever-present danger of 'spontaneous combustion'.

In contrast, seventeen-year-old Vera's 1911 diary about the school holidays is cheerful and enthusiastic. After a trip on New Year's Day to Manchester with their neighbours, the Ellingers, to see the pantomime *Cinderella*, the week continues:

> Wednesday 4th
> We had an 'At Home' in the evening for grown-up unmarrieds and 'flappers'. The first thing was a treasure hunt & the second a musical romance competition. Douglas Spafford won the treasure hunt.
>
> Sunday 8th
> Douglas Spafford came to call in the afternoon & I spent the rest of it reading about Wagner's glorious operas. Read Tennyson after supper to the accompaniment of Edward's violin, which he played better than usual

– thought a good deal about the dream-world of the future with its longed for independence and wider life.

Monday 9th
Started a design for a painted scarf for mother. Went with Edward in the afternoon to a competition party at Mrs Brutton's. Quite jolly, especially the later part. I did not quite get a prize but very nearly. Edward went to Miss Dodd's dinner party [Lena Dodd, Vera's headmistress at the Grange].

Tuesday 10th
Dentist [the family dentist at Newcastle-under-Lyme], wrote letters, Margaret Shipton called; played bridge after dinner.
Wednesday 11th
Dentist again (good long visit!). Did good bit more to scarf. Played bridge in evening.

Thursday 12th
Painted scarf. Went to town. D. Ellinger came to tea. Daisy Whitehead also called. D. Ellinger sang to us; she has such a sweet voice. I talked to her about Garretts Hall [Dorothy's school in Manchester] and told her about St Monica's.

Friday 13th
Edward & I went to tea with Miss Harley & enjoyed it immensely. She was so funny….we were in fits of laughter the whole time. Returned to have dress fitted once more.

Saturday 14th
Toothache.
In the evening my new evening dress (ninon over soft satin) came & I went to Mrs Ellinger's dinner party and dance. (<u>Enjoyed it</u>). Dorothy had on a new dress and looked very sweet.

Sunday 15th
Stayed in bed for breakfast. Got up at about eleven & went to meet them coming from church. Read in afternoon. Had hair washed after tea & wrote in the evening.

Monday 16th
Dentist for the last time these holidays. Mother went to see *Mrs Gorringer's necklace* at the Opera House.

> Tuesday 17th
> Went to London with Daddy. Went to National Gallery & saw *Charley's Aunt* at the Savoy Theatre... roared with laughter the whole time

The 1911 Easter holidays continue in the same relaxed vein: a shopping trip in Manchester with Edith; Arthur's birthday (Vera gave him a silk handkerchief, her mother a box of cigars); helping her mother turn out Edward's room ('roared with laughter over reminiscences of infantile days'), a day reading, and a trip in the motorcar to Topley Pike & the Cat & Fiddle. On Sunday 9 April Vera enjoyed the sermon at St John's. After tea, Edith sang, and Vera practised the piano accompaniments. The following day 'New navy coat and skirt arrived. Very smart; also two hats .... I chose the silver-grey straw with the trimming to match coat collar. Finished 'Daniel Deronda'. On Tuesday, Vera 'spent most of the evening trying on muslin dress'. A motor ride with her father 'round by Macclesfield and Capesthorne Hall' was followed three days later by another to Matlock and back via the Chatsworth Estate which 'looked lovely'.

A staple of provincial life was the middle-class ritual of leaving a visiting card to signal an intention to call on a designated day, a tradition established in the nineteenth century. Sometimes there might be up to ten male and female callers, although not all stayed to tea. From a young age, Vera was expected to accompany Edith in receiving and calling on neighbours. In keeping with convention, she was given her own cards when she turned eighteen. On one occasion, Edith's younger sister Lillie persuaded them to 'let the "At Home" day take care of itself' and, as Vera noted, 'naturally ever so many people called while we were out!', including Mrs Lawson, wife of the headmaster of Buxton College and one of the few Buxton women Vera really liked. Still, it had been worth it: after playing a 'total of 36 holes [at golf]; it had been a simply perfect day & not a bad record for a beginner!'[21]

In the hard-to-imagine days of no texts, social media or emails, and equally hard-to-imagine four daily postal collections and deliveries (including one that arrived before breakfast!), women like Edith and Vera did a great deal of letter writing; Edith's would have included household administration as well as correspondence with family and friends. In later life, especially when she became famous, Vera would handwrite up to 12 personal letters every morning while her secretary typed the rest.

Much Edwardian middle-class social life centred around various 'at home' entertainments, such as dances and dinner parties:

> The dinner [at the Ellingers] was a competition & each gentleman moved round & everyone voted at the end for their nicest partner. Miss Arrowsmith

got the ladies' prize and Cyril Johnson the gentleman's. Afterwards Daddy came for the dance which I enjoyed very much, especially with Mr Pettit [the headmaster of Holm Leigh] and Maurice. Maurice & I had a long sit out in Mr Ellinger's study.

Board and card games with prizes were extremely popular. Vera records enjoying bridge, Khun-Khan, and Empire (where players had to trade with the colonies). Other competitions included a 'Potato Tea' which 20-year old Vera enjoyed in 1913, where 'we had to dress up potatoes as dolls…mine was a little negress in a white dress with pink sash & bonnet, all done in crinkled paper'.[22]

The most popular 'At Homes' were musical evenings at which people sang and played the piano and violin:

Monday January 6th, 1913
Edward and I played a round of golf in the morning but it was very cold and the ground too hard to be really good. In the afternoon mother, Edward and I went to a musical party at the Harleys'. A person was there who professed to play the piano well but really played very badly, as Mrs Ellinger said, with a little [illegible] and a great deal of affectation! Bertram Spafford sang quite well; his voice is sympathetic & he has much improved. Miss Harley also attempted to sing & the pianist to recite [illegible] a rather weak performance….Edward was quite the redeeming feature; Mrs Ellinger told Maurice so. He really played the violin excellently and I accompanied him in the Pietro Mandarin Sonata… It rained when it was time to leave & Mrs Ellinger, Lady Vaudray, mother and I drove back together. Mrs Ellinger…looked very smart in a purple velvet Henry VIIIth hat.

Music was a particular joy for Vera, and she wrote often in her dairy about its emotional effects, such as the overture to Parsifal:

….that product of Wagner's last days, which came to a height almost incomprehensible to us his life-long ideal of love & purity triumphant over sensuality…without comprehending its true meaning, I know I must both hear it many times & grow older before its true message will dawn on me.[23]

Vera maintained that music was the only thing preventing her family and the atmosphere at Melrose from being, as she would later describe to her future husband, 'uncultured and commonplace'.[24] All the Brittains loved music. Edith was an accomplished singer, Vera was a competent pianist and Edward came to play the violin with increasing professionalism and the church organ, and to compose music. For Vera, music was a crucial bond with her brother:

> Tuesday November 25th, 1913
> …[music] is too valuable a means of self-expression and I think everyone ought to train & use every means of self-expression that is given to them – the possession of a talent ought to be a sufficient reason for cultivating it…music is too great a relief to my often over-burdened feelings to give up; besides, it is my best means of keeping really intimate with Edward. That I should be good at it is necessary to his complete success; I must play his accompaniments & compositions & the fact that he with his musical judgement thinks me good is sufficient reason for me to study for my own & art's sake!

A highly talented singer at Buxton musical evenings was Maurice Ellinger's cousin Dorothy who lived in Manchester. A 'tiny dark doll of girl', she was the same age as Vera, who was in awe of her voice:

> January 5th, 1913
> …Maurice & Dorothy came to tea…Edward & I played the violin and piano and Dorothy sang. Oh! how I envy such a glorious voice – it is like one's dreams of Heaven. There is no gift that I would place in preference to this one – this voice that can not only win fame but more hearts as well. How I would love it! I cannot understand her being undecided about going on the operatic stage when she is implored by everyone to do so & knows she would be at the top of the tree almost immediately.…

In 1915 Dorothy had a professional engagement to sing in the Buxton Gardens but was destined for greater things. As the well-known musical comedy singer 'Desiree Ellinger', the *Stage* magazine praised her in 1921 as the 'possessor of a wonderful dramatic soprano'.

For all her criticism of Buxton society, Vera also enjoyed discussions with some interesting, eminent people she met at the Ellingers' dinner parties, including Sydney John Chapman, the Stanley Jervons Professor of Economics at Manchester University, who was staying for the weekend:

> Sunday May 11th, 1913
> I wore my new grey coat and skirt and my brown hat with flame wings and Bulgarian embroidered blouse…I quite expected Mr Chapman to be old & pedantic & was very surprised to meet a young, dark, earnest man

of about thirty-five. Mrs Chapman, who doesn't wear stays and looks like it, was rather plain & shapeless but had nice blue eyes. She was garbed in some sort of greeny blue 'High Art' robe… We got into a very animated discussion on women's suffrage; the Chapmans & I were very much in favour and seemed to convince everybody… Afterwards we talked politics a little more and I accompanied Mrs Ellinger in one or two songs.

When Vera met Chapman, he was renowned for his work on labour economics, state aid and public finance. He was gaining a reputation for innovative research into the cotton industry which drew on the expertise and real-world experience of businessmen and manufacturers. This is probably how he met Barnard Ellinger. Chapman had a similar background to Vera's Buxton circle. From a fairly ordinary middle-class background (the son of an estate agent) he attended Manchester Grammar School and the University of Cambridge before marrying the daughter of a wealthy ship owner. It seems he had progressive views about education, teaching for the Museum and Workers' Educational Association. This had grown out of Oxford's extension movement before the First World War as a response to its limited success in achieving its goal of appealing to working-class students.[25]

Vera did meet a few other interesting people, including a woman Edith engaged to speak on Christine Rossetti for the Buxton Mothers' Union. During lunch at Melrose, this 'very interesting woman was interested in my literaryness'.[26] At another Ellinger dinner party, Vera met Sir John Matthews, an eminent lawyer and, until 1911, Chief Justice of the Bahamas. The 'Woman Question' and marriage were again hot topics:

Sunday February 22nd, 1914
I had supper at the Ellingers', & put on my black dress, which Mrs Ellinger was immensely taken with. They all would talk of literature & my going to Oxford. They seemed amused when I said I wasn't going to get married, & called upon Sir John Matthews, who is a lawyer, to put it down. Mrs Green said people wouldn't let me embrace a literary & virginal career. But they needn't be so confident, for it takes two to make a match, & whatever disadvantages women may have to endure in the present society, the option of refusal is always theirs. Mrs Ellinger contended a woman couldn't be a great writer unless she was married as otherwise she could never know a man properly. I said that could only apply in the case of novelists, & it was questionable if it applied to them. We didn't come to any conclusion, & afterwards the conversation turned on the Woman Question, & as to whether physical force, the source of man's superiority, was not still, in

spite of the veneer of civilisation, the real test to-day. I sat & listened to this, saying little, as, though I have my own very decided opinions, I felt too young & that the ideas were too idealistic to be exhibited to the very worldly-wise and experienced company.

Vera's temporary reticence soon abated when, according to social convention, the women went to a separate room for coffee. In a lively discussion about the Brontes, George Eliot and Christina Rossetti, Mabel challenged Vera's ideas about literature. She held her own:

Before the men came in Mrs Ellinger & Mrs Green were talking to me in a strain that inferred that great books could only be written after great experiences by the author. Mrs Ellinger always seems to try & make me feel my own inexperience & youth, & sometimes she succeeds, but she didn't tonight. I believe I have advanced too far now to lose a certain amount of faith in myself; young & experienced as I am, I *have* thought and studied. I wonder if one of the consequences of increasing years is to try to crush the youth that they have lost, & to belittle it in the light of their advanced experience and ideas!

At one of Lady Vaudray's parties, Vera also met the famous dramatist and writer Laurence Irving and his actor wife, Mabel Hackney. When they both drowned in the sinking of the *Empress of Ireland* in May 1914, she noted in her diary, 'it is a great loss to the world'.

By April 1914, Vera's plans for escape to Oxford were firmly in train and life in a fashionable town was now merely a pleasant temporary diversion. In any case, whatever intellectual stimulation she gained from dinner parties and debates with neighbours was soon to seem very lack-lustre. At Easter, Vera's 'home of many comforts' hosted Edward's school friend, Roland Aubrey Leighton. Charismatic, highly intelligent and interested in feminism, Roland could not be more different from the men Vera knew in Buxton. Within three months, she was to find 'he shares my faults & talents in a way I have never found in anyone else'. Roland would become her first and greatest love.

Chapter Six

'A Good Strong Splendid Man, Full of Force & Enthusiasm … There Must *Be* Such!'

Infatuation And Love

'I refused to be … impressed by this person, but such equanimity was difficult'

On 18 April 1914, 19-year-old Roland Aubrey Leighton and his friend Edward Brittain travelled by train to Buxton from Uppingham in Rutland. Roland was looking forward to getting to know Edward's intelligent, pretty sister, and spending Easter in a town he had never visited, with a family somewhat different from his own. Coming down to dinner that evening, Roland was slightly surprised to find Vera not yet at the table but, with his usual assurance, was quite at ease chatting with his hosts while they waited. Having deliberately absented herself when Roland arrived, then delaying her arrival for dinner and taking great care with her appearance, Vera affected an air of courteous indifference towards Edward's handsome, confident friend. After supper, she went to see an amateur dramatic group perform the popular comedy 'Between the Soup and the Savoury', having been persuaded by Douglas Spafford to write a review for the *Buxton Advertiser*.

Vera first heard of Roland in April 1913 when Edward was 'sitting in his bedroom … surrounded with loose sheets of music, setting to music a poem of 'L'Envoi' written by the captain of his house in honour of boys leaving Uppingham'. At Uppingham Speech Day on 27 June 1913, Vera

Roland Leighton (left) and Victor Richardson at Uppingham, 1914. (*McM*)

'A Good Strong Splendid Man, Full of Force & Enthusiasm' 85

met Edward's house captain, noting that he was greatly admired by other boys for his academic ability and great confidence; 'he seems so clever & amusing & hardly shy at all!' Edward, Roland and their friend Victor Richardson were members of the school's Officer Training Corps and were all planning to go to Oxford together.

Roland was fifteen months younger than Vera who normally liked 'a man [to be] about thirty & really can never see the attraction of young boys'. Despite the age gap, she realised that 'in maturity and sophistication' Roland was infinitely superior to her and Edward, and to any of the Buxton men Vera knew. He wrote poetry, read widely, was deeply interested in philosophical and theological ideas, sympathetic to feminism and had won a scholarship to Merton College.

Vera was especially fascinated by Roland's parents. Both were well-known writers: Marie Leighton was the flamboyant, best-selling author of melodramatic romances, serialised in the *Daily Mail* and *Mirror*, and the family's main source of income; his father Robert wrote boys' fiction and between 1896 and 1899 was literary editor for the *Daily Mail*. Vera was intrigued by what sounded like a very unconventional lifestyle in the exotically named 'Vallambrosa', a rambling, disorganised house in north London and a summer home on the

Uppingham OTC, 1913, Edward back left, Roland middle left. (*McM*)

cliffs at Lowestoft in Suffolk, noting that 'Bohemia is always appealing to aspiring provincials.'

The day after Roland arrived at Melrose, Vera tried to avoid writing an honest review of the play she had seen because 'I thought the whole affair rather rubbish but it will certainly not be polite to say so'. He helped by 'dictating … what I had written when I was copying it out again'.[1] After going to hear Edward play the organ at St Peter's Church in Fairfield, Vera and Roland had the first of what would be many intense discussions:

> Saturday April 18th, 1914
> We had a most interesting conversation, a good deal of which was about our ideas of immortality. He is interested in me now, though I can't make out whether he likes me very much, or dislikes me very much. After dinner I was reading Thoreau's Walden (Leighton told me this morning a good deal about it, having read it) which he bought in town, & when I had finished the chapter & said I liked it he asked me to keep the book, much to my astonishment, so I did.

The next day, all three attended Reverend Ward's morning service at St Peter's:

> Sunday April 19th, 1914
> E. & Leighton & I went up to Fairfield to hear Mr Ward. It was quite a good sermon…Leighton liked it alright, though he suggested some of the 'florid' passages would stand a little pruning. I don't think I agree about that – not in a church like Fairfield.

After tea, Vera, Roland, Maurice Ellinger and Edward went for a long walk in the Goyt Valley. She and Roland resumed their philosophical debates. Vera teased him for what she called his 'Quiet Voice', telling him it was patronising:

> Leighton is a funny boy; he was very depressed & would hardly speak a word for about half the walk … I criticised him all day with most open frankness, telling him that there must be something wanting in his intellect if he could not see the intellectual beauty in music & also accusing him of adopting an artificial instead of spontaneous appreciation of Nature because he thought it a literary attribute.

The next day, with Edith dusting and Edward at organ practice, Vera and Roland went to Corbar Woods, where they sat on a tree stump and talked about his mother and Edward, whom they agreed was too orthodox and proper in his opinions. Time flew by. Roland was disappointed that Vera was leaving the next day to visit her father's sister Muriel who was married to Leigh Groves, heir to a wealthy brewing family. The Groves lived on the Hole Hird Estate near Windermere.[2]

While Vera was away, Roland wrote his first letter to her:

Dear Vera,
Edward has commanded me to address you in this way. I hope you do not object. Here is The Story of an African Farm, but such a wretched little edition after all, that I feel it is hardly worth sending you. I find it is the only one not out of print now. Please forgive it & me. The spirit was willing, but the publishers unaccommodating. When you have read it let me know what you think of it, and whether you agree with me that Lyndall is rather like you – only sadder perhaps and not so charmingly controversial.

I am so very sorry you had to go away just as I was learning to renounce the Quiet Voice and had begun to feel less shy. It sounds very selfish of me to say this; but I have enjoyed my visit to you (as you put it) immensely. Now that the greatest attraction has taken herself off I shall be free to devote myself to the neglected Edward. Not that he seems to mind very much.

I am very disappointed about the book. I hope you don't mind. Meanwhile – till Speech Day.
Yours very sincerely
Roland Leighton (or Aubrey if you prefer).

Roland and Edward returned to Uppingham. On her return to Buxton, Vera wrote:

Dear Roland
Thank you so very much for the 'Story of an African Farm', I am delighted with it. I cannot think why you should despise the edition, as it pleases me, for though the ornate bindings look very elegant in my bookcase, the plainer ones are the kind I *use*.... When I have read it I will write and tell you what I think of it. Probably I shall be unable to see any resemblance to myself in Lyndall, but doubtless that will be owing to my lack of skill in *self*-criticism.

I too was very sorry to go away on Tuesday, though I have had such a delightful time that I need not complain ... I have motored round all the Lakes except Westwater [sic], and I have never in my life seen anything so lovely – 'Earth has not anything to show more fair'.

I hear you & Edward managed still to live quite comfortably in spite of my departure, and that you were dragged off somewhat unwillingly to a dutiful inspection of our magnificent Manchester – once seen, always avoided!

I shall make every effort to come to Speech Day, & shall look out most carefully for the Quiet Voice, especially if you are well laden with prizes as the result of the occasion. The Quiet Voice, you perceive, is intensely symbolic, – at least to me.
Yours very sincerely
Vera M. Brittain[3]

Spring and early summer 1914 was an exciting, optimistic time. Walking home after playing tennis all afternoon:

Saturday May 16th
From being much below zero as they were yesterday, my spirits jumped up degrees & ended at a pretty high elevation …It was a simply perfect evening, the very houses, half in deep shadow, half in brilliant sunshine, seemed to sleep. The distance all round was a sort of misty blue & we could hear the calls of the birds in the stillness. It was a joy in those four hours to be alive. I did not get home for dinner till 8 o'clock.

There is nothing in Vera's diary about Roland during this time, but they exchanged a few friendly letters, discussing books and ideas, and bantering with each other. Three months later they were to recognise their mutual attraction.

'I am no longer perturbed in that direction'

Roland Leighton was not the first man to interest Vera. Since 1907, she had been infatuated with Adrian Stoop, one of the most highly regarded players in English rugby history. The eldest of nine in the extremely wealthy Dutch-Scottish family of Vera's school friend Cora, Adrian was 24 when he met 13-year-old Vera on her first visit to their home. She noted in her diary that he was 'the most interesting member of the West Hall community'.

Adrian had made his debut for the England rugby team against Scotland in March 1905. Garnering newspaper headlines like 'Stoops to Conquer', his exceptional mastery of tactics and skill made him an instant hit. As captain of the national team from 1910, Adrian, with his brother Freek (Frederick), went on to play for England until 1913. Lauded in the media for the whole of his career, Adrian's captaincy of the Harlequins turned them into the greatest English club before the First World War. Their ground, the Stoop, is named after him.[4]

In 1913, 30-year-old Adrian was dropped for the international against the Springboks at Twickenham, leading Vera to wonder whether the Rugby Football Union had made the right decision:

Saturday January 4th
Today is the great international rugby match England v the Springboks. Freek Stoop is playing for England but not Adrian – it seems hard that with Adrian's athletic skill & prowess he should be thought to be too old now to play in international rugby football matches. Thirty seems absurdly young for a man to stop playing a game, but I suppose the reasons for so doing are good.

A dance partner at the Brittains' sponsored ball was probably surprised at Vera's avid interest in rugby:

Adrian Stoop, c.1910. (*Ian Cooper*)

Wednesday January 8th
I had a very interesting dance with Mr Anderson, he talked all about the England International against the Springboks, which he watched and said he thought Adrian Stoop whatever his age ought certainly to have been in the team. Needless to say I <u>quite</u> agreed! He also informed me that poor Freek has been chucked for the next international.

A few days later Vera searched *The Times* to find the results: 'England, it appears, was beaten in the Rugby International ... by 9 points to 3. Freek, the papers say, was not always reliable.' She wondered whether Stella Sharp 'means anything to Adrian' and 'couldn't help reading about Adrian in Cora's letters with eagerness'.

By the time Vera went to a dance at Byfleet that summer, her infatuation had faded: 'I saw something of Adrian during the weekend. I am not now so perturbed in that direction – luckily, since he and Estelle Cox are practically hooked. I spent one day with him & Cora fishing.' She considered making Adrian a character in a novel but never did. There is a final brief diary mention in September 1914 when he enlisted for war.

'Marriage to any man I then knew, would have rooted me ... among the detested hills and dales of Derbyshire.'

As Vera's infatuation with Adrian Stoop faded, a Buxton man was becoming increasingly smitten with her. Aged 29, Bertram Spafford was nine years older than Vera. The eldest of four children, he worked for the family cotton trading company in Manchester. After Vera returned to live in Buxton, Bertram developed a habit of waiting by his garden gate hoping she might pass by on her way to and from town. The Spaffords' home at the entrance to The Park opposite the Devonshire Hospital was a good vantage point. If Bertram did not happen to meet Vera this way, he would wander round the Gardens in case she was promenading or listening to music. Failing that, he could hope to see her in church, or at an 'at home' musical evening or bridge party. And there was always the tennis club where Bertram enjoyed playing with his fiercely competitive partner and opponent. Fortunately, he was unaware of what Vera thought of his tennis:

> Tuesday June 24th, 1913
> He plays the most unsporting game … as soon as he begins to lose, he pelts the lady the whole time, not by placing but by hitting very swift shots straight at her; it may be quite a clever game but it is not quite what one likes to see a man doing.

A week later, Vera talked to Bertram for the first time, after he 'insisted on accompanying me all the way [home]; he is most amusing. I wish he were not quite such an idiot.' She learned later he had first noticed her at St John's church when she was 14 and, once Vera was presented formally to Buxton society as an eligible marriage prospect, Bertram assumed she would be open to a proposal. In September 1913, he wrote to her:

> My Dear Vera
> The night I took you down to dinner at your house 16 months ago, I first knew I loved you – and since then you have been everything in the whole world to me. I was intending to wait until I could afford to ask you to be my wife, before I told you this; but I realised last time you went away the awful risk I was running of losing you and I can't face this possibility.
> Is there the faintest chance of you caring for me even a little – and will you give me a chance of winning you, by waiting for me for a year, because by that time I shall be able to come forward and ask your father to let us be engaged openly.
> Sincerely yours
> Bertram Spafford
> You are of course free to show this to your parents.

Vera recorded in her diary that she 'sent B.S. a very cold & decided refusal … Daddy called it presumptuous and an insult.' Her letter was characteristically unequivocal:

Dear Mr Spafford
Your letter came as a great surprise to me and I was very sorry to receive it.

I cannot for a moment entertain the idea of accepting your proposal, and I must beg you to consider this as final, as I have no doubt whatsoever of my feelings on the subject. I do, and always have, regarded you merely as an acquaintance, and to the best of my knowledge have always treated you as such.

I regret the necessity of hurting your feelings in this matter and trust that you will forget about it as soon as possible.

Believe me.
Yours sincerely
Vera M. Brittain.

Edward offered a feminist understanding, with a little teasing thrown in:

Dear Mrs Vera Spafford
Thank you very much for your letter. I can stand 4d so you needn't have bothered about the stamps but thanks v. much all the same. I think it is quite exceptionally priceless you receiving a proposal at your age. Don't be too hard on the wretched man. If he really does love you I suppose he has a right to say so, so to speak, though as you say, I daresay the money question is not far in the background. If I were you I wouldn't be too rude because it is more his misfortune than his fault that he wants to marry you. Of course I know Father must be very annoyed but you should point out to him that the fault is not so much with the creation as with the Creator. Plenty of people before to-day have conceived impossible unions for themselves with another, without it being any fault of theirs. I daresay it has been a good thing in a way. It is always desirable to learn a thing early and everyone needs a little practice in the gentle art of rejection of suitors. You will doubtless have to repeat the process many times in future before you find the right man, if you ever do, as there are far too many men who consider themselves only in the marriage question. It is always 'she will suit me alright', never 'Shall I suit her alright' as well.

I hope you have started regular work [reading for Oxford] now; I want you to write and tell me what you are doing and where you are in a certain book etc. from time to time. Have you got Palgrave's Golden Treasury thing yet?

With much love,
Your affectionate
Edward.[5]

Bertram Spafford was completely out of his depth. Vera regarded her besotted would-be lover with a mixture of amusement and scorn, tempered by the allure of being admired, even adored. She found it hard to resist playing with his feelings:

> Tuesday November 18th
> I went this evening to a Progressive Bridge at Mrs Whitehead's. Crowds of people were there ... B.S. ... avoided me studiously, & I tried to be as alluring as possible to tease him. I managed to go from table to table on small scores till I finally caught up with him at the end of the evening. Poor thing! I am afraid he was very sad and uncomfortable, as he kept turning round so that he would not have to look at me, which was rather a difficulty as he was sitting opposite. I suppose it is wrong to sear people's feelings so, but oh! the temptation!

A week before her twentieth birthday, Vera yearned for a relationship with someone more impressive than the young men she knew:

> Saturday December 20th
> We went to a little dance at the Briggs'. Although I danced every dance hard & had what I suppose everyone would call a good time, it leaves me with a very unsatisfied feeling to have met so many stupid & superficial men, with whom all the girls are obviously so pleased. How I wish I could meet a good strong splendid man, full of force & enthusiasm, & in earnest about his life! There must *be* such!

Over the next nine months, she allowed the unfortunate Bertram to believe she might relent, whilst sanctimoniously hoping 'his small soul will grow through the suffering caused by rejection of him'. They had many tennis matches and awkward conversations:

> Friday May 29th, 1914
> As I approached the Spaffords' house I saw B.S. standing at the gate; wonderful to relate he did not go away ...& as I am determined somehow to stop this silly constrained business I stopped & spoke to him. He seemed as depressed as usual though he did answer; I looked at him very keenly & found that his eyes are honest & steady. Gwen appeared & spoke of tennis & asked him if we not get some up ... When she asked him when it should be he said rather stiffly 'Any time Miss Brittain likes' ... Miss Brittain talked to him in a very kind voice and smiled at him most sweetly when she said 'Good evening.' Next time the opportunity may arise for a more intimate conversation – perhaps an explanation of sorts.

Bertram's attempts to understand the complicated object of his infatuation were repeatedly confounded:

> Thursday June 4th
> … He said he could well understand why the ladies didn't like me & when I asked 'Why?', quite unsuspectingly he said 'You're too good-looking'. I got quite worked up talking of popularity; I said I thought it was a sign of weakness … I said I wanted to stand alone & live up to my ideals, that I did not, & never had, depended on anybody, & I added, with full regard for effect, 'Perhaps I never shall'. He suggested that I might change, but I replied that I might modify but the foundations would always remain the same. He said good-afternoon at the corner & hurried back very fast. I couldn't make out whether he was very upset or merely very annoyed.

Frequently bored, Vera tested the novelty of someone being in love with her:

> Tuesday June 9th
> The days are more interesting when I talk to B.S. To fall in love with him would be a perfect impossibility but it is very easy to be in love with love. To hear a man's voice say 'you' in a tone which he uses to no one else on earth, is in itself a gigantic temptation to make him go on saying it like that & to go on listening. It is wrong of me to think of such things, still worse to take pleasure in them, but then I am not good, & in spite of high purposes, only a very human girl. Still, that's no excuse!… I am doing very wrong, yet cannot prevent myself, & fate seems to give me all the assistance in its power. I wonder what the result of it all will be. (I really have no idea myself now.)

After being unable to walk home from the station with Bertram because her parents had come to meet her, Vera mused on whether 'one can really feel physically attracted towards someone with whom one is intellectually quite at variance … I thought myself quite free from it, but if so I don't know why I was so distracted because I could not walk home with my would-be lover.'[6]

Summer 1914 was a heady time. Vera was acutely aware of her attractiveness. She found Mr Railton, who directed 'Raffles', 'very attractive & interesting & I should like him to know a little more of me than the mere name & part I represent to him'. At a concert on 17 June: 'Close behind me was sitting a goodlooking man of about forty, a stranger to Buxton, who looked both wealthy & refined … he could scarcely take his eyes off me the whole time … I hope he will know me again when he sees me!'

When Arthur's second sister Edith visited Buxton, she advised her niece to empathise with Bertram's difficulties:

> Sunday June 28th
> … she appeared most anxious to have the man who wanted to marry me pointed out. We went into the Gardens after they had had the waters, & I pointed him out … he gave me one of his semi-shy smiles as we passed him & she said he had a 'nice kind face'. He hovered round me all the time … Aunt Edith … said he was obviously deeply in love with me & very wretched. She did not blame me at all (though she certainly would if she knew of some of my experiments in that direction) and did not see what I could do, but said that men feel this kind of thing very much & I must be careful not to hurt him worse. I protested that it was not so certain that he felt so much about me as all that, as he never came & talked to me. She said that of course he didn't as once he had been told he wasn't wanted it would be a most ungentlemanly thing to force his presence upon me, but that he seemed too attracted to keep quite away. I must say that never struck me … I began to wonder if what I have been secretly despising as half-heartedness & stupidity is really a stress of emotion too great to dare to trust itself too far. If he really suffers so, I am a hard-hearted little brute to tease him as I do; I really ought to put right away from me the temptation which is brought by the power to give pain.

Vera's contrition was short-lived. Her next flirtation with Bertram was over a review in the *Buxton Herald and Gazette* of her performance in 'Raffles':

> [it] said I looked so bewitching in my white frock 'that it was a wonder all the male members of the cast had not succumbed to my charm'. He said 'oh, it doesn't matter what you <u>wear</u>!' … He chided me for sitting up til 12.0 and getting up at 6. I said it didn't affect anything except one's beauty, & he laughed and said it certainly hadn't done that yet, & asked me if I ever looked in the mirror.[7]

'Until I have loved purely, passionately & selflessly, my character will always lack something.'

Vera's rejection of Bertram Spafford's advances, the beginning of her attraction to Roland Leighton and, as we shall see in Chapter Seven, her infatuation with Reverend Joseph Ward led to frequent reflections on love and marriage:

Wednesday July 1st
As I was passing the Spaffords' house the thunderstorms broke... Mrs Spafford...beckoned me to shelter ... I was there for nearly 2 hours! As soon as I came in, Bertram came racing down to talk to me & I talked to him & Mrs Spafford for some time... After a bit she went out & Gwen came in & we began a really interesting conversation...we discussed books & evolution, in which Gwen more or less agreed with me, & we pretty well squashed Bertram, who seemed to think England the only country & Christianity the only religion in the world. Finally our conversation drifted as usual into the position of women, especially with regard to marriage. We – espec. I – spoke of the new era of the companionship of woman, no longer the angel, set up on a pedestal, & shut out of everything, & no longer the toy, the sort of soft cushion or hot-water bottle for the husband to soothe himself with after having spent the day seriously. I said it would be a veritable hell to me, but that I believed a heaven was possible even in this generation, & that I would wait for that or have nothing. I said I did not believe that the intellectual woman 'went down' except by flirting and pretending she was not clever, but Gwen said she was certain that kind of woman always found her counterpart. She talked sensibly all the time, I was very surprised, & looked pretty & intelligent too... the whole family...were <u>most</u> charming to me...[B.S] actually appealed to me once or twice to know if he was correct on certain literary or historical points, a thing I have never known him do before.

Thursday July 2nd
To-night I stood by the open window & looked right out into the great wide space before me. I felt more alone than tongue can tell, but I felt a kind of bitter exaltation ... It was a very sultry night; thunderstorms had been about all day & the air was hazy with steam from damp hot ground. The lights from the houses were mingled with the still vapour, so that everything seemed to be wrapt in a kind of luminous mist.... I longed as I gazed into that dim expanse for something to worship, & respect with all my soul, something to which I can turn for counsel, before which I can kneel in reverence. I spend much time wondering whether I, who so desire to stand alone, shall ever find that something or someone the reverence of which is not dependence.

Two days later Bertram and Vera had a furious argument:

> I insisted that my ambition was a spiritual ambition and asked him very quietly what he thought it was. He said bitterly that I wanted to be famous & make a name for myself, but I should be none the better for it ... I gently but firmly insisted again that I had no care for the material glory even of fame but he did not believe it and said that the best thing for me to do was to learn to be a woman, as he could not see that I was acting like a woman at all at present. That really roused me, and I said that far from not being a true woman, I was essentially feminine but 'I suppose you think that because a person wishes to stand alone, to develop her intellect & make her will strong, she is not a true woman', I burst forth angrily ... He has done me great harm ... I don't care what the people who dislike me may think, but I am sorry that one, even such a one, who loves me should so utterly misjudge me as to imagine me a slave to ambition.

Bertram's criticism that worshipping someone would not bring happiness led Vera to reflect later, 'I know that until I have loved someone purely, passionately & selflessly, my character will always lack something'.

'Oh! How much I have discovered makes me long to know more!'

Before Vera's dalliance with Bertram Spafford, she developed an infatuation reminiscent of the 'grand passion' she once felt for Edith Fry at St Monica's. Longing for a friend in Buxton she could truly relate to, Vera became fascinated with Mrs Harrison, the organiser of the Oxford extension lectures. In May 1913, a break during a tennis match enabled them to have their first proper conversation:

> Tuesday May 27th
> I don't know whether she has taken a fancy to me as I have supposed, but I know she does attract me; there is an undeniable fascination about her. She was telling me her opinion of most of the Buxton people, with whom you never get any further though you meet them again & again, & who have so large an idea of their own importance & so little to have an idea about. She was, she told me, blackballed when she first wanted to enter the tennis club. It is disgraceful the way people here – the snobs! – have treated her simply because she had the courage to marry Mr Harrison, who being the proprietor of St. Ann's Hotel was lower in the social scale, & of course with these parvenus the fact he is clever & well-educated doesn't count at all.[8]

Thursday May 29th
...she certainly gets to attract me <u>more</u> & more. In fact (foolish as it may seem, afterwards, but I have set myself the task of chronicling the honest impression of each day as it passes so must not try & deceive myself). I am by way of feeling quite a G.P. for her... How she must have suffered from the unkindness & snobbishness & neglect of these people here! No wonder she has tried to pretend she does not care a jot...When I got in I found an invitation from Mrs Lawson to tea & tennis... so I pray for a fine day.

Mrs Harrison (we never learn her first name) was probably in her early 30s when she met Vera. Before marrying, she had studied music in Paris for three years. John Milligan Harrison was a Buxton resident who took over the lease of St Ann's Hotel from his father in 1904, but we do not know how the Harrisons met.

Vera's idol offered her a different image of womanhood from other Buxton women and they both felt alienated from the snobbishness of Buxton society. Vera was impressed by Mrs Harrison's organisation of the Oxford lectures and moved by her love for her two children and her 'sweet' relationship with Milligan.

In October 1913, Stella Sharp came to stay and after meeting Vera's idol, 'quite fell in love with her'. Vera reported Mrs Harrison's 'attraction for me is still going very strong', and noted 'everything she puts on she adorns', admiring her 'glorious eyes... so blue & brilliant & full of expression & intelligence'. That month, Mrs Harrison invited Vera to join her lecture committee.

Vera also liked Mrs Lawson, the wife of the headmaster of Buxton College; 'dear Mrs Lawson seemed sweeter than ever...I only wish she took half the interest in me that I take in her!' Another long and exhilarated diary entry noted how the two women had transformed Vera's feelings about Buxton:

Wednesday November 5th
... after nearly two years of peevish discontent, I love this place at last! I revel in the wide open spaces, open to so large an expanse of earth & sky. I feel as free as the racing clouds or as the wind that blows them...I realised too that loneliness does not depend on the absence of many people, or its reverse...one may be as lonely in a crowded room as out solitary upon the wind-swept heath... I cannot of course deny that the acquaintance of Mrs Harrison & in a lesser degree of Mrs Lawson has made all the difference to me in what I feel about this little town. So with them here, & the hills & winds & spaces to keep me free, may I love it long just as I love it now.

Monday November 17th
I have had the most thrilling afternoon. We gave a truly fashionable bridge party, to which fifteen of the most interesting of all the people in Buxton came. Nor to mention the one…What really overjoyed me was that between the hands she asked me if I would come up to her house one day & help her send out over 200 circulars (part of the Lectures business) and stay some time. I took some of the many opportunities I had of studying her to-day. What a mixture she is of good & evil, & how strong in both! There is strength in the firmness of her chin, the uprightness of her head & whole figure, & even in its slim grace; her lips are so thin & firmly closed that they express much of hardness & cruelty & a sort of fierce, unyielding, unforgiving vigilance, yet in her eyes there are untold depths of idealism, & loveableness, intelligence, sweetness – & mockery too! Her thin sensitive hands seem to show how very much she is alive & awake to all that goes on – nothing escapes her. Oh! how what I have observed makes me long to know more!… her dress was a dark blue velvet with white round the neck & she had a black hat….I did not notice every detail, but Mother and I both agreed how well she had looked. What I did notice were her lovely rings…she has such nice shaped hands.

Two days later, Vera went to help Mrs Harrison send out publicity leaflets for the lectures. From another impassioned diary entry:

Wednesday November 19th, 1913
Well, I am not likely to forget this afternoon; how I wish instead of its being all over, that it was all to come. I arrived at Mrs Harrison's about 2.30 and we started straight away to work, I writing addresses on envelopes & she reading out the names to me, & folding up circulars and putting them inside envelopes. Mr Harrison also was there the first two or three minutes; they are always very sweet together… Then we two were left alone & got through simply heaps, tho' we might have got through still more if we hadn't talked hard all the time. I only wish I could remember all the conversation, it was all precious, & got more and more intimate as time went on. She said somewhat pointedly that, while you always had an antipathy to some people, there were others with whom you felt on the same plane at once & she went on to tell me that she had noticed me first at the Hunt Ball two years ago, when Mrs Ellinger pointed me out as a debutante. I don't know whether that remark meant anything I wanted it to mean, but you don't generally trouble to think where you first met people unless they interest you a little…. Oh! I am glad I went,

for great as I knew the good to be in her, it is already even greater than I thought... I do wonder if I am one of the people with whom she seems to be on the same plane at once. Oh! How I pray for opportunities of knowing her more & more!... I love her way of talking with her eyes as well as her lips. I always feel depressed though when I say goodbye to her & go away feeling that having seen so much of her I am no nearer ....to her real self...I suppose such an intimacy as I hope for is too good a thing to happen.

But for all Vera's yearning for friendship, she met Mrs Harrison only occasionally and there was little opportunity to talk. By the beginning of 1914, there was no progress:

Thursday January 1st
At midnight I lay in bed & listened to the bells ringing for the New Year. This morning I tobogganed with Tom Lace & the Cawleys; the day started beautiful but about midday a thaw began & soon everything was drippy water. We started on Manchester Road, then to The Park, & back to Manchester Road. Finally we gave it up. I walked back with the Laces and met Mrs Harrison and her sister going home. The former, who still looks very pale, gave me one of her enigmatical smiles after some ordinary remark of mine about the weather. Strange how few opportunities I get of really seeing much of her – but the possible is ever with us!

Friday January 2nd
I seem to be writing to-night with hardly any of my circumstances changed from last year, when I sat here and wrote at the same time. Mrs Harrison, B.S. & Oxford are the only really important things that have come into my existence since last Jan. 2nd. Otherwise – the same surroundings, the same friends, the same hopes, the same objects in life, & perhaps a still greater number of unfulfilled wishes! Shall I be writing here, I wonder, next Jan. 2nd with all the circumstances still unchanged? Truly we count time in events, not years.

A fortnight later, Vera's enjoyment of the annual ball at Corbar Hall was marred by the appearance of Mr Harrison without his wife. At the end of a long, animated diary entry about the décor, music and dance partners, Vera reported: 'The evening was delightful & we stayed right until the end. It needed only Mrs. Harrison's presence to make it perfect but her not being there gave a slight feeling of incompleteness which made me almost sad as I went home.'

This is the last affectionate mention of Mrs Harrison. Following a few fleeting references to seeing her at some occasion or other, she appears for the final time on 22 April 1915:

> Mrs Harrison called this afternoon; she was as attractive as ever but looks older & more lined since the baby came. We talked chiefly about Oxford & the war. She said she supposed I should find a little time for tennis even if I was nursing & reminded me with amusement how had all pressed her to play so eagerly last year, & she had had to make up excuses!

Although Vera's longing for friendship never came to anything, Mrs Harrison inspired 'Mrs Hastings', a central character in *Not Without Honour* ('Her face, though pale and delicately lined, was amazingly young when she smiled'). Ostracised by Torborough (Buxton) society because she is married to a dentist, Mrs Hastings is suddenly in huge social demand after the obnoxious matrons discover she is the daughter of an esteemed Liberal peer and compete to receive her calling cards. Mrs Hastings and Christine Merrivale share feelings of alienation and frustrated ambition. As well as lampooning Buxton society, Vera used her heroine to voice progressive (and, in those days, controversial) ideas about the need for working class women burdened with too many children to have access to birth control.

The Harrisons were to run St Ann's until the late 1920s. We do not know what happened to them after that. Perhaps Mrs Harrison came across her fictional incarnation in *Not Without Honour* but if she did read *Testament of Youth*, she would have found the most cursory reference: 'a cultured woman, needless to say on the fringes of the Buxton set'.

'As soon as I saw his plain, intelligent face & dark expressive eyes again'

Against a backdrop of widespread public ignorance that war was looming, Vera spent two gloriously hot July days with Edward and Edith at Uppingham's 1914 Speech Day and re-met Roland Leighton:

> Friday July 10th
> We went along the dark quad past the lighted windows until Edward tapped at Roland's and said a visitor wanted to see him. The window was opened and I leaned in. As soon as I saw his plain, intelligent face & dark expressive eyes again, I knew I had not overrated their attraction for me

– the call up of mind to mind & sympathy to sympathy made itself felt immediately. I stood teasing him & telling him I would look out for every atom of conceit ... He said he would think of me when he went to receive his prizes & knew he would fall over the steps & make a fool of himself.

Sitting apart in the rose garden while everyone else milled around, the pair resumed their philosophical conversations. Next day they continued long 'abstract discussions' and talked about their own characters. Roland was due to receive the school's seven most important prizes and his friends joked he had a wheelbarrow at the ready. Vera was impressed: 'so marvellous an intellect & not-easily-understandable personality. The reserved conceit ... which never boasts, but subtly reveals itself in those attributes which make the boys call him "The Lord".'

To Vera, Roland had several irresistible attractions: he was interesting and intense, he declared himself a feminist and the pair shared feelings of alienation, intellectual superiority and distinctiveness from their peers. They were similar in other ways too: diffident, uncomfortable showing emotion and believing in the importance of self-control. Both knew they were admired but not popular; Roland confided that Vera made him feel less lonely because she admitted to being isolated too. He said his fellow pupils found him 'haughty and conceited'; Vera told him, 'I was very conceited myself – he agreed he was too.' And she felt a great affinity with 'a sort of depression that resembles my own kind very much... I said goodbye to him with more indifference than I felt. I could not help wondering whether & when I shall see him again'.

A fortnight later, Vera reflected again on the sort of man she might marry:

Friday July 24th
Maurice, upon my saying I was quite heartless ... said that I should probably marry a very masterful sort of person who would rule me utterly. I cannot imagine that happening but I would a thousand times rather do that than be bound to someone my inferior in intellect – for that would indeed be a loss of freedom.

Vera and Edith had one of their heart-to-heart conversations, this time about Bertram:

Sunday July 26th
Mother & I actually had a long & animated discussion after supper about me, my lack of heart. I told Mother I discussed B.S.'s affection for me quite freely with him; I hoped she was not shocked but I wouldn't alter myself

even if she were. She did not appear shocked; she seems to grasp modern conditions quite well ... she managed to sympathise quite respectably with me.

By August 1914, Bertram had finally realised his feelings were completely unrequited. Ten days after war was declared, Vera reflected for the final time on their awkward relationship and her treatment of him:

> B.S. was in the shadow of the bushes as we passed their house, but neither moved nor spoke. When I think how generously yesterday he said that though I was a flirt I had not flirted with him, and that all that had happened had been entirely his fault, I feel much more kindly towards him than I ever have before. Considering the intentional provocation I have given him, he has been remarkably patient with me. I only hope that he may some how, some day, be rewarded for the love that 'suffereth long & is kind'.

Meanwhile, Mrs Harrison was not the only Buxton person to intrigue Vera: from November 1913 when her 'grand passion' was at its height, the charismatic, controversial Reverend Joseph Ward was fast becoming another focus for one of Vera's intense fascinations. He was to be an important inspiration for her ideas and beliefs.

Chapter Seven

'More Influence Upon Me for Good and Strength than Anyone'

A Very Unorthodox Friendship

'The church which once used to be so empty, was simply packed'

Putting the finishing touches to the sermon on the first Sunday in 1914, Reverend Joseph Harry Ward knew his adoring congregation would, as usual, enjoy his eloquence and passion even if his repeated warnings against present-day indifference unsettled them. Today he had based his sermon on the text 'Arise, wake out of sleep', planning to stress that virtue did not consist in churchgoing and piety, but in daily work for the sake of right. And he would remind those who kept telling him he did not preach comforting sermons that he was not in Fairfield to be comforting but to arouse people from their apathy.[1]

Ward was proud of his skills as a preacher and his talent for crafting a well-honed sermon. After leaving school at 13, he supplemented a stint as postmaster with avid reading. In his twenties, self-taught proficiency with the English language led Ward to become a secretary to a steel magnate in Sheffield where he was much in demand for speech writing amongst the city's aldermen and steel bosses.[2] After completing four years' theological training at Cambridge University, his first curacy when he was 32 had been in a very poor part of Nottingham. The Bishop of Lichfield, in whose diocese Fairfield sat, had decided that Ward's beliefs and his impoverished background as one of six children to a Nottingham builder made him a perfect fit for a parish which, after 25 years with the vicar Joseph Eayrs, was in a very poor ecclesiastical and spiritual state. When he

Reverend Joseph Ward, date unknown. (*Mark Bostridge*)

arrived in January 1913, the *Buxton Advertiser* had given 34-year-old Ward a glowing welcome.³

Strains in the relationship with Eayrs became apparent almost immediately. At his interview with the bishop, Ward had warned he might be too radical for Fairfield. Three months after he arrived, the situation had become intolerable. Joseph had gone to see the bishop, intending to resign, but was persuaded to stay. By January 1914, Joseph Eayrs was frequently using his own services to criticise his curate who was no longer allowed to officiate at burials or baptisms, or even visit ill and bereaved parishioners. Ward knew most of his congregation had signed a petition asking him to stay, but others supported Eayrs' campaign to remove him. Joseph and his wife did not know how much longer they could stand it.⁴

Still, on that first Sunday of 1914, there was a service to give. Donning his black liturgical cassock and white surplice, Ward prepared to leave the house. In many ways, Fairfield had worked out well: he was extremely popular; his services were packed; the school was flourishing; 260 men had joined his Bible class, an unprecedented number, and his innovation of 'open Sundays' had been a huge success, with wives and friends attending too. He told his men's class that Christianity should make them 'not superior, nor sanctimonious or cringing, but manly'.⁵ And Inglewood, a pretty, red-tiled semi-detached villa on a tranquil lane, with a front garden and far-reaching views at the back, was much nicer than the Nottingham home had been.

Crossing the lane, the Wards went through the side gate into the churchyard. As Joseph greeted his congregation, he saw a dark-haired young woman resplendent in expensive Sunday clothes, sitting at the back of the packed church with a tall young man who was obviously her brother. Ward was intrigued. Middle-class Buxton residents never ventured to St Peter's: it was over a mile uphill from town and, in any case, social class usually determined people's choice of church.

This was Vera's third attendance at St Peter's. Accompanied by Edith for her first two visits to Fairfield, Vera had no difficulty persuading Edward. With 'the wind blowing great guns', they strode up to the village, pausing on the green to hear the joyous cacophony of church bells ringing out across the town below. As Vera waited for the service to start, she was struck again by how much she liked the 'enthusiasm and sincerity' of the plain, solid church, musing that no other Buxton church had that feeling. Its stained-glass depiction of St Peter in jail had the angel's robes in the purple and green of the women's suffrage movement. Vera was intrigued by the contrast between the Fairfield congregation and the wealthy people she usually mingled with at St John's. Several had brought small children who were by no means silent, and she was surrounded by coughing and sneezing.⁶ Edward was looking forward to hearing the organist.

'A sort of Robert Elsmere'

Vera first came across Joseph Ward nine months after he came to Fairfield when she read two pages in the *Buxton Advertiser* about the religious controversies he was stirring up in the town. From a much longer account in her diary:

> Saturday November 15th, 1913
> This morning ...was a continuation of the religious controversy started last week by Mr J.H. Ward, the new curate of Fairfield, who is a sort of Robert Elsmere. He wrote then to ask for justice with regard to a statement made at a Bible Society meeting (at which all the narrow & evangelical clergy of the district were present) that he had denied the Bible to be the Word of God. To-day there are four letters in answer, three from Fairfield men, testifying to the excellent work done by Mr Ward, & the sort of religious wave that is passing over the village; the other & longest was from a regular narrow old-fashioned evangelical parson. He condemns Mr Ward right & left as a heretic – and then goes on to ask Mr Ward to answer certain statements, taken down in writing from Mr Ward's teaching – such as 'The Garden of Eden is a myth', 'There is nothing miraculous about the birth of Christ', 'I decline to believe in a God who requires me to be washed in blood', 'There is not Hell except in this life'. It rejoiced my heart to read them & feel that there is at least one in the Church of England who is moving with the new thought & new truth of the age.
>
> Mother and Daddy read the letters, & Mother more or less agreed, in her mild way, with Mr Ward. Daddy, somewhat to my surprise, went on like anything, saying that such men as Mr Ward were dangerous to the Church, that it would be a good thing if he were tumbled out etc. I was too indignant to speak & all my powers of argument promptly left me; I did try to argue ... but he seemed to think it terrible heresy, & argued on the lines of the usual threadbare superstitions & traditions – i.e. that any science or discovery that proved the Bible different from what he had always believed it must be wrong *because* it told him different from what he had always believed ... Finally he ended up by saying that I didn't know what I was talking about, & that it was ridiculous a little slip of a girl arguing with him about what I didn't understand etc ...
>
> I do not for a moment believe that I have found the truth (what, indeed, is truth?) but I do think I have found a glimmer of it, & have entered upon

a train of thought which will develop and modify as long as I have mind & spirit ... Thus I believe that the faith I hold now (which is what I have thought out for myself, certainly not which I have been taught, except in a few instances) ... is of true & lasting value to me, is, I <u>know</u>, of more real truth, is at least more able to be proved, than the dogmas of superstition & worn-out incorrect doctrine, with which the majority of Church of England parsons fill my ears every time I go to church.

A week later Vera saw 'young Mr Ward' for the first time, in town:

Friday November 21st
He has a pale, rather sad face & very thoughtful eyes, & a firm jaw. Mother was talking to old Mrs Bennett about the letters in the paper; Mrs Bennett has great faith in Mr Ward although she is old & might have been old-fashioned, & says she heard an address of his that was most inspiring. She does not understand how any enlightened being of the present day can dare to contradict him, but said that there were so many people in the world who never troubled to think & her advice was to let them be ... She says she knows from experience that a person's views may become quite unbalanced & leave them with no faith at all by a modern overthrowing of all their traditional beliefs... I don't agree that people ought to be left alone in their blindness; I don't think one ought to *force* one's own convictions

Fairfield parishioners, early 1900s.

on other people, but I do firmly believe they ought to be aroused to think things out for themselves & come to a conclusion which would be of value because of their own making.

Two days later, after an 'appallingly dull service' at Burbage, she and Edith went to the evening service at St Peter's:

Sunday November 23rd
To-day has been more interesting than Sundays are as a rule ... [St Peter's,] which once used to be so empty, was simply packed. They were nearly all poor people & he was talking to one of them in the aisle when we got there, moving, with his pale thoughtful tired face, like a leader among them. The service was short & very simple, such a contrast with this morning, & when Mr Ward began to preach all the discomforts of our crowded pew were forgotten at once. He took as his text those most wonderful of words (which have so often served as an excuse for wearying people with all sorts of obvious & platitudinal remarks), 'I am the Light of the World' ... it is impossible to reproduce his sermon in a few words, or to give any idea of the originality with which he treated his text ...

You couldn't exactly have heard a pin drop while he was speaking ... But he seemed to rise quite beyond the undercurrent of noise, & held everybody tense & spellbound till the burst of enthusiasm with which he ended. Afterwards he shook hands with everyone at the church door. I do hope soon to get to know him.[7]

Sunday November 31st
...his eloquence is great – not only does his sermon excel in depth of thought, beauty of expression, wealth of illustration, but it is also full of that strange power of spiritual & intellectual imagination which holds audiences spellbound.

Ward brought politics into his sermons, castigating politicians who prophesised 'the end of all things'. Vera summarised his sermon approvingly:

Sunday 14th December
...people want something to hope for, a vision... the end of one thing implied the beginning of another, the end of powerlessness, the beginning of power, the end of weakness, the beginning of strength, the end of sin, the beginning of righteousness etc. The end is not something to be dreaded & feared but rather to be worked for as the end of the old thing & the beginning of the new.

Ward had strong similarities to the hero of *Robert Elsmere* which Vera read at St Monica's two years earlier. This best-selling novel by Mrs Humphry Ward presented the deep theological rifts of late nineteenth-century Anglicanism to a mainstream audience. At the heart of Victorian philosophical and literary circles, Mrs Ward's uncle was Matthew Arnold. The novel reputedly sold a million copies, a phenomenal sales figure for the time. Such was its significance that Liberal prime minister William Ewart Gladstone published a lengthy rebuttal of the novel in the May 1888 issue of *Contemporary Review*. To 17-year-old Vera, the book was gripping and disturbing. It made her doubt orthodox Anglican observance and, as her diary shows, Ward sparked a deep lifelong interest in religious and spiritual questions.

Robert Elsmere is now almost forgotten and, even among scholars of Victorian literature, remains largely unknown or unread. It tells the story of a clergyman who trained in theology at Oxford and, during his first curacy, experiences a profound and unsettling de-conversion from traditional Anglicanism. Unlike many Victorian sceptics, Elsmere does not abandon the superstition and dogma of the Anglican Church for atheism but instead adopts a gruelling life of Christian social service in the East End of London.

The hero must confront profound questions raised by a movement called 'higher criticism'. Influenced by European intellectual movements, it was first popularised in England by Samuel Taylor Coleridge and then George Eliot. Supporters questioned traditional teaching about the miraculous elements underpinning the Bible which were presented to worshippers through sacraments. Higher critics proposed that, like any text, the Bible should be studied to understand what its authors meant in their own context. Advocates challenged the idea of God and Christ as divine and the Bible's stories as factual accounts of miracles, arguing instead, that man created the idea of God to express the divine within himself.

For Elsmere, it was the Bible's account of the Resurrection that most engaged his attention and ultimately undermined his faith. In his deconversion, he comes to believe that Christ is a man amongst equals and that much of the Bible's teaching is from a different stage of learning and civilisation: 'the imperfect, half-childish products of the mind of the first century'.[8]

It is difficult for contemporary secular readers to appreciate the popular nineteenth century appeal of *Robert Elsmere*. It is a wordy, theologically complicated story, in which the main characters offer didactic religious expositions through lengthy speeches. The story's popular impact came out of a world wrestling with insights from Darwin's *On the Origin of Species*, discoveries in geology and astronomy and new radical ideas in German philosophy and political thought. The 'Victorian crisis of faith' in the Anglican and Catholic

'More Influence Upon Me for Good and Strength than Anyone'   109

church emerged from fierce disagreements generated by these new insights. They posed deeply unsettling questions for traditional Christian orthodoxy.

'The usual sleepiness – I may say boredom – in church'

The Brittains went to church every Sunday, often twice, either to the early service at Burbage where Edith did the flowers and helped with the Mothers' Union, or St John's just down the road from Melrose, where Arthur often did the weekly collections. Its graceful Italianate building was paid for by the fifth Duke of Devonshire and built between 1802 and 1811. It was, and still is, Buxton's most Anglo-Catholic church and, in Vera's day, the Devonshires attended services there.⁹

A couple of weeks later, Vera enjoyed another ball at Corbar Hall and prayed afterwards for friendship. The following day, she and Edith visited the Wards:

> Friday January 16th, 1914
> Heaven ... won't help those who don't help themselves ... I persuaded Mother to come to Fairfield with me & call upon his wife – hoping they would both be in. A little maidservant showed us to a very small sitting-room & then left us alone for some time so I studied my surroundings. The house is

Joseph Ward and his family (Ward is standing next to his wife, on the right of the second row), early 1900s. (*Mark Bostridge*)

quite near the church, & though tiny is much better than the places where some curates have to live. The front …looks on to Fairfield churchyard, but at the back …there is a view right across the valley. It looked very dreary and miserable on such a grey foggy day as this, but sometimes must look beautiful in the brightness of our occasional clear skies. The room itself was just like the sitting-room of a lodging-house but more homely.

After …some time Mrs Ward came in, obviously rather frightened of us at first & not knowing quite how to take us. She is a very small woman of the insignificant type that one would never notice out of doors, & was dressed in dark blue. She is considerably older than he, & looks forty, but probably judging from her sad expression & worn look, has grown prematurely old. She addressed us very nervously, using our names a great deal, but became much more at her ease as we explained our sympathy with Mr Ward & eulogised his teaching. She, like he, was probably one of the people, most likely a district nurse, & has not risen as far from the ranks as he…Apart from her nice blue eyes…the whole effect is plain & rather pathetic – clearly her husband goes beyond the exterior in his judgements…I liked her.

Arthur and Edith did not pressurise Vera to attend a particular church, but Joseph Ward reinforced her dissatisfaction with traditional services. She was especially critical of Reverend Charles Elliott Scott-Moncrieff, who had trained at Trinity College, Cambridge and came to St John's in 1911. His religious teaching epitomised the Anglicanism Robert Elsmere rebelled against:

Sunday January 19th, 1913
Felt the usual sleepiness … in church. Oh! 'Church of England', 'where is the *King*, that I may worship him?' After supper I read from the book Miss Heath Jones lent me, *Christ and Human Need*. In spite of its unusual sensibility & clearness in dealing with the historical Christ from the orthodox point of view, I closed it still with the same belief, namely that Christ, though among the most wonderful & the greatest – perhaps *the* greatest – that has ever lived, was man even as we are, & that his Divine nature was the same in quality – though greater in degree & realisation – as our own.

On Thursday 22 January:

Edward and I met Mrs Ward in Boots today … I introduced her to Edward; he was very surprised to see her as he thought I was merely talking to somebody's maid. She had a little girl of four or five with her, whom she told me she had adopted from a poor family.

Later that day, after a very enjoyable afternoon of bridge, Vera and Edith went to a lecture at the town hall by Dr Bennett of Liverpool College on 'The Bible in the Light of Modern Scholarship'. The controversy Ward had stirred up resulted in a packed hall:

> It was an excellently tolerant lecture ... the main point the lecturer urged throughout ... was that it is the spirit of the Bible not the letter of it that is our strength & inspiration & to which we must cling. The hall was packed & the audience very interested & attentive, except for a few giggling schoolgirls who should never have been there. There were several men on the platform including Canon Scott-Moncrieff, who took the chair ... Mr Ward never spoke at all; I half suspect the lecture was arranged on account of the letters in the paper and no doubt he felt it concerned him too nearly for him to begin to take an active part in it ... and his expressive face showed very varied emotions of which humour was not the least frequent ... he looked very tired & worn, & as usual rather sad.
>
> I think the whole affair was splendid ... a very difficult subject was treated in such a way as to offend no denomination or holder of independent opinion ... the spirit of toleration that pervaded all [was] certainly a step in the right direction ... [it] is an advance which the Church, leaving her narrowness & bigotry aside at last, must do to imitate and continue.

As Vera became interested in the community served by St Peter's, she increasingly disliked the social circle attracted to St John's. Edith's experience of a tea party at Mrs Scott-Moncrieff's led Vera to observe:

> Monday February 3rd
> ...she seemed to have invited all the wealthy, influential & swells ... It does not seem entirely diplomatic in a parson's wife to choose out the swells & not only from her own parish, & leave out the less wealthy & showy. Such is an act of the Church but not the Kingdom of Heaven!

Long reflections on religious questions and Vera's own deeply felt idealism competed, in typical Vera fashion, with more frivolous interests:

Tuesday February 4th

I had quite a gay bridge at the Whiteheads' this afternoon. I was most rash and doubled all I could and went 'no trumps' on both possible & impossible hands, but just missed the prize. I finished Felix Holt after dinner. How George Eliot's books do inspire me; they make all good seem worthwhile. How I long to be such a character as Felix Holt, to have no regard for failure, to hold an ideal for humanity high enough to be forever leading further onward & yet applicable to the smallest things of life! How I yearn to follow pure and heavenly aspiration, without the alloy of a desire for self-glory or of personal ambition, to heal some little part of the sore burdens of mankind!

Friday March 1st

Good Friday – which in spite of its solemnity brought a fresh excitement. I went first to church with Daddy & then to the first part of three hours service with Mother, which led to one of my not-infrequent spiritual conflicts as to 'what is truth'. It would be easy – or rather, so much easier – to accept religion in a form in which the church doles it out – beautiful enough but to me, I will by no means say incorrect, for I dare not, but not complete enough, not satisfying enough. Yet, when one cannot accept what is given only, it is hard to find fresh paths for oneself. Yet is not this very difficulty the inspiration of the determination 'to strive, to seek, to find & not to yield'! Heaven grant me at least to be true to, honest with, myself & work from right & just motives. May it grant me also never to be self-satisfied, never to reach that pleasant state of complacency which lulls the spirit to sleep! Gladys Lathbury rang me up at the telephone [*sic*] while I was at church. I rang her up when I returned & learned that she wanted me to act in the play *The Amazons* which they are getting up.

Saturday March 8th, 1913

I went to the Hippodrome [Buxton's picture house] tonight to see that extraordinary cinematograph 'From Manger to Cross' or 'Jesus of Nazareth'. I did not quite know what to expect, the story of Christianity is a somewhat unusual subject for a cinematograph – but I was very impressed. Somehow the fact of seeing it pictured – & the pictures really were beautiful, made the reality of it all seem so much nearer. What a strange combination of mythology, beauty & history that great story seems to be & yet it is all so wonderful and the Spirit, which is what really matters, is so loving & embodied in all that we can define, of the forms in which it is pictured, however exaggerated or imperfect ... Somehow beyond all else it seemed

'More Influence Upon Me for Good and Strength than Anyone' 113

Buxton Hippodrome, early 1900s.

to dwell upon the awful loneliness of that sublime figure. How can we but help, before that marvellous patience, to grow patient & in the light of that self-denying love to grow ourselves more loveable![10]

'A guiding and transforming power in one's life'

With preparations for Oxford in full swing, the first few months of 1914 were an exciting time. Visiting her dressmaker Mrs Fowler at her tiny cottage in Fairfield to talk about dress patterns, Vera sat 'in the corner of a deliciously warm kitchen' and the women shared their admiration of Ward. She walked home in one of her idealistic, almost euphoric moods:

> There was an influence in the air which made me feel I loved all the world & every person I met. I realised absolutely how much more [people like Mr Ward], the strivers & strugglers of our indifferent age, or the comparatively poor & kind & unassuming are nearer to my soul than the kind of people I dance with & play bridge with. It is with those whom so-called polite society despise or laugh at that I feel alive ... But courage

– tonight I have chosen – chosen poverty, loneliness, scorn, the way of trial & sorrow, before comfortable words & congenial things.[11]

Vera became more impatient with 'the droning platitudes of the conventional platitudes of the conventional parsons that leave us where they found us'. In contrast, Joseph Ward preached 'simply indescribable' sermons, and Vera was enthralled by 'his mighty gift, how the personality of the man (if it *can* be separated from his gift) influences one'.

But Ward was clearly weighed down by his situation in Fairfield:

Sunday March 29th
[Mr Ward] looked very pale & miserable, & read the lessons in that nervous way he always has when something is up … I think he was trying to persuade himself as well as us that the blessings [of] suffering overcame its miseries … Mother told Mrs Ward we wanted them both to come to tea, & that we would have music. I do hope we cheered her up as she seemed so despondent & there seems to be no doubt that *he* is. Oh! they will drive him away from his people – his poor & his work.

By this time, Edward was being taught by St Peter's organist and sometimes played at services there. On one occasion Vera accompanied him to his practice and 'tried out what it felt like from the pulpit … I should not mind at all speaking from the pulpit – it is a fine place!'

Two weeks later, Ward and his wife came to tea at Melrose.

Tuesday April 14th
… I was very agitated inwardly about it & when they finally did arrive, I felt hot & shy at once. Just at first they were both a little uncomfortable; she, in fact, was the less nervous of the two … Luckily they were neither of them too shy to eat; they both enjoyed their tea, he especially. I told him I was nervous of playing because I had not practised for so long, but he said they were not critical. I mentioned as we were getting ready that Edward was very ambitious in trying to compose sonatas. 'It is a relief to find someone who is ambitious', he said, so I replied 'We are both somewhat afflicted that way, for Edward tries to compose & I write poems, & Daddy thinks us both mad.' He roared with laughter & then said he was sure he would like both to hear the music & read the poems. I managed to play the Grieg sonata much better than I thought I could. Somehow when he is close by, a kind of force *impels* one to give one's very best.

He was very pleased to hear I got my Somerville Exhibition without any coaching, & told me that he coached himself for everything except

Euclid lessons, to get which he walked 7 miles there & 7 miles back. Such courage as it was – to leave his profitable business & start examinations & present himself at Cambridge at the age of 28. He told us that Fairfield suits him & he doesn't mind the struggles on account of his health; it is the restraint & the lack of independence that drive him to distraction … I said 'But the very fact you're opposed shows how much you are needed here.' I looked at him very intensely, & he turned suddenly & fixed his penetrating eyes on my face.

He is so perfectly natural & delightful & his sense of humour is very keen. There is no affected manner, no hushed voice when he speaks of things religious; religion & life are not separable to him, which is as it should be – & he does *not* wear a cross on his watch-chain. A cross on a watch-chain always typifies the effeminate & inefficient parson to me – specially when it has a text on it! He went on to say 'You see, I have thrown a good deal of the old theology overboard.' 'I shouldn't come & listen to you if you hadn't,' said I … I felt so strangely happy & content all the time he was near me. When I went downstairs to them as they went, we happened to mention my coming exam. & my mathematical difficulties. 'Oh! you'll do it,' he said, & half raising his hand, 'Rise,' he said to me quietly. 'Achieve'… & having thus spoken & smiled a smile of extraordinary sweetness at me, he turned & went down the drive.

After attending one of Ward's services, Arthur had dismissed the curate as 'playing to the gallery' and a 'pleb talking to plebs', protesting that he preferred to be amongst his 'own kind'. Nonetheless, when the Wards visited Melrose, Arthur joined in a discussion about the social make-up of Fairfield, the economic hardship of Ward's parishioners, and the difficulties created by Joseph Eayrs.

In May 1914, Eayrs had a stroke and replaced his and Ward's ministrations with a locum. It was the final straw. Ward accepted a post in Bournemouth as association secretary to Dr Barnardo's Homes, a charity for orphaned boys, and planned to leave at the end of August. On 27 May, Vera wrote at length about visiting the Wards with Edith. She and Joseph were left alone in his study to talk about literature, the need for self-reliance and his feelings about being pressured to leave Buxton. When Edith and Mrs Ward 'came up & disturbed us…I had forgotten everything but his magnetic personality & the joy of discussing things with one so exceptionally understanding as he'. A few days later, Ward's sermon was despondent:

I simply longed to comfort him, to give him some strength in return for some of that which he has poured out so freely for me & others. Whatever it is I feel toward him rose stronger than ever & seemed to swamp all other feelings; I don't care whether the cause of his trouble was personal loss or some less worthy motive such as wounded pride ... I would have given ever so much to have been able to remove it.[12]

Vera and her mother went again to St Peter's and Edith invited Ward to lunch. During his visit, he mentioned that he had seen Vera perform in 'Raffles' on both nights, commenting that 'we all wore lovely dresses', and stayed all afternoon till tea:

> Monday 22nd June 1914
> He told me ... that I was both artistic and scientific & ... nearly as original as Maggie Tulliver in The Mill on the Floss as I said I had a fellow feeling for her. When Mother went out of the room ... he started telling me all about Mrs Ward, how she was brought up a strict Calvinist & that, though she had grown up under his tuition, something that he had taken two years to build up could be knocked down in 2 minutes by an ultra-orthodox person. He told me that he felt at times very spiritually & intellectually lonely. Why he elected to tell me I can't think.

Vera was inspired by a recurring theme in Ward's sermons, on the need to be independent:

> ...not to depend on systems, authorities or friends... we must be [self-reliant], stand alone. If we see too much of those who can help us, we begin to lean on them...they cannot give us salvation... Redemption is from within, & neither from God or man!

When Vera heard Ward was leaving Buxton, she recorded: 'But oh! It is hard to lose his influence just when it was becoming a guiding and transforming power in one's life.' Two weeks after war broke out, she and Edith went to hear Ward's farewell sermon. From a diary entry of eight pages:

> Sunday August 30th
> ... a crowd came to hear him greater than I have seen before...I could not help thinking of all the novels I have read dealing with clergymen, like Robert Elsmere & Richard Meynell, who rouse the minds & hearts of men & women. Mother whispered to me 'It's just like a story book'... when Mr Ward came into the pulpit a sort of electric shock went through the church & he became the centre of everyone's emotions. I expected his sermon to be very personal, as I have noticed before that his chief fault is

a tendency to talk about himself in a distinctly appreciative strain. But I was wrong. He made no personal reference at all except to say that he had failed in so many directions in which he hoped to have succeeded there, but that no one beside himself & God knew what that failure meant to him. He had always bidden us consider three great questions – what we are, why we are here, & whither we are going…we were not mere bundles of matter, mocked by moral insight & longing… but divine spirits, full of the power to do great deeds, think great thoughts, range over spiritual worlds …We were here to develop our high mental qualities, & to increase our sensibility to emotion…to unite our wills with the power for righteousness that runs through all things & all ages…

He spoke very seriously of the War, & the non-realisation, especially by the working classes, of its meaning. We did not realise, he said, that God was calling us by this terrible calamity from our life of sensation & self-indulgence…

Outside the church we waited for a few moments for me to bid goodbye to him. He stood there in the porch, saying goodbye to each member of that large congregation, with a cheerful smile & a kind word for each, as they all came crowding out …I do not think I shall ever forget the scene – his slight figure in its white surplice showing dimly in the faint light from the church, & all his people, working men and women mostly passing into the night, but still crowding round him & loth to leave. He must have been worn out but stood there with his expression of gentle loving sadness, kindly patient with each one who would gladly have monopolised all this time for themselves.

He gave me a moment after saying goodnight to all, in which I could only say how sorry I had been not to see him the day before. 'You shouldn't go off playing tennis,' he said smiling, half reproachful & still clasping my hand in his warm grip … He [said] he would write to [Edward] & would be able to keep in touch with me that way too. I begged him to come & see me …if his work ever took him to Oxford – 'You will not forget that', I said & he replied 'I will remember'. Then we had to go. All through the churchyard people were talking about him. Two women were clamouring for photographs of him to a man who evidently had been taking some. One woman, when asked if she was going to see him off next morning, replied 'Eh no! A'm not. If A' went, A' might disgrace meself by throwing me arms round his neck'.

So closes the religious & emotional movement which awoke Fairfield from its indifference & may have prevented its sinking back again for ever …

A *Buxton Advertiser* editorial, 'A Useful Ministry', reported Ward's departure on 31 August 1914. In place of the heated controversy the newspaper proclaimed in November 1913, it had nothing but praise:

> A smiling countenance, and cheery words, have brightened many a dark hour and lightened many a heavy burden…something akin to a spiritual wave has been passing over [Fairfield] during the past few months … working people in particular have received his whole-hearted attention. His short stay …will long be remembered by them. Evidence of this may be found at the Men's Class … and at these gatherings his discourses … are listened to with rapt attention – the true indication of the value of Mr. Ward's teaching. It is now about fourteen months since the inception of the Class, and … the growth has been such as must have gratified all concerned …
>
> The Class is indeed a brotherhood in the best sense of the word.…we quote the words of a member of the Fairfield congregation …'Every time I hear him preach, some difficulty is removed from my mind' …Mr. Ward has endeared himself to many; by his example large numbers have been influenced for good. His departure will cause no little regret in all quarters of the town…

'I am interested in that marriage for many reasons'

What are we to make of Ward and Vera's friendship? In a socially conservative Edwardian town, it was certainly unorthodox: Vera, Edward and Edith supported Ward's controversial views publicly, attended a working-class church outside the town and socialised with the Wards. The pace and intensity of Vera's diary also suggest that her fascination for Ward went beyond mere spiritual interest, admiration, and appreciation of his empathy.

Two months after meeting Ward, Vera noted in her diary that he was to be the centre of a new plot in her 'Buxton story'. The result was highly charged scenes of ardour and longing in *Not Without Honour*. Ambitious, argumentative, attractive Christine Merrivale has a strong sense of her intellectual superiority and rebels against a destiny as provincial society matron. Arthur Clark, a fascinating, intellectually gifted, lonely young curate, married to a plain, dull wife, arrives to serve a working-class village near the town. Despite being popular with his parishioners, he is eventually hounded out because of his radical beliefs. The two central characters fall in love, but Clarke rejects Christine's suggestion that they should run away together. When her parents find out, they force her to go to university in Oxford to avoid social scandal. Both characters have a mutual aspiration after martyrdom; Clarke achieves it when he is killed in the war. Christine learns of his death at Oxford, where she is finding her way to independence and self-fulfilment and to the maturity that both characters have lacked.

Does Vera's claim in 1937 that 'so often one can put the real truth about people in novels' suggest her romantic feelings and perhaps Ward's too? Amongst her many fervent diary reports is the time-honoured, cliched arrogance of an attractive, vivacious young woman intrigued by an older married man, who dismisses his wife rather unpleasantly, as 'plain' and 'worn', an 'insignificant' woman unworthy of such a complex man:

> When I get away from the sound of his voice I still remain within the magic circle of his predominating individuality. I was thinking actually tonight that it is a pity that his wife is so much older than him & seems so unworthy of him. One cannot feel that she was an object of great passion to him & great passion he is assuredly capable of feeling. I should like to know the story of that marriage for many reasons.[13]

In *Not Without Honour*, Clark/Ward:

> ... looked at the slender figure, bright with vitality and enthusiasm ... it had become inevitable that he should contrast her with that other figure, to whom his library was so much more familiar and yet so utterly strange. 'I'm afraid "Home Gossip" is more in poor Gertie's line.'[14]

This melodramatic scene in Clark's study leads to their first passionate embrace.

Nonetheless, whilst it is tempting to read all this through a twenty-first century lens, it overlooks the strength of Edwardian morality and young Vera Brittain's own sensibilities: as we shall see in Chapter nine, she was sexually innocent, found what she did know about sex somewhat distasteful, and had a very strong sense of propriety. In contrast, the thirty-year-old Vera Brittain who wrote passionate scenes for *Not Without Honour* was making her name in a flourishing post-war market for melodramatic women's fiction and had experienced the ardour and loss of romantic love and sexual desire. In Buxton, Vera's literary aspirations must have influenced how she regarded Ward, and how she wrote about him in her diary.

There are further caveats to inferring romantic feelings for Ward. The diary's streams of consciousness about him have all the hallmarks of Vera's earlier 'grand passions' for Mrs Harrison and Edith Fry. She had a propensity to form extremely intense attachments to the few people she liked and admired before, as she herself admitted, moving on without further thought. For all Vera's impassioned narrative and Ward's warm promises to meet if he came to Oxford and to write to her and Edward, there are no surviving letters nor any further mention of him in her 1913–1917 diary.[15] Just like Mrs Harrison, Ward disappears completely from Vera's diary after their final meeting.

The timing is also significant. Lonely and alienated from people in Buxton, lacking friends her own age, and with hopes for friendship with Mrs Harrison receding, Vera felt Ward 'knows too much & sees into me & everyone else in a way we people who would fair conceal their feelings are not accustomed to'. Vera said he helped and comforted her loneliness. The first half of 1914 was also an unsettling yet exciting time: war was looming, Vera was becoming attracted to Roland Leighton, still dallying with Bertram Spafford, and excited about going to Oxford with Roland and Edward.

Yet there is no doubt Joseph Ward had a very significant influence on young Vera Brittain. The deep sense of moral purpose and idealism she had in Buxton was to last all her life. Ward was the first religious dissenter and visionary she had met, and she was affected emotionally and intellectually by his impassioned preaching, his commitment to social action and his spiritual courage in the face of fierce opposition. Vera admired Ward's dedication to an ideal, in which he walked 7 miles for the Euclid lessons he needed for admission to Cambridge as a mature student, supported himself by teaching in a village school and studied until the early hours. She liked his vigour and passion, describing him as 'so strong, so vital, so full of the fierce & passionate joy of life'. Ward was the only person in Buxton with whom she shared interests in literature and writing, and a love of music. In later life, Vera would once again be inspired by the power of a charismatic, courageous religious dissenter in the form of Canon Dick Shepherd who, in 1937, persuaded her to campaign for pacifism through the Peace Pledge Union. As we shall see, Vera's own courage and her commitment to controversial beliefs in the face of fierce opposition were to last until she died.

What about Joseph Ward? It is easy to see how a beleaguered, 34-year-old man would be flattered by the attention of an unusual, clever, attractive young woman, and intrigued by her intellectual energy and spiritual seriousness. Vera also shared his feelings of alienation and spiritual isolation. If he was an unusual figure in Edwardian Buxton, so was she. Given that he went twice to see her perform in 'Raffles', perhaps there was a hint of personal interest too.

Not Without Honour portrayed Ward (Arthur Clark) as brilliant, but ultimately weak, self-centred, and prone to exhibitionism. In *Testament of Youth,* he merits just a cursory sentence:

> Two things alone prevented me, during Edward's school terms, from dying of spontaneous combustion – my diary … and the appearance in a neighbouring village of a rationalist curate, whose unorthodox dissertations on the Higher Criticism I took for the profoundest learning, and whose florid, dramatic services, to which every Sunday I walked three miles to listen, seemed to me the most inspired eloquence.[16]

It seems unlikely that Ward came across *Not Without Honour* but perhaps he read *Testament of Youth*. We shall never know.

For his parishioners, Ward's brief sojourn in Fairfield had a sobering endnote. Conservative Edwardian Buxton arrived late to the Anglican controversies Ward brought with him in 1913 but they would become horribly significant for his parishioners:

> With the awful experience of the War…some will have lost their faith totally; others will have rediscovered their need of traditional Christian faith just to get through. The optimism that lay behind the liberal explorations of the 19th century was trashed on the Western Front.[17]

For Vera too, war would trash all the liberal optimism inspired by her friendship with Ward.

Chapter Eight

'A Terrible Moment When the Great Movements of the World Enter Like an Earthquake'

The Outbreak of War

'Edward's and Maurice's keenness to do something definite.'

On Saturday 1 August 1914, Vera pored over newspaper reports that Germany was mobilising and hopes of peace were seeping away, and then went up to the tennis club. Bertram Spafford walked home with her as usual. Over the previous few weeks, Vera had noticed he sometimes looked 'forlorn and absolutely wretched'. But today he was greatly amused by her clever mimicking of people they knew, until she informed him gaily that she took him off too because he was so funny. 'You might least have spared me that', Bertram said glumly, before pent-up confusion finally got the better of him: 'Were you annoyed when I told you I – liked you?' She replied, 'I was.' 'Why?' he asked, and she retorted 'Because I didn't like you'. He fell silent. Again, Vera felt sorry, because she had said what she felt and because, she recorded later, 'my lack of feelings leads me so often to be so very callous about other people's'. This was to be their last proper conversation.[1]

The pair were not the only ones going about their lives as if nothing was happening. Buxton already seemed remote from turmoil elsewhere in Britain. During the first half of 1914, industrial strikes and growing militancy in campaigns for women's suffrage and Irish Home Rule had been threatening the established order, although Vera's diary makes no mention of them, other than one criticism of suffragette 'barbarity' (see next chapter). She did note briefly the build-up of tension in Europe but thought this seemed far away. In the run up to the Bank Holiday, while politicians discussed what to do if the Germans invaded Belgium and pledged support to France if it were attacked, most of the population were more concerned about whether bad weather might spoil the weekend. Two days later, with record numbers visiting seaside resorts, the main topic of conversation was the possibility of war.[2]

Everywhere was a strange mixture of deep foreboding and determination to carry on as normal. The *Buxton Advertiser* hoped that impending conflict would not diminish Buxton's status as a flourishing spa town and tourist destination, while the *Catering and Hotel Keeping Gazette* singled out the Buxton Hydro as a shining example of new commercial opportunities created by the closing of German spas to British visitors:

> …our own inland watering places….yield not a jot to such overrated spas as Hamburg, Nauheim, Weisbaden and Karlsbad. Diabetic clinics in the continental plan are sure to be installed, and particulars of one such kind are to hand from the Buxton Hydro Hotel… the only extras being medical fees, medicines, and wines and spirits. We have no doubt the Hydro…will find due reward for its enterprise.[3]

As Bank Holiday Monday dawned, it was clear war was imminent. From one of Vera's many extensive diary entries over the coming week:

> Today has been far too exciting to enable me to feel at all like sleep – in fact it is one of the most thrilling I have ever lived through….I sat this morning after breakfast reading various newspapers for about two hours….I should think this must be the blackest Bank Holiday within memory. Pandemonium reigned in the town. What with holiday-trippers, people struggling for papers, trying to lay in stores of food & dismayed that the price of everything had gone up, there was confusion everywhere….Paper money is useless and the majority of trains are cut off.[4]

On the brink of Britain's military intervention, the government tried to prevent a disastrous run on the banks by extending the Bank Holiday to 6 August. Vera's diary entries are a complete contrast with her proclamations of ignorance about the war in *Testament of Youth*, and her claim in the memoir to be 'afflicted with hysterical exultation'. Her diary reveals palpable jingoistic excitement:

> Late as it is & almost too excited to write as I am, I must make some effort to chronicle the stupendous events of this remarkable day. The situation is absolutely unparalleled in the history of the world…It is estimated that when the war begins 14 millions of men will be engaged in the conflict…& the destruction attainable by the modern war machines used by the armies is unthinkable & past imagination…I went up to the tennis club this afternoon, more to see if I could hear anything than to play, as it kept on pouring with rain. No one knew any further definite news, but

we all discussed the situation...The war will alter everything &, even if I pass my exam., there would probably be no means to send both Edward & me to Oxford at the same time...

Edward had procured an evening paper with the startling news that England had sent an ultimatum to Germany, to expire at midnight to-night, demanding the immediate withdrawal of her troops from Belgium...Stupendous events come so thick & fast...One feels as if one were dreaming, or reading a chapter out of one of H. G. Wells' books like *The War of the Worlds*...Daddy says the key to the whole situation is the British navy, & that as that stands or falls the fate of Europe will be decided. ...Immediately after dinner I had to go to a meeting of the University Extension Lectures Committee. Small groups of people, especially men, were standing about talking, & in front of the Town Hall was quite a large crowd, as on the door was posted up the mobilisation order, in large black letters, ordering all army recruits to take up the colours & all Territorials to go to their headquarters. Edward has been reading the papers carefully & says that at present only the trained army & the Territorials are wanted & there is no demand for untrained volunteers...

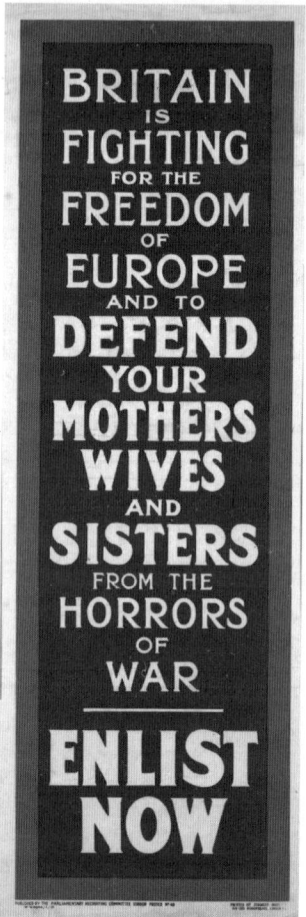

Recruitment poster. (*IWM*)

While Maurice and Edward wondered how to get a temporary commission until October when they were due to start university in Oxford, Mrs Kay, the Melrose cook, was confiding to Edith that Tom, one of her four sons and chauffeur to friends of the Brittains, had been informed he was required immediately because he was in the Army Medical Corps. Already caring for three tiny children, his young wife had given birth only a week ago and was beside herself with worry since she would only receive an allowance of two shillings a day (about £7 a week today). Mrs Kay said she would have to help look after them, adding that all her four sons were Reservists and had volunteered for foreign service, so she would probably lose all of them.

Wednesday August 5th
... groups of people were standing about talking & one or two Territorials were passing through the streets. Several Territorials & one or two Reservists were going off by train... & there was a small crowd on the station seeing them off... As we came up from the town I met Maurice & went down again with him. Though excitement & suspense are wearing, I felt I simply could not rest but must go on wandering about...

The *Buxton Advertiser* reported a 'stirring speech' by the Duke of Devonshire in which a band played stirring patriotic music while he asked the assembled crowd 'the one question which you have to ask yourself is 'Is there any reason why I should stay behind?'

A few days later, Maurice saw an announcement in the paper that 2,000 temporary commissions had been offered in the regular army. He rushed by train to Derby to find out how to join, returning to report to the waiting families that he had seen 'enough of the type that enlist as privates to make quite sure that he would not join the army in that way' which Vera said had been a 'mad idea' in the first place.

Maurice's parents were proud of his desire to enlist but Edward had to contend with Arthur's angry objections. A fervently patriotic Vera thought Edward must enlist and, after initial reluctance, Edith agreed. The atmosphere at Melrose was 'quite intolerable', with daily arguments and Arthur's furious outbursts. Edward reminded his parents about the speech by Uppingham's headmaster a month earlier, in which he had admonished pupils and parents to 'Be a man – useful to your country; whoever cannot be that is better dead'. Edward explained to Vera that, since Arthur had never been to a public school himself, he could not possibly understand what duty to one's country meant.

There were tensions between the Ellingers and Brittains. At a First Aid class:

...Mrs Ellinger sat just in front of us & was quite rude to Mother, saying... Maurice intended signing on for 3 years, that he could easily go to Oxford after, that we should give our sons to fight for their country, etc. etc.[5]

A week later, there was an air of surreal unreality. Vera played tennis at the club where the only topic was war, and recorded details of matches in characteristically assiduous detail. Later she walked with Edward in the Goyt Valley:

The cry of the startled bird, the soft swish of the long grass in the breeze ... as we came home it was almost impossible to believe war was on the world; the peaceful sky through which an occasional shooting star flashed

& the sleeping hills seemed to enshroud our little earth in a field of perfect peace...The news of the loss of thousands is now regarded with philosophical calm...My beloved brother! What will become of him? But as I told him... dreary as life is without his presence, & dreary as the prospect of what may lie before him, yet I would not have his decision back, or keep him here.[6]

After reading about British losses and the 'call for 500,000 men to take arms', Edward was 'feeling depressed & miserable because Daddy withholds him from doing his duty, but being only 18, can do nothing without Daddy's consent'. Edith wrote to Arthur's business partner, Frederick Haigh, 'asking him to use his influence on Daddy ... [Haigh] said he had tried to'.

Edward after dinner definitely asked again if he might go. Daddy was distinctly hostile, saying that if Edward went, it would be the death of him, and that he thought Edward very unkind after the education he had etc. etc. Both Mother & I talked it over & made him see it from the point of view of honour... he has promised to consult Dr Hannah about Edward's health & general stamina.

Recruitment poster. (*IWM*)

Vera's admiration for the values of duty, heroism and honour made her lambast Arthur for his lack of 'manliness' and 'courage', writing in her diary 'Daddy does not care about Edward's courage or honour, as long as he is safe'.

Eventually Maurice and Edward gave up their plans for Oxford and enlisted alongside young men with whom Vera had played tennis, danced and acted in amateur dramatics. Six Uppingham masters joined up as soon as war started, and Harry Lawson, headmaster of Buxton College, a year later. Edward went to tell the Ellingers he had decided to join the Army rather than go to Oxford. Vera recorded 'Of course they were thoroughly delighted, & Mrs Ellinger informed us she really had to kiss him, though Edward of course never mentioned that'.

Government poster. (*IWM*)

'It is quite disturbing to see so many men & women absolutely idle'

As soon as war was declared, antagonism towards those reluctant to join up appeared in towns around Britain. Vera was very unimpressed with her thwarted would-be lover:

> August 4th
> I mentioned Edward's & Maurice's keenness to do something definite & ... [told] Bertram Spafford that the fact of a strong healthy man like himself being absolutely ignorant of military tactics was a proof that our military system was at fault somewhere. He said that at the Manchester Grammar School, where he went, they had no [Officer Training] corps, & that many men were in the same case as himself.

Ten days later, Vera helped move equipment at the Red Cross headquarters and walked home through the Gardens, noting 'it was quite disturbing to see so many men & women absolutely idle, sitting in an illuminated place listening to the band'.[7] She criticised men 'who will be branded for life because they have not taken part in the greatest struggle of modern times'. Seeing Bertram 'strolling past pushing his mother's bathchair through the Gardens', she and the Garnetts 'all looked at him, contemplating his obvious strength & suitability for military work'.

As for middle-class women, they were not expected to work but instead to create a calm, loving home for soldiers to return to, learn basic First Aid in case of emergency, and encourage each other to show solidarity and forbearance. From *The Lady* magazine:

> The fact that one cannot bear arms does not excuse any one from helping their country's cause by fighting such foes as misery, pain and poverty... If we cannot in our innermost hearts feel really hopeful, we can at least pretend we do, and talk hopefully to those about us, write hopeful letters to distant, anxious friends and do our very best to inspire a calm, courageous view of the situation among all those with whom we come into and mothers whose anxiety equals our own.[8]

Vera planned excitedly for university and there were some remnants of the old life:

> Mother, E. and I went to the Opera House to see Martin Harvey in 'The Breed of the Treshams', one of those melodramatic plays which seem to be dying out but which are rather a relief after the problem & rather plotless pieces that hold the stage just now.[9]

For a short time, it seemed as if Roland might not have to fight after all and would go to Oxford as well:

> Friday August 21st
> I heard this morning, to my joy, that Roland Leighton, owing to his defective eyesight, has not passed the necessary exam for serving in the army, & therefore cannot go. I am glad because I didn't want that brilliant intellect to be wasted & that most promising career to be spoilt at the outset.

Other aspects of Buxton's cultural life carried on as usual. The town's four orchestras performed a special matinee on 26 August, guests continued to stay at Buxton's luxury hotels and even the Hydro's 60 permanent residents had no thought of leaving. Meanwhile, Vera, her mother, and Mabel Ellinger took their First Aid examination at the town hall:

> It did not begin until 6.00 & all day long I studied both the book & the bandages & tried the impossible task of drilling into Mother's head things

which went straight out. We certainly don't inherit our brains from her, & she is so utterly unable to control her nervousness that an exam is almost an impossibility…I thought I did not care whether I passed or not, but I do very much now…because of the general principle such an exam. as this involves. One of my aspirations is to succeed in whatever I undertake, & to undertake nothing unless I do it well.[10]

She worried she would soon hear she had 'failed badly' in the Oxford Senior… & my chance of Oxford postponed. I must again arise, & stir up my inexhaustible fount of enthusiasm, energy & will once more'.

A few days later, Vera enjoyed sitting in the Gardens reading George Eliot's *Middlemarch*. But under this veneer of normality, life in Buxton was changing fast and irrevocably. The town's newspapers adapted their cheerleading for a booming resort into patriotic morale boosting. The *Advertiser*'s reviews of concerts and reports of cricket scores were now accompanied by news of Buxton's first wounded soldier, German atrocities and enlistment figures. The paper encouraged men to enlist, residents to raise money for the Buxton War Fund and women to knit: the *Buxton Herald and Gazette* reported that 'Mr E. Stott has given sufficient wool to knit 100 pairs of socks for those who are on active service, and there are many ladies in Buxton who are clever with the needles – it is hoped that the wool will soon be used up'. Vera had already started knitting sleeping helmets:

> …as I have forgotten how to knit & was never very brilliant when I knew, I seemed to be an object of some amusement. But even when one is not skilful, it is better to proceed slowly than to do nothing to help … all day long I knitted away.[11]

On 26 August, Vera heard she had passed her Buxton First Aid examination, noting it was not such a great feat as only six failed out of the 98 who entered. The next day, she was overjoyed to hear she had passed the University of Oxford's entrance examination:

> At least before me is the prospect of enthusiastic & no longer lonely, work & though the absence of small luxuries at Somerville, & the oppressiveness (to me) of women together & the uncertain uncongeniality of some of them – I shall count these as jam when they are part of the intellectual work I love & the companionship of one or two at least with whom I can share my thoughts without dread or misunderstanding.

Vera's Oxford plans were almost derailed when an irascible Arthur told her that with war making the future of business precarious, he could not support her at Oxford. Vera was beside herself with fury at his lack of pride in her achievements, but this merely stiffened her resolve to go and she could 'not remain dismal for long':

> The inward joy was too strong to be repressed…[it] proves I have the intelligence to adapt & apply myself in a short time to subjects for which I have little aptitude… and use them to serve my own ends.[12]

She wrote to Somerville to accept, and Roland wrote to congratulate her:

> Sunday August 30th
> …. though all his [letters] have been a strange source of comfort to me through everything, I have never received one which impressed me with quite such a sense of joy as this. He begins 'I am so glad – so very glad. You do not know how wretched I would have felt if you had failed… And I look forward to facing a hedge of chaperones & Principals with perfect equanimity, if I may be allowed to see something of you on the other side'.

That evening Vera and Edith went to Ward's final sermon. A couple of days later, Vera made a charity visit with Edith to collect Red Cross shirts sewn by women in Burbage, went to a First Aid class and then to St John's to hear Edward practise the organ:

> As I sat there in the dimly-lighted front row & looked at the long shadows filling the solitude & heard the organ's solemn tones echoing amidst the roof & arches, I felt a sudden acute consciousness of the sorrow of life… felt too, almost immediately, the grand compensation of such a sorrow. To be afflicted & to endure, & to help others to courage by one's endurance, is a far greater destiny than to enjoy never-ending satisfaction or complacent supremacy, rousing others to irritation & envy, but never inspiring nobility or moving the better instincts of human nature.[13]

Vera's very detailed diary for this period intersperses details of the latest war manoeuvres or other news with her conflicting feelings about the future:

> And yet every letter I get causes a great deal of pain as well as of joy. Oh! Roland! Why did you ever come & make me love you? I could have done so well without love – before it came – I with my ambitions & life work &

occupations. I shall ever again be able to work towards worldly triumphs with the same disinterested concentration.[14]

Between the outbreak of war and 1918, over 250,000 Belgian refugee families would be housed in towns across Britain. The *Buxton Advertiser* praised donations to the Belgian Fund, and the town's generosity towards wounded and convalescing soldiers through well-attended weekly concerts with 'long and attractive' programmes ... greatly enjoyed by our Belgian guests and our Soldiers.'

Despite mounting casualties (some 15,000 by early September), local newspapers fuelled the national wave of patriotic fervour with lurid reports and images of German atrocities in Belgium. The *Advertiser* published a drawing of a German soldier with a sword threatening a Belgian woman with a small child whilst proclaiming 'Massacre of Civilians... women were confined in convents whilst hundreds of men were shot. A hundred prominent citizens were shot in the Place d'Armes.' Around the country, newspapers used German barbarism to keep up the momentum of recruitment. Lord Kitchener had asked for another 100,000 volunteers and by the end of 1914, some 600,000 across Britain responded. By September, Buxton and surrounding villages had set up war funds. Affluent residents donated substantial sums and Buxton's newspapers changed their pre-war lists of hospital subscribers into lists of war donors.

Amidst all this turmoil, and despite news of Buxton acquaintances wounded at the Front, there was still occasional enjoyment:

Wednesday September 8th
Between tea and dinner, Mr & Mrs Busby came in & Mr Busby played piano & violin – Shuman [*sic*], Grieg & Beethoven. It was delightful; it is not often we get the chance of really good music at home.

Yet these vestiges of genteel normality could not obscure tensions over the presence of 'aliens' in towns around Britain. Buxton was no exception. Five days before war was declared, Vera reported that 'the German cousins who are staying with the Garnetts, one of whom Edward and I were playing in the big tennis tournament have been sent to come home immediately'. Buxton's decades of dependence on German, French and Swiss hotel staff, prized for their conscientiousness, efficiency and pride in service, was threatened when Oscar Weiss, a German employed by the Harrisons at St Ann's, was charged at a special court with, as Vera noted, 'failing to register himself in accordance with the regulations'. Although Oscar had been living in Britain since 1900, suspicion of foreigners was running high:

Thursday September 9th
Six Germans with ammunition belonging to them have been arrested in Buxton. Two are Wenzel the hairdresser's men who is said to have cut part of a lady's hair off in vindictiveness and to have cut a man's head with a razor. Two others belong to the town band.

Friday September 10th
Several more Germans have been arrested in Buxton. Pfander the grocer … was one; he has been railing for a long time against the English, & said he hoped to see Spring Gardens red with British blood!

On 11 September, Edward departed to join the University of Oxford's OTC, and 'left home laughing with a delighted sense he is not to be one of those young men who will be branded for life because they have not taken part in the greatest struggle of modern times'.

Saturday September 26th, 1914
Maurice to my great joy came to Buxton today for two days' leave. I went to meet them as they came back from the station, & was delighted with Maurice's appearance in his officer's uniform. He has grown a small moustache, & looks much older & has an air of confidence & self-respect which he never seemed to trouble himself about before. He also seemed to have grown taller & held himself splendidly without any suspicion of laziness…I am afraid there is a little jealousy on [Mother's] part, for there is no doubt the Ellingers have gone one better than we this time, though when Edward *does* get his commission he will be even more a figure to be proud of.

Edward's studio portrait taken in Buxton, 1914. He sent one to his and Vera's former Macclesfield governess, Miss Newby, who replied to say how fine he looked and that his country should be proud of him. (*SC*).

The rituals of leisured Buxton society, such as promenading in the Gardens, became opportunities to shame those who had not enlisted. By this time, Vera's remorse for her shabby treatment of Bertram Spafford had been replaced with contempt for his unwillingness to enlist:

> Sunday September 27th
> ...it would be good for [Bertram Spafford] if I walked through the Gardens with Maurice in his uniform, appear both interested & pleased with Maurice and cut B.S. with obvious intention. This plan I accomplished with perfection & saw him looking disconcerted...I went out with Maurice. We looked most smart together, especially as his khaki & my pale blue went excellently together. We went to the Gardens... [then] into the Ellingers' for some violin playing after supper. Maurice & Edward played Edward's own composition... and Mr Ellinger was delighted with it.

'This is an important step – perhaps the biggest I have taken'

Arthur's objections to sending Vera to Oxford were short-lived, and she was delighted about being able to control her finances, starting 'a banking account in my own right... for the first time. Daddy went down... and paid in £100' (about £8,000 today). Having her own college room to decorate and furnish as she liked would be another genuine symbol of independence. But she feared Roland might not be going to Oxford after all:

> [It] will not be the same if he is never there. The glamour will all fade from my college dreams. How much this terrible war has wrecked beside the lives which are exacted in its toll![15]

The next day Roland wrote that he would soon know if he could get a commission:

> His letter – or rather that part of it which suggested he might never go to Oxford – filled me with a kind of inexplicable, mute despair... He is certainly longing to take part in the war, considers it a fascinating thing – even finds 'something, if often horrible, yet very ennobling & very beautiful, something which elemental reality raises it above the reach of all cold theorising'. I could have written emotion & passion into my answer, but instead I made it express tranquillity... There are some feelings which we dare not begin to show.[16]

With her tremendous capacity for fortitude, Vera set aside gloomy thoughts and looked forward to an independent, purposeful future:

> This is an important step, the biggest since I have left school, perhaps the biggest I have ever taken….It is a step to freedom & liberation of thought, work & endeavour… Surely now…I may begin to *live* & to find at least *one* human creature among my own sex whose spirit can have intercourse with mine.[17]

Fervently patriotic and believing in the moral justification for war, it would be nine months before Vera's life crashed into chaos. In Testament of Youth she captured this with a quote from George Eliot's *Daniel Deronda*:

> There comes a terrible moment to many souls when the great movements of the world, the larger destinies of mankind, which have lain aloof in newspapers and other neglected reading, enter like an earthquake into their own lives….[18]

Chapter Nine

'A Nature Restless With Search And Strife'

On The Brink Of A New Life

'There was very little of the halfway house of popularity.'

By September 1914, with Vera's much longed-for escape from Buxton imminent and her 21st birthday just three months away, what sort of person was she, and how had her cosseted provincial upbringing shaped her ideas, beliefs and sense of self?

Photographs show Vera as small (5' 3"), slender, dark haired, with beautiful hazel eyes. Some images hint at the liveliness, enthusiasm, and frivolity we have seen in earlier chapters. Others suggest the steely determination that must have made Vera somewhat intimidating to her Buxton peers. She noted in her diary that a petite stature and feminine appearance 'don't inspire people with fear because ...people [assume] there is nothing behind the smallness & daintiness'. Vera's feminine appearance belied the unconventional ideas she was developing about her future, and her fierce resolve to be 'an exceptional & brilliant person... to succeed in whatever I undertake... and to always come out on top in the end'. Vera's school career, her success in winning a scholarship to Somerville College, her love of literature and great interest in philosophical and spiritual questions, highlight her intelligence and intellectual curiosity. Vera believed in the

Vera and friend (identity unknown) at Melrose, 1914. (*McM*)

dictum that a 'person of real intellect can do anything he or she chooses' and saw 'love of learning [as]the very essence of my being'. Her 'rather full-blown opinion of my own intelligence' alienated her from those she regarded as intellectually inferior. She told Roland that one reason she felt such an affinity with him was their shared conceitedness about their own brilliance, and their belief that, as a rule, 'popularity implied mediocrity'.

Vera's diary has many searingly honest assessments of her character. Sometimes she berated herself for the negative impression she created. At other times, she was defiantly indifferent to people's opinion of her and celebrated her temperamental, restless personality. After a reunion with Stella Sharp and Cora Stoop:

> Monday February 24th, 1913
> Yet, dull as it is here & though she [Stella] finds life a bed of roses & I often find it something closely allied to a bed of thorns, not for anything would I change a nature that is restless with search & strife, hard & often bitter though it be, for one that is passive, complacent and easily satisfied with the small things of life.

All her life, Vera was volatile and intense. As a young woman, she desribed her spirit as 'divided between idealism and the frivolity I hold so dear'. In Buxton, her frivolity was evident in her huge enjoyment of dancing, music, games and clothes, and being admired for everything from her dress sense to being good at drama and tennis. She had an admirable capacity for throwing herself with exhilaration into everything she attempted, no matter how difficult. Beautiful surroundings, interesting people and inspiring literature lifted her spirits. Yet frivolity and gaiety could give way suddenly to moody pessimism, prickliness and introspection, and vice versa. Vera noted 'disappointing & dispiriting days which will creep in among the smiling ones & make you feel the future holds nothing very bright'.[1] In one long, unflinching analysis of who Vera liked and disliked, what they thought of her, and why a woman she is interested in did not reciprocate, she wrote:

> Saturday June 28th, 1913
> It may all be in my imagination – when one is tired & depressed one is apt to imagine many things… It is quite amusing to have a nature like mine; now I am so down life seems hardly worth living; probably before long I shall be so bubbling over with the joy of being that my heart will be raising itself in gratitude to Heaven simply because I am alive!

'A Nature Restless With Search And Strife'

'If only I had someone to really love & be friendly with, what a different place Buxton would be!'

Vera's feelings of alienation, her lack of real friends and her propensity for 'grand passions' for people she admired, would last all her life. In Buxton, these traits led to bouts of acute loneliness. After an argument with Arthur:

> November 15th, 1913
> I feel now as lonely & far removed from my present surroundings, in all but material form, as the evening star, shining alone in the dim sky…I feel like Shelley, that
>> 'My spirit's barge is driven
>> far from the shore, far from the trembling throng
>> Whose sails were never to the tempest given!'

When it came to friendship or just getting on with people socially, Vera knew she stirred up very mixed reactions. A neighbour reported what she had heard about Vera's reputation at St Monica's:

> Monday November 17th, 1913
> … everyone was talking about Vera, & saying how I had been Head, & how popular & how clever I had been. I said I was sure it couldn't be true, & I never knew I had that reputation, as I thought they all hated me. (That to be exact is not quite true; some of them did hate me & others had violent adorations for me, there was very little of that half-way house of ordinary popularity.)

Vera's bravado and resolve to be self-sufficient belied periods of deep insecurity and a lifelong tendency towards hyper-sensitivity. Having no friends when she moved to Buxton, and making none at the Grange, Vera's relationships with Cora and Stella were loving but fraught. Vera swung between anxiety about whether they still loved her, and defiance. Frequently cast down

Vera and Cora Stoop, c.1910. (*McM*)

by 'comparatively unimportant things that weigh on our spirits more than really serious things', Vera was also, as she told Stella, sometimes overwhelmed by the strength of her feelings:

> Things weighing on my mind kept me awake at night & unbalanced my brain. I told her all the shadows of the greater things of life & my wish to write about them.[2]

After a reunion with Cora and Stella, Vera reflected:

> Friday April 3rd, 1914
> ...But I am always alone, & they, who are used to the constant companionship of one another, cannot realise what so rare a thing as companionship means to me. It often seems to me queerly ordained that, lonely as my mental qualities make me in any case, I should be placed by circumstances in physical solitude also. But solitude is a source of strength, & the strength that grows in solitude is the property of the Messiahs of this life!

A week later, a fractious day with Edith who told Vera she was 'fed up' with hearing about her Oxford examination, led Vera to note another bout of 'extreme aloneness which comes on me more and more'. She yearned for friendship:

> I fear I am going to bed in the sort of depressed mood mother often mistakes for discontent which is really of longing unsatisfied, I don't quite know for what but I think for more fullness of life and love! If only I had someone to really love & be friendly with what a different place Buxton would be!

Vera's difficulties in finding someone she could truly relate to in Buxton were not helped by her tendency to be dismissive of women. In *Not Without Honour*, she ridiculed the 'jealously domesticated wives of unenterprising businessmen', censorious, staid 'matrons' who looked down on the 'lower orders', and girls only too keen to marry one of the lacklustre, self-satisfied men on offer in Buxton. *Testament of Youth* was only slightly less harsh. Vera noted in her diary and to Roland that she did not like women very much and preferred the company of men. Yet her early life also shaped a strong sense of what sort of woman she wanted to be, developing a lifelong admiration for women such as Edith Fry, Mrs Harrison and Mrs Lawson who combined femininity with strength of character and aspirations for independence.

With young women her own age, the rivalry and snobbery of a competitive marriage market could be a barrier to genuine friendship, even with Vera's close friend Stella Sharp. Meeting a 'dowdily dressed' Stella and her mother for afternoon tea in London brought this into sharp relief. Vera reflected in her diary: 'The fact I am pretty (and I am pretty, I had a good examination in the glass before dinner!) probably only strengthens in [Stella's mother] the determination not to associate me with her lumpy daughter'.[3] Noting that Mrs Sharp wanted to find eligible men for Stella before her younger sister made her social debut, Vera recorded indignantly that the woman did not regard the Brittains as 'old family' or wealthy enough to cultivate because they had no useful social connections.

'The suffragette movement in which I was so deeply interested'

Vera's 'equal rights' feminism began in Buxton as a protest against a family and wider environment in which women's subordination was taken for granted. Vera never sought solidarity or fellow feeling with other women, nor was she especially interested in equal rights for working-class women. Instead, like many feminists of that era, Vera wanted the same opportunities and privileges enjoyed by middle-class men whilst resisting assumptions that an attractive woman who loved clothes and dancing could not also be idealistic, clever and independent.

She loathed being patronised, railing against men, such as an acquaintance of her father's, who treated her as a 'being of utter irresponsibility & inconsequence, to whom no confidence or affairs of importance could possibly be imparted'. Such men were, Vera said, more 'deadly to the cause of women's freedom and independence than its most ardent opposer … women to him have always been inferior as a matter of course!'

After Vera left Buxton, she presented her youthful feminism as a single-handed revolt against the oppressive Edwardian mores of provincial society. In a 1928 article for the *Manchester Guardian*, Vera reports being forced to listen in 'furious silence' during 'bridge drives' and 'provincial tea parties' to a 'vocal variety of witch-burning' against 'those awful suffragettes'.[4] *Testament of Youth* reports that Vera's feelings of alienation from Buxton were created by the 'feminism … being developed by the far-away suffragette movement in London… in which I was so deeply interested', adding she was outraged by the notorious 'Cat and Mouse' legislation of 1913.[5] In *Testament of Friendship* she claimed she 'followed the militant campaigns with the excitement of a sympathetic spectator.'[6]

Yet these spirited narratives bear little relation to Vera's diary in which there is no hint of having to suffer a 'vocal variety of witch-burning', nor, apart from just one note to condemn militancy, any mention of suffragette campaigns:

> Tuesday March 10th, 1914
> Surely there was seldom such barbarity as that of the Suffagette who in the National Gallery this morning slashed & cut with a hatchet Velasquez's famous *Venus*! They say the damage is serious but not, they hope, irreparable. Poor artist & genius!....It shames the glorious cause for which the best women are fighting that one should act like this under cover of their standard. But I suppose every great cause, like every religion, has its fanatics who do not stain its truth, though they may cast a shadow upon it.

It is also intriguing that Vera's diary does not mention women's suffrage activity in Buxton. In 1909, Emeline Pankhurst, leader of the Women's Social and Political Union (WPSU), stayed at the Hydro and addressed a meeting of 250 people in its luxurious lounge. Buxton had three suffrage groups: the Church League for Women's Suffrage, run by Frances Sutcliffe (also a member of the moderate National Union of Women's Suffrage Societies (NUWSS); a branch of the NUWSS run by Mrs Ashwell Cooke; and a Fairfield branch of the more militant WPSU. The *Advertiser* reported well-attended, lively events on women's suffrage, including an open-air debate in front of the Town Hall in 1913 in which angry tensions erupted over militant and moderate methods before the crowd voted unanimously for women to be given the vote.

'The longing for the harder, less comfortable but more idealistic life I would choose'

Young Vera Brittain was also formulating her political ideas. St Monica's had introduced her to radical thinkers such as Thomas Carlyle and William Morris, although she had little time for Morris' criticisms of capitalism. Her 1911 diary mentions that the wave of strikes sweeping the country was the 'subject of my passionate editorial for the school magazine'. In Buxton she enjoyed John Marriott's lecture on Chartism and social movements:

> Wednesday March 19th, 1913
> Of course Mr Marriott absolutely demolished state socialism but admitted it possible when love was extended among men & each worked for others as he now worked for himself, only in that case when socialism becomes possible it becomes at the same time superfluous. Love Socialism! Ah! What a grand ideal!

Joseph Ward's dissenting beliefs and spiritual vision also inspired Vera's idealism and interest in social inequality. If her diary is anything to go by, she seemed to show little interest in the lives of working-class servants at Melrose, but Vera and her parents did learn from Ward how a few families owned Buxton's profitable quarries, hired and fired with compunction, and controlled the lives of their workers. And while Vera's own experience of Fairfield was relatively sanitised, for example seeing Ward's parishioners in their Sunday best for church, and visiting the tiny cottage of her dressmaker, she did become aware of her gilded privilege. Sometimes she railed fervently against it:

> ...clothes wear out, brown hair goes grey, bright eyes dim & perfect skin loses its freshness but the soul & the mind are among the immortals for always. How can I choose the material joy the world offers me & think I care about them more than anything else?[7]
>
> I understand now why our great religious geniuses & leaders have been poor. How blinding & atrophying are material possessions, the homage of custom, the paths of congenial conventionality. Oh! may I be poor, simple in tastes, never luxurious. May I learn to renounce all those comforts... with which I have been indulged. My sphere is among the poor & striving & thwarted (as I realised walking back from Fairfield the other day)...I intend to have as little apparent part as possible with the opulent & luxurious who float on the surface of their own complacency & self-satisfaction![8]

Reluctant participation in Edith's charity work opened Vera's eyes to the deleterious effect on women's health of having too many children, and led her to dislike what she saw as the detached, patronising philanthropy of the Anglican Church and Mothers' Union. She criticised these organisations in *Testament of Youth* for their belief in the sanctity of marriage, 'no matter how unhappy this made families'. Nursing at the Devonshire Hospital in 1915 gave Vera an insight into the drudgery and exhaustion working-class women endured all their lives.

Vera's dislike of Buxton's snobbishness sharpened her belief in meritocracy. She admired how Mrs Harrison organised her lecture committee:

> She seems to bring out to the full her power of tact & social charm ... there is no shade of difference in the manner in which she treats everybody, whatever their actual distinctions of age, position, intelligence etc. in 'the democratic spirit of the age' which judges people for their merits alone.[9]

Seeing the motorcade of the queen and duke of Devonshire pass through Buxton to cheering crowds in 1913, Vera reflected again on merit and privilege:

Her Majesty looked very portly…her large & rather expressionless features are not remarkable in any way for aristocratic distinction…How thankful I am that I don't belong to that class of society; if I am to have any distinction I want it to be that of intellect & talent – so far, far more worth having than the pomp & circumstance that comes from being the possessor of wealth…Expensive lunatics that are kept in motors & sables by an industrious nation's toil![10]

Nonetheless, Vera could be quite snobbish herself:

Tuesday February 24th, 1914
I went to bridge at Mrs Heathcote's… no one of any interest there – they seemed to be rather a highways-and-hedges lot. There were two appalling people, a mother & daughter, the height of vulgarity. Both were dressed in several bright colours, with large hats overflowing with feathers. They had gold purses & card cases galore, & the mother had a gold wristwatch studded with diamonds… In view of such examples, one is led to hope fervently one will never have much money.[11]

'I could not endure to be constantly propitiating any man'

In stark contrast to Vera's claims in *Testament of Youth* and *Not Without Honour* that her parents expected her to marry the first suitable man who presented himself, her diary does not suggest this. Rather, Vera had time to develop her ideas about what sort of woman she wanted to be and to consider who she was prepared to marry, and to recognise her own unique qualities.

Six months before Bertram Spafford's proposal, a discussion with Edith enabled Vera to understand the constraints that had trapped women like her mother:

Thursday April 23rd, 1913
Poor Mother must have had a dreadful time in the midst of poverty & struggles & inefficiency (as she tells me) of my grandfather, & too many children in the family. [Daddy] moved heaven and earth to get her; I can't imagine him passionate about anything, but no doubt he set his mind on her, wanting a wife, & as he wanted her particularly he was determined to get her. I seem to have known all along that she wasn't reconciled to it at first, but a home of her own must have attracted her & made her agree, & she probably was glad to escape from the poverty and sordidness which surrounded her for a life of steadily increasing comforts. It is not

for those things that *I* should count the world well lost, I don't feel I could marry a man if there was no romance attached to him, especially if he were impatient & intolerant like Daddy was with Mother. But then I have never known the sting of poverty, so I can't imagine the great joy that release from it must be.

When Bertram did propose, Arthur said indignantly it was an insult to the family.

Vera would never lose her enjoyment of male attention and being admired for her appearance. As a young woman, she did not reject the idea of marriage; rather, she wanted freedom to choose a husband who would take her career as seriously as his own and match up to her romantic ideals. Vera wanted financial independence from her father or a husband and had no time for men who were not clever or were indifferent to literature, existential questions, and women's rights. She often wondered about what made a marriage successful, on one occasion speculating about Mrs Ward:

Sunday March 8th, 1914
I have taken a liking to the plain, simple, rather timid little woman because I feel some of her unselfishness, her tenderness, her many little sacrifices. If only I could get her not to feel afraid of me, & to talk to me without timidity…I am sure it's some fault of mine that she seems in awe of me… though from an intellectual & character point of view she is not good enough for her forceful husband, yet I am sure she supplies a sweetness & sympathy which a stronger willed or cleverer person might not be able to give.

A letter from Stella Sharp about a schoolfriend married, as Vera said scathingly in her diary, to 'someone who is not up to much', led to further reflection:

She is evidently one of those people who has exchanged all that counts in life, all the precious things for gold and material comfort. At the age of 22 she has shut out all romance from herself, probably for ever. I envy no one less than her, in spite of her wealth & child. They say her husband is much older than she; I should imagine that a rich man, who has lived in India, & reached the age of forty or so without marrying would not be the most desirable man in the world to marry.[12]

On another occasion, meeting an acquaintance who had recently married, Vera observed that despite 'wearing a beautiful mauve dress, she seems to have coarsened & to have lost a good deal of her unaffected charm; all her words & movements are less spontaneous'.[13]

As Vera prepared for Oxford, she continued musing on a suitable husband:

> Monday September 7th, 1914
> I do not think I am likely to marry as I am too hard to please and too difficult to understand thoroughly. I would be satisfied with nothing less than a mutually comprehensive loving companionship. I could not endure to be constantly propitiating any man, as Mother seems to have spent her life doing or to have a large range of subjects on which it would be quite difficult to talk to him

> Thursday September 24th
> [I had a long talk with Cora] about marriage & our ideals of it. I said that once I had thought I could not endure to marry a man unless he was older than I, but that now I felt much the most perfect thing would be to marry someone about my own age & start life together, & share its development instead of stepping into a place ready-made by a man older who would only consider me an addition & not an integral element in his life.

Young Vera Brittain liked children, was always enchanted when they seemed fascinated by her, and assumed she would eventually have her own. Nonetheless, she was sometimes overwhelmed by the idea of motherhood:

> Mrs Lawson always moves me to a sort of emotion with her affection ... but what she shows is not nearly as moving as Mrs Harrison's depth of joy in her child; her love for him seems somehow intoxicating & passionate & carries one away with the idea of the most deeply felt, fully realised kind of motherhood there can be...I could scarcely bear to look ... her motherhood is something to be treated with reverence & passion.[14]

'Being afraid of my own ignorance in sexual matters'

Like many Edwardian middle-class young women, Vera was, as she recounts in her diary and memoir, confused about male attention, extremely ignorant about sex and repelled by what she did know. In 1913, she fought off Maurice Ellinger and Ernest (his and Edward's Uppingham friend) after they all returned to Melrose from a ball. Like young women through time immemorial, she felt guilty:

Alas! I fear dances have the effect of turning both Ernest's & Maurice's heads. Ernest, after several sentimental remarks, seized hold of me at my bedroom door & tried to persuade me to come with Edward & talk with them in his room while they smoked. Maurice was taken the same way last night... he murmured something that sounded like 'Darling' & tried to put his arm around my neck. Oh! they have no right to behave so to a girl much weaker & smaller than themselves. When they behave so I feel ashamed both of myself & of them. They have left me feeling very tired & depressed tonight; I feel surely they would not take such liberties unless there were some element in me not altogether admirable & worthy of respect.[15]

A couple of months later, confusion led Vera to ask her mother about 'sexual matters which I thought I ought to know, though the information to me is always intensely distasteful to me & most depressing'.

A profound challenge to provincial respectability and to Vera's understanding of sexuality came in June 1913 when Maurice Ellinger and some other boys were expelled from Uppingham for 'immorality'. Vera noted in her diary that Barnard Ellinger had written to Arthur and Edith mentioning 'the fact of Maurice's disgrace because of the long intimacy between the two families'. The headmaster

Vera with Maurice Ellinger on a trip to the Peak District, c.1912. (*McM*)

helped secure a private tutor so that Maurice could study for a scholarship to Oxford. In 1914 he gained one to read History at Worcester College.

It is clear from Vera's very long diary entries about the incident and its aftermath that it was a while before she understood what the 'immorality' actually involved. Edward told Vera it was the one transgression Uppingham would not overlook, reporting that Maurice had told him he 'was the worse for drink' and so was not responsible for his actions. Vera remonstrated in her diary 'oh! what an excuse for what an offence', adding that 'every offence is atonable...as George Eliot wrote, "if we knew ourselves, we would not judge each other so harshly"'! Vera thought Maurice's 'great unhappiness' was existential but also that Mabel Ellinger was to blame, through the 'steady neglect of all that a mother should mean to her son'. But Vera was confused: earlier that year Maurice had shown her he was attracted to her, and also confided his attraction for some girls at a Buxton dance. The event caused Vera a great deal of distress and uncertainty about sex:

Wednesday June 25th, 1913
Edward & I both agreed that Maurice's lack of ideals & moral standard – which is really religion, the broadest kind – was responsible in a great measure for his downfall.... Being afraid of my own ignorance in sexual matters I entered after Edward had gone into an intimate discussion with mother about the 'open secret' – now I know. I feel as if I don't want ever to marry – it is all such confusion, the union of our physical & spiritual nature, & to know [illegible] where longing becomes temptation & is wrong. Oh! I wept for the war of physical inclinations with spiritual aspiration & for the frailty of our poor human nature!

Maurice in tennis gear, outside Melrose morning room, c.1913. (*McM*)

Unknown to Vera and her parents, Maurice's expulsion reflected the darker side of his and Edward's renowned public school. When they went to Uppingham in 1908 as twelve year olds, it had a new headmaster but under his predecessor, 'all that was worst in public schools, militarism and immorality, [came] to Uppingham...'.[16] There was a pervasive dormitory tradition of 'beastliness' in which, seemingly unknown to teachers, older boys inflicted various forms of bullying, including sexual acts, on younger boys. According to the artist C.R.W. Nevinson, 'I was kicked, hounded, caned, flogged and hair-brushed... I possessed at the age of fifteen an extensive knowledge of "sexual manifestations".'[17] Between 1900 and 1908, some first-year boys found it so unbearable, they persuaded their parents to remove them, and several older pupils were expelled. Records do not show how many.[18]

There were similar problems in other public schools. At Uppingham, things did begin to change under the new headmaster, but Maurice's expulsion indicates that 'beastliness' was still prevalent. Sadly, he would later develop serious psychological problems, resulting in an attempted suicide in November 1914 and again in May 1915.

'My practical, realistic and stoutly middle-class Staffordshire family'

Vera never shook off her conviction that her upbringing made her uninteresting and conventional, and put her at a disadvantage with people she regarded as better educated and more culturally sophisticated. Both *Not Without Honour* and *Testament of Youth* presented her parents as conservative, philistine and 'robustly low-brow'.

Vera, Edith and Arthur, 1913. (*McM*)

In notes for her third novel, *Honourable Estate*, Vera embellished this characterisation: 'my practical, realistic and stoutly middle-class Staffordshire family had no contact with highbrow circles which they disliked socially and despised financially'.[19]

An exception to Vera's criticisms were two uncles, Edith's brother Bill and William, the husband of Arthur's sister Edith. Both were very supportive of Vera's university and literary ambitions. Thirteen years older than his niece, William recommended books and sent her his own poems and plays; in 1913, Vera was impressed with 'a very good review' in the *New York Post* of his 2-act religious play, reporting that 'he seems so much more refined & intellectual than the rest of the Brittain family'.

The Brittains had the typical frictions, affections, big and petty annoyances of any aspirational family. With a dominant father and wider social expectations of female subordination, Vera was often exasperated by her parents' assumptions that the privileges of better schooling, the promise of an Oxford education, and greater freedom of movement were necessary for Edward but not her.

She criticised her father's snobbishness: after Arthur attended one of Ward's services, he told her indignantly he preferred to sit in church with people of 'your own class... a good congregation of a better class of people, not these common louts'. Vera railed in her diary 'mind & character ... to Daddy seem not to count at all, unless it is allied with position', concluding 'what is the use of such a long report of human limitations, especially alas! by such a close relationship allied to myself?' On another occasion, religious differences led Vera to observe 'he & I will never find a meeting ground on anything but the most trivial of subjects'.

Arthur was an affectionate, generous father but irascible and prone to outbursts of temper, especially if routines and expectations were disrupted. Similar temperaments and different aspirations could lead to stormy arguments. Sending Vera away to school had taken her ideas for the future in a totally different direction from the advantageous marriage he and Edith hoped for. St Monica's had also made Vera look down on her parents' background and attitudes, while it is also possible that elocution lessons in the carefully enunciated tones of 'received pronunciation' made her look down on Arthur's Staffordshire accent.[20]

Whatever their differences and occasional altercations, Arthur was very fond and proud of Vera:

March 25th, 1914
This evening Daddy showed his appreciation of my work in general by a long and confidential conversation about my prospects, the works & various

other matters. He told me he felt inclined to put more & more confidence in me as I was showing myself more & more worthy.

Her portrayals of obdurate, unsympathetic parents in *Testament of Youth* and *Not Without Honour* are one-sided to the point of caricature. Again, Vera's diary tells a very different story. While *Testament of Youth* narrates Vera's 'furious battle royal' to be allowed to go to university, Arthur and Edith soon accepted her university aspirations and supported her wholeheartedly by arranging and paying for tutors. They were extremely proud of her: according to Vera's diary, Arthur boasted to Buxton acquaintances about her success in getting into Oxford.

Vera's public depictions of her mother are especially unflattering. In *Not Without Honour*, Mrs Merrivale is a staid, embittered provincial matron, concerned with what acquaintances think and constantly disappointed that her daughter has rejected 'all the work' put into her social debut. Vera's third memoir, *Testament of Experience*, published in 1957, tells readers that 'during my rebellious girlhood, having little in common', [she and Edith] 'had been constantly at loggerheads'.[21]

They did have the sorts of occasional acrimonious exchanges many mothers and daughters will recognise:

Tuesday April 8th, 1913
Mother of course found fault with everything she saw at home & seemed to think everything a complete muddle if she was away. It is characteristic of Mother that though I always want her to come home she always upsets me when she does come ...When Mother wants to be particularly nasty to me she impresses upon me how like I am to the Brittain family; thank goodness, thank goodness I am! *They* at least have a little courage, reserve, self-control, determination and staying power!

Yet, sporadic wrangling and mutual irritation apart, Vera's diary and her and Edith's frequent chatty letters over many years, reveal a close relationship. Contrary to Vera's later protestations about never being allowed any freedom, the diary shows that Edith permitted a good deal more than one might expect for that time. And, perhaps unusually for the time, they had intimate conversations about marriage, sex, family dynamics and Vera's complicated emotions:

Thursday April 23rd, 1913
I managed to drag from [Mother] a little of the closed book of her early life. It is so true that nobody's life is humdrum & everybody's life is tragic

– how little everybody knows about everyone else! I have not been touched directly yet either by the thrill of joy or the darkness of tragedy; mine has been a very sheltered life, so I suppose it is all to come...

The story of all these things made it clear to me why Mother finds me difficult to understand & get on with, because the part that *is* understandable is like Daddy's side, which she always objected to, rather than hers. The sense of loneliness quite overpowered me; there seems so often to be *no one* here to turn to; Daddy of course is hopeless, far too shrewd, business-like & limited, & Edward is the baby that boys of seventeen nearly always are. So I began to cry weakly at first & then more miserably & entered with Mother into a variety of rather heart-rending explanations concerning difference of temperament. She did seem to want me after all, & to want to make me less lonely. A few hours ago I couldn't have imagined myself either confessing my loneliness to Mother or letting her see my distress, but I am glad of it instead of sorry if only to prove how great a darling I always knew she could be.

Edith did, undoubtedly, want a conventional life for her unconventional daughter. Yet she was extremely proud of Vera, encouraging her interests and enthusiasms, even when these went against the grain of provincial expectations. Not only did Edith mount a staunch defence of Vera's university ambitions with women in their social circle but, with genuine enthusiasm, she also encouraged Vera's essays for John Marriott and her highly unorthodox friendship with Reverend Joseph Ward. She was sympathetic to Vera's difficulties with Bertram Spafford, and to her feelings for Roland. And while Vera did often feel intensely lonely and confused, she did not endure those feelings alone, or without Edith's comfort and reassurance.

'What I do possess is essentially mine – a quality peculiarly & intensely individual'

Vera was fiercely ambitious, idealistic and convinced she was exceptional:

Friday 13th February 1913
The smallest intellectual success always brings back to me the longing for the hardly less comfortable but more idealistic life I would choose .... how all material things seem to lose their brightness beside one successful & idealistic thing.[22]

Friday 28th November 1913
I wonder more & more how I sprang from the family stock. I can only hope that is as I am always longing – that perhaps in very truth, I am destined to be a genius – or at least something removed from the everyday…What I do possess is essentially mine – a quality peculiarly & intensely individual, rising back no further than myself & leading oh! Whither?

Vera maintained her unshakeable belief that 'all that was exceptional in my character and intellect… everything that was best was due neither to heredity nor environment but was so absolutely my own'. Comparisons with Edward confirmed her feelings of exceptionalism:

Saturday November 29th, 1913
When we were talking about exams. & fame etc. this evening, Mother told me she has always felt I shall succeed in everything I undertake & Edward will always just miss. Well, time will show! Edward, whatever he does, has at any rate the power of making himself agreeable to anyone, which will carry him far & keep him happy and popular. The exceptional and remarkable people seem always to be the unhappiest & the loneliest, even theirs at times is the joy which nothing else on earth can replace.

Friday December 19th, 1913
Edward seems shocked at the idea of playing [bridge] for money, & also moralises against my love of argument. I am afraid he is much more naturally virtuous than I am. But I would not give up what is my own though it has to be accomplished in solitude. He forgets that his placid temper finds it easy to let an argument drop, while to my pugilistic one it is well-nigh impossible. So many people make allowances for outside circumstances & forget the difference in nature of temperament, which counts more than all.

In the face of Edith's occasional disappointment with her ambitious daughter, Vera was determined to make her mark on the world:

Friday January 22nd, 1914
She admitted today that she would much rather have an ordinary daughter – living & sleeping & dying & leaving no impress behind! I suppose I have all the share of [the Brittains'] enterprise & ambition. After all I may leave no impression behind than the most abject parasite that ever lived

on someone in this country – but I am determined anyhow to have a good attempt, for failure will be less ignoble than never to try.

One of young Vera Brittain's most endearing characteristics was, as she described, an 'inexhaustible fount of enthusiasm and energy'. As she set off for Oxford at the beginning of October 1914, this character trait would foster Vera's naïve illusion that war would not disrupt her life too much. She was about to spend the next six months under that illusion.

Chapter Ten

'Oxford I Trust Will Lead to Something, But Buxton Never Will'

To University and Back

'I live in an atmosphere of exhilaration, half delightful, half disturbing, wholly exciting'

Oxford is beautiful at any time of year, but when the low autumn sun illuminates the reddening vines that cover its lovely old buildings, and the city is alive with new students excited about starting university life, it is perhaps at its most stunning. From the moment Vera arrived at Somerville, she loved the graceful red-brick Arts and Crafts manor house on Woodstock Road, with its gracious flower borders, the splendid wood-panelled dining room, and tranquil library with Delft tiled fireplaces, cushioned window seats and heavy oak tables lit by brass lamps under an ornate plaster ceiling. During her first week, Vera was taken with other first year students to sing hymns to

View of Somerville quad from the Maitland building, with library building on the right, early 1900s. (*SC*)

patients at the Radcliffe Infirmary next door, went into town to buy 'still more necessaries' including a notebook and lacrosse stick, bought furniture at a college auction, and arranged to rent a piano.

She was especially pleased with her 'light and sunny' room in the Maitland building. Reporting delightedly to Edith that 'this is the loveliest room to be in', Vera's room looked over the lawned quad with its enormous spreading yew tree and summer tennis courts, with the library on the right. It was customary for new students to find out the colour of their room and bring their own furnishings. Vera's appreciation of style led her to cover cushions with a stylish black patterned fabric greatly admired by her fellow students. She wrote to Edith asking her to send some more material for curtains; lined in 'rose pink silk', these would look good, she said, 'with a black rug with a pink patten…no one else has black draperies'. Ten days after arriving, she was proud to serve tea in her room to Edith and Edward, who had begun his army training with the Officers' Training Corps at New College.

Eulogising about the loveliness of Oxford, Vera threw herself with customary enthusiasm into college life, staying up until the early hours at 'merry & noisy' cocoa parties gossiping about other students and tutors, and having philosophical and religious discussions. In 1914, Somerville was in the throes of a 'ghost craze', where students told psychic stories into the early hours and played practical jokes. Vera enjoyed church services and concerts in the Cathedral, renewed her love of acting by setting up a first-year amateur dramatic society, joined the Bach Choir with Dorothy L. Sayers (who would go on to become a famous novelist), wrote for *The Fritillary*, the magazine for Oxford women's colleges, and joined her first women's suffrage group.

Other aspects of Vera's new life took more getting used to. While college servants cleaned students' rooms, cleared and laid their fires, students had to undertake personal tasks for the first time, such as buying their own toiletries and sanitary towels and having their hair washed at a local hairdresser.[1]

For the first few weeks, Vera found it hard to keep ahead of her studies:

> …which always makes me feel depressed & unequal to being the exceptional & brilliant person I am determined to be. As a rule, when I hear brilliant people like Miss Barber & Miss Rose spoken of, I feel determined even to out-do them in glory, but on depressing days I feel I can never get near their standard. But I can![2]

Vera continued to be fascinated with women's appearance and character, musing in her diary about the model of womanhood she aspired to. She thought the 'dowdily dressed' spinster dons were as unappealing as Buxton's society matrons.

Instead, Vera admired women who combined intellect, attractiveness and womanliness, this time a tutor she greatly admired:

> ...she is very far from sharing the donnish disregard for dress, & though she is certainly plain, as most dons seem to be, the fact ceases to be obvious beneath the intelligence, humour & sympathy of her expressive face... Perhaps she is nearer to the ideal type of woman – to the woman we hope the future will bring – than at any rate any [other] don I have ever met. She is an instance of a woman who has spent her life in the pursuit & imparting of knowledge, & whose daily round is one purely concerned with intellect, without losing any atom of her womanliness & feminine attractiveness, without having her humaneness warped or her sympathies blunted.[3]

Some of Vera's Somerville peers, including Dorothy L. Sayers, shared her scathing dislike of the anti-fashion, anti-frivolity ethos of suffragette and socialist students who prided themselves on wearing unflattering, eccentric clothes and were contemptuous of vanity and feminine attire.[4]

Vera's propensity to attract and alienate people continued alongside her unflinching yet unrepentant self-assessments. She noted that a combination of reserve and a habit of holding forth in 'my customary dogmatic fashion' on subjects like religion (a sensitive topic in a non-denominational college) was an impediment to close relationships. Writing to Edith, she said people 'thought me pretty and talked a great deal about my eyes but wished I would not make my mouth sneer when I talked!' She observed in her diary:

> Wednesday October 14th
> I am the kind of person who is either adored or hated...I am quite indifferent to people's opinion of me....I do not think that one feels enough for one's fellow creatures. I am such an egoist anyhow that I seem to take like anything to the all-for-self atmosphere.

> Thursday November 12th
> I have of course got my usual reputation of being insufferably conceited, hard & cold, without a scrap of sympathy or kindness. Alongside of this goes the usual interest in me, & I seem to be a much-discussed person. But if the majority do not love me, at last they cannot say I am mediocre & seem to find me original. I wonder if I shall ever have the warmth under the hard crust aroused here.

Vera at Somerville, 1914, 5th left third row. Novelist Dorothy L. Sayers 1st left third row. (*SC*)

Saturday 28th November 1914
…most of them say they cannot make me out & wonder if I am sincere or not. I tried to convince [a fellow student] that I really am, though I often deliberately act, & sometimes even deceive people.

For all Vera's enjoyment, her relief at leaving Buxton, and her defiant bravado about the impression she made, her old life turned out not to be the main cause of her bouts of discontentment and loneliness after all. Noting 'it is a queer thing that it is here more than anywhere that I am least myself & most a stranger', Vera agreed with a friend's observation that she had two personalities. She continued:

College really is a dreadful place for causing me ups and downs of feeling – as though I were not bad enough anyhow…Lonely I always am – in spirits, not materially – for my detachedness makes me so, and sometimes the loneliness oppresses me utterly.[5]

Ten days later a disagreement with one of her tutors led Vera to describe herself as 'the kind of apparently bumptious person people in authority are fond of taking down – at any rate at first'.

'Keep as high as possible England's standards of intellectual and moral life'

In her first autobiographical novel, *The Dark Tide*, published in 1923, and *Testament of Youth* ten years later, Vera recognised she was one of the first

Somerville dining room, c.1925. There is no photograph from 1914. (*SC*)

generation of educated middle-class women to achieve the goals of nineteenth century feminists. The Edwardian era was a time of great social change: while it was still unusual for young middle-class women to choose university, new opportunities had arisen from a combination of women's suffrage campaigns and wider demands for universities to train a new professional middle-class.

When Vera went to Somerville, it was just 35 years old and she described its third principal, Emily Penrose, as 'the first genuine scholar among women principals'. Penrose had built up a highly trained tutorial staff of university women and planned for the eventual admission of women to full degree status which came in 1921.

While Vera's determination to go to Oxford was neither as clear cut nor the lonely struggle against opposition she depicted in *Testament of Youth*, her success was undoubtedly a huge achievement. Vera was not a typical university student. To herself and others, she appeared too financially fortunate and attractive to need a university education or to earn her own living. In 1914, it was harder for women like Vera to get into university than women like Winifred Holtby (who Vera was to meet at Somerville in 1919). Winifred's father was a wealthy, influential farmer in the East Riding of Yorkshire, her mother the first woman county councillor. The Holtbys had always regarded university and a career as more realistic for their shy, socially awkward, not conventionally attractive daughter, whereas Winifred's younger sister Grace was always destined for marriage.

Women faced other obstacles, not least the extremely variable quality of girls' schools and the prohibitive cost of university. Amidst the economic uncertainty of the First World War, Somerville cost Arthur Brittain almost three times as much as St Monica's had. Despite his complaints about money, he added an allowance to Vera's scholarship. Many years later it would become clear that financial concerns rather than objections to women's education in principle, lay behind Arthur's ambivalence about Vera's university aspirations: his will made a 'generous bequest' to poor students at Somerville College in the event of her dying without having children.[6]

Vera never acknowledged the part class and wealth played in her own achievement. Less affluent middle-class women such as Storm Jameson, who went to Leeds university and would become part of Vera's literary circle in 1920s London, faced much bigger barriers. And, of course, the situation for working-class students was much worse. In 1910, fewer than a thousand attended university from grant-aided schools. By 1939, it would be more than 4,000 but it was not to be until the Robbins' report of 1963 and the establishment of five new universities that significant numbers of working-class students of both sexes had better opportunities for higher education.[7]

Most university educated women went into teaching. Vera's own literary ambition had been boosted by a suggestion from Edith Fry that 'being a secretary to a literary man, preferably a well-known one, would be a better way of launching myself into the literary world than any other'. When Somerville sent Vera information about how to increase her chance of obtaining a good teaching post by studying certain courses, she noted indignantly in her diary 'rather than being a dreary downtrodden teacher at a small school, I would give up working'.[8]

During her first term, Vera believed student life was a valid contribution to the war effort, explaining to Edith:

> I heard a splendid sermon ...from the Bishop of Oxford to-day...He spoke especially to students & all engaged in the intellectual & artistic rather than the practical kinds of employment, & said that the part of those who could not fight or take an active part in the war was to keep up as high as possible England's standard of intellectual & moral life so that those defending her might feel she was worth fighting for. He said that if one assumes we're fighting for righteous & honourable ideals abroad it was our duty to see that we did not let those ideals slip at home.[9]

At this stage, Vera, Edward, and Roland supported the war wholeheartedly. While Edward trained with the University of Oxford's Officers' Training Corps, Buxton began its transformation into a garrison town. In October, the 6th Sherwood Foresters were billeted at The Empire, where they would stay until January 1915. In November, Edward was gazetted as a Second Lieutenant in the 11th Sherwood Foresters and sent to Surrey where he spent a frustrating period supervising the building of defences. Before he left, Vera enjoyed showing him off at Somerville, telling Edith 'he looked so nice in his officer uniform & he created great interest in the minds of those working at their windows by walking up & down with me in the garden'.[10]

In November, Buxton life intruded into Vera's Oxford idyll when Maurice Ellinger was sent home from the army after attempting suicide by ingesting a mixture of veranol and sulphanol. Vera wrote it was his second 'nervous breakdown' after being 'threatened with one before', telling Roland 'Mother thinks he was leading a life of it and that his breakdown is caused by more than work alone'.[11]

Before the Christmas holidays, Vera discussed with Miss Penrose her hopes of becoming a secretary to a literary man and Penrose advised that English was the best preparation. Vera's diary recorded atrocious conditions in Poland which had fallen to the Germans, and her great trepidation when taking examinations in the Sheldonian Theatre.

In Buxton for Christmas, Vera met Maurice who had resigned his officer's commission before the army could throw him out:

Friday December 18th
Maurice looks very well – almost too well, & does not show much trace of nervousness, but of course he is more natural & less shy with me, according to his own telling, than with anyone… he is going to a small health-resort in the South to live with a doctor. I keep trying to think of things he can do, such as playing the piano & writing stories, that he may not feel his time is wasted or he is useless.

A few days later, Edward arrived by the last train from London:

Wednesday December 23rd
It was 50 minutes late, so we wandered up and down the cold platform with Daddy getting more inwardly irate every moment. …I always love a railway at night, the lights in the distance, the shunting & the red steam – even if it is cold & damp. At last the train came in & he appeared, looking so fit & good-looking, in spite of having got up at 4.0 this morning. He

seems so tall & absolutely grown up ...I shall be proud for anyone to see him, he really is a fit object of devotion. He has never looked so well as he does in his military clothes. When I read & read about the tragic deaths of only sons, of brothers & husbands, I cannot think there is any reason why our one beloved representative of the Army should be spared.

Across Britain, fears that reports about the realities of war might deter new recruits led to a shift in government recruitment tactics from 'your country needs you' to moral pressure on reluctant men. Women organised national 'white feather' campaigns and persuaded others to hand out the traditional symbol of cowardice. To offset hostility towards men in necessary civilian jobs, the government had to issue badges confirming their status. In Buxton, Bertram Spafford was being harassed to enlist. The Brittains went to the Christmas service at Burbage:

Edward in khaki enlivened the scene somewhat. He was the only soldier [there] & almost the only man, except Bertram Spafford, who looked quite out of it in civilian clothes...Every young man of officer standing has gone from here except B.S. who has received various anonymous letters & white feathers which seem to have no effect. It is impossible to say whether he is most afraid of getting hurt or of losing what money he has.[12]

On 6 January, the *Buxton Herald and Gazette* noted the passing of another year. Observing how war overshadowed all aspects of life, it noted optimistically that 'the New Year opens brighter in that respect. We are all hoping that the war will be over, and Prussian militarism defeated, before another New Year is celebrated'. Just a month later, Vera was glad to hear rumours that the Empire hotel was to reopen after the Sherwood Foresters who had been garrisoned there went to the Front.

These hopes quickly evaporated. The Empire remained closed, and casualty lists began to take up more than one column in the *Advertiser*, although the newspaper was keen to reassure readers that 'the enormous proportion of complete recoveries testifies to the humaneness of the modern bullet and to the great skill of the surgeons'. It added 'if the war is of a long duration, the majority of wounded men will return to the front'.

Clamour for new recruits continued apace. With more able-bodied men enlisting, farmers had to employ old age pensioners and boys. The *Advertiser* reported an appeal from the Buxton Voluntary Aid Detachment (VAD) for billets lasting no more than three weeks for convalescing officers who would not require special nursing. A letter advised readers that 'nothing stops a bullet like a bag of loose sand and therefore as the weather warms up, sewers should turn their attention to sewing sandbags rather than warm clothing for the men'. In anticipation of large numbers of wounded soldiers expected shortly to arrive, the Red Cross Society appealed for a further 3,000 VAD nursing assistants and the Home Guard advertised for more volunteers from the over forties.

While Buxton became ever-more embroiled in the war, Vera's interests remained with Oxford and Roland. A few weeks into term, despite feeling unsettled, Vera soon resumed college life:

Friday February 5th, 1915
I put on my new blue & grey dress, in consideration of the fact that Miss Fry was arriving – also that there was a lecture on "The Way to Permanent Peace" by a Mr Trevelyan whom I had not heard about before but seems a famous person. I got pleasure out of the dress… Quite an embarrassing number of people came up to me specially just to say how pretty it was, so it must really be strikingly pretty as things have to be striking here to be noticed at all.

Without servants to do personal tasks, Vera relied on those at home. At the start of war, large numbers of domestic workers emigrated to Australia. In Buxton, the Melrose servants left. Edith had managed to find replacements but seemed to be having discipline problems. Vera wrote:

I shall probably be sending one or two garments for washing this week… will you please tell whoever the housemaid is now to mend the camisoles if they are mendable…I am really quite amused about the housemaid trying on my clothes in the attic. I did not…leave much behind that could be spoiled, else I do not suppose it would have been very good for them.[13]

Vera took part in another acclaimed dramatic performance, this time in 'Goodnight Babette' and 'The Dear Departed' on 26 February:

In the evening we did our plays, in candle-light with a flickering fire behind. I forgot myself quite soon…I sang quite confidently too…I think it went down well especially with some of the more artistic people. I rushed away and changed to Victoria, to the great joy of the audience from the point of view of my appearance. I tied my hair with a little ribbon at the side & left it flowing…The laughing was so vociferous that we sometimes had to wait quite a long time & occasionally our cues were drowned.[14]

But Vera was finding it harder to justify scholastic isolation, telling Roland:

> I think it is harder now the spring days are beginning to come to keep the thought of war before one's mind – especially here where there is always a kind of dreamy spell which makes one feel that nothing poignant and terrible can ever come near.[15]

'Hard work is the only way of coming through these troubles.'

While Vera began to consider whether she should continue studying and volunteer for some sort of war work, some aspects of Buxton life continued much as before. The Hydro still hosted distinguished guests, including Ottoline Morrell and Bertrand Russell, and offered the same rich programme of recreation and entertainments it always had.[16] Easter 1915 was another commercial success; some of the Hydro's wealthy guests had been visiting for 25 years, many for over a decade, and 60 still lived there permanently.

Other staples of Buxton life were fast disappearing. The *Advertiser* reported the end of cricket matches; the cost of maintaining the ground and hosting matches was prohibitive now that so many subscribing members of the club had enlisted, and players from the previous summer were already at war. During May, numbers of casualties grew and pressures on men to enlist were stepped up: Buxton tradesmen received notices to release men aged 19–38 and to guarantee employment when they returned.

The town's once-rich array of entertainments was now essential for fundraising and morale-boosting. At the end of one performance, Lieutenant Brindley of the Gordon Highlanders took the stage to appeal for further volunteers, explaining that it was the last day of his one week leave from France. The government issued War Saving Loans (bonds) and warned the public that there would be financial problems when war ended so they must save for the future.

By spring 1915, it was becoming harder to encourage men to serve. Some wealthy employers paid rent for soldiers' families and kept their jobs open, including the Johnsons whose chauffer Tom Kay was the son of the Brittains' cook, and had a wife and four young children. Yet for poor families, deaths of a father or son meant a complete loss of income. Organisations like the Buxton War Relief Fund offered assistance but as the *Advertiser* observed, cases for support were not always straightforward:

> The deaths of three soldiers killed in action were reported… The cases of their dependants were brought to the notice of The Royal Patriotic Fund Corporation, who at once sent a grant for the widow. In the third case, as

'Oxford I Trust Will Lead to Something, But Buxton Never Will' 163

the deceased soldier had not made an allotment of his pay, and had not otherwise contributed a regular sum towards maintenance, as required by the regulations, the Corporation were not able to make a grant.

To spur more men to enlist, the *Advertiser* announced the formation of a new battalion to be known as the Chatsworth Rifles, proclaiming lower standards for eligibility:

...the fact is patent that there are hundreds of fit and capable young men in the towns and villages and amongst the hills and dales who have not yet seriously thought what the "call" means. Height standard no longer serves as a barrier, it is now the chance of those from 5ft 3in. to 5ft 6in. to show of what grit they are made.

The loosening of criteria for fitness to fight heightened tensions over men who did not join up, and growing calls for women to contribute to the war effort. While some of Vera's Buxton acquaintances volunteered, she continued to regard war service as irrelevant to her:

The temporary Red Cross nurses such as Leslie Duncan and Nancy Garnett were selling programmes. It is an excellent thing for these idle people to have something as strenuous & useful to do as scrubbing floors

Soldiers garrisoned in Buxton 1914–1915 arriving at the railway station. (*PtP*)

& carrying dishes…at the Devonshire Hospital…I quite envy them for the experience, for it must be most useful & interesting in spite of the hardness & monotony of the work. Now that I am so busy it is quite impossible for me to do anything of the sort, especially as they have more helpers almost than they want, but if the war had come two years ago, I should have been almost grateful to it for providing my unoccupied & unprofitable hours with employment.[17]

In May, the *Buxton Advertiser* reported 'a stirring little scene …at the Midland railway station on Tuesday morning, this being the send off of the Misses Cox and Duncan, whose services as nurses at the front had been offered and accepted'. Vera went to see the Devonshire Hospital matron Miss Hyland, who she knew from church, to volunteer for the summer holidays. She wrote to Roland:

Work for the long vac is fixed up… It is a splendid place, and most excellently managed; they have extended it to take in 150 wounded as well as the usual patients. I would rather go there than… the temporary Red Cross Hospital where the discipline is not nearly as good. If one must be under authority, it is preferable to have it as strict as possible.[18]

Telling Edith 'hard <u>work</u> is the only way of coming through these troubles…', Vera decided to take a year's leave of absence and joined other students and some of her tutors in weekly 'Invalid Cookery' classes. After discovering that 'very few qualifications are needed' for nursing in France, other than a month's training at a provincial or London hospital, she told Edith she was considering doing this. She was increasingly weary:

Tuesday May 18th
Every estimate of the length of the war both by The Times & other people seem to get longer, while as it is I feel I cannot stand much more of it sometimes.

A couple of weeks later, news that Italy had joined the war raised Vera's hopes that perhaps it would soon all be over. Her optimism was misplaced. Local and national newspapers were again full of German atrocities and seeing Oxford day-trippers who Vera thought should be fighting for their country, heightened her jingoism. She wrote indignantly to Roland:

…[the Germans'] treatment of the women and children is the worst of all. If they ever get over here I shall go about with a revolver – not for them but for myself. I don't know how any man can read it and not enlist. It makes me feel I could do anything to the German soldiers if only I had the power...I want to say to you and everyone else at the front I know, 'once you get hold of them, do your worst'.[19]

Vera was 'longing to begin' nursing because 'the only way to stop suffering one's self is by alleviating even if it is so only little and indirectly, the sufferings of this unhappy stricken world'.[20] Somerville students took part in entertainment for wounded soldiers, and Vera wrote to Roland:

Most of them were crippled and bandaged and I don't know when anything has made me feel so sad as the combination of the music, the lovely gardens on a glorious afternoon, and these fine specimens of humanity with their once-strong bodies broken and helpless. Most of them were Tommies, some as young as sixteen.[21]

In May 1915 Maurice Ellinger's psychological problems reappeared. After attempting to shoot himself in the head during a train journey, he was put on 24-hour suicide watch at a convalescent home in Reading, where Vera visited him. In an era when attempted suicide was regarded as a sign of moral cowardice, she wrote to Edith to criticise the opprobrium she assumed would be rife in Buxton after the news was reported in the paper, adding 'he informed me of the real reason why he left the army... But it was not really to

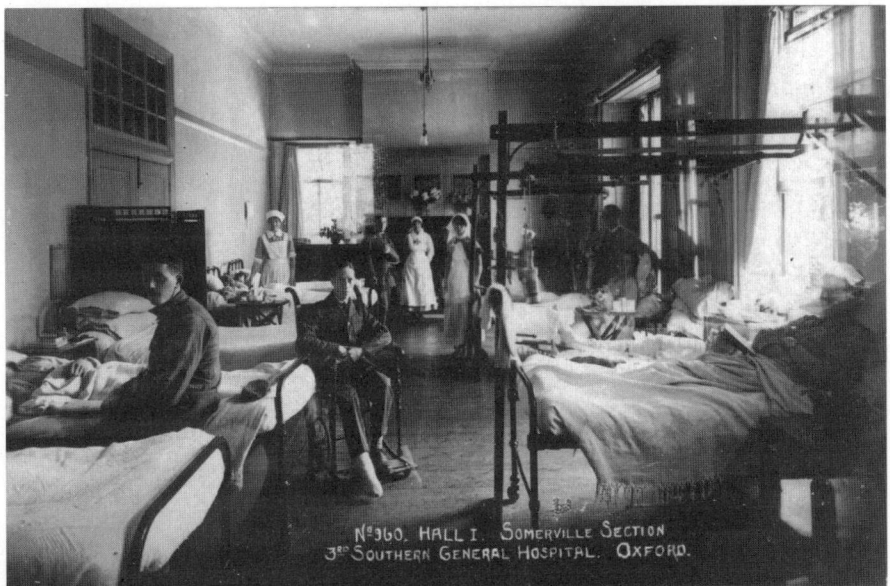

Somerville section of 3rd Southern General Hospital Oxford. (*SC*)

his discredit at all, & was the result of mental rather than moral instability'.[22] She noted in her diary:

> He told me he suffers from a form of insanity – suicidal mania… the fits come on him in a kind of deep depression, which at present nothing can keep off. In his normal moments he does not want to commit suicide at all… it was one of those fits which led to his removal from the army.[23]

Vera urged Edith to reassure Miss Hyland that she was suitable for nursing, adding 'you need not be ashamed to own that Maurice was my friend'.[24] He told Vera he was working at law, and writing stories and poems, some of which had been accepted for publication. He would eventually recover and go on to become a fine concert pianist in later life.

War was now intruding more often into Vera's life. Amongst the death lists in *The Times* was Murray Drummond-Fraser, a friend from Buxton:

> He was only 21 … I have often played tennis and bridge with him, & always liked him very much … so they are all departing; fulfilling, like the Acheans of Homer's Illiad, a cruel fate – "the eloquent, the young, the beautiful and the brave"… words of grief become almost meaningless these days, they have to be used so frequently. But one does not feel any the less. Sorrows do not grow lighter because they are many'.[25]

Roland was moved to a different line of trenches in the Somme and a couple of days later Vera met Edward in Oxford. Still waiting with growing frustration to be sent to the Front, he commended her decision to nurse. Vera worried about his fate:

> Saturday June 12th
> Edward…seems to have a queer sort of premonition that he will fall – he says it will be part of the irony of life if he does, because he so loves peace. He says that he dreads death for purely egoistical reasons, as he feels very ambitious sometimes, but really it has not any very great terrors for him….I sat listening to all this feeling rather chilled. Every time I see the dear lad I seem to love him better; he is growing into so much finer a person than I ever supposed he would be….sitting beneath the trees in the gathering twilight, the feeling was so strong as to be almost a conviction that once Edward gets out he will never come back.

There were more Buxton casualties:

Monday June 14th
...a Lieut. F. Helm, of the 8th Manchester Regiment., was killed in the Dardanelles. I think it must be Frank Helm with whom I acted in The Amazons and Raffles. I begin to feel I shall soon have no more male acquaintances left – to say nothing of friends.

Vera spent her final evening in Oxford:

Tuesday June 15th
Miss Hughes & I went on the river this evening & took dinner out. I like her ever so much better than I ever have before; I suppose with one's friends it is the same as I am finding with Oxford – that everything seems so much more precious when there is a possibility of leaving it. We punted home as the sun was setting – or rather I lay on the punt, exulting in the light of the sunset on the water.

After sitting her final examination with four women and fifty men and watching an extremely entertaining 'going-down' play, Vera walked round the dark quad for the last time. Despite everything, she was still optimistic about her future:

Saturday June 20th, 1915
My year at Oxford – how much I have learnt in it! How I love "old Oxford with its spires so grey"! And yet...I have by no means done all I meant to do...conspicuous for scarcely anything – unless it be for prettiness & athletics, which are the two things I care about least of all. Only a very few... are at all aware that I have an intellect or character. Scarcely anyone knows of my literary attempts & ambitions...And yet – somehow I feel the reputation will be mine some day, even at College.
 ...I went to the Cathedral, for perhaps the last occasion for a very long time. There I looked at the crimson & purple reflections of the stained glass window on the grey stone, listened to the music & thought of Roland, with vague scraps of poetry running through my mind, wakened by the day's emotions to creativeness. The anthem was glorious. I did not hear the words of it till right at the end, & then it seemed to me significant that what I was regarding as my hymn of Au Revoir to Oxford should close with the words 'And sorrow, and sorrow, shall flee away.'

It would be four years before Vera resumed her studies and six before she graduated. In 1948, when her daughter Shirley Williams was successful and happy at Somerville College, Vera wrote:

> Although in the circumscribed Buxton existence, Oxford had meant the realisation of an early dream which once seemed unattainable, its achievement was never complete until Shirley went to college. There she experienced the…gorgeous normality that in a wartime and post-war university had never been mine. Her three years at Somerville proved that everything I had believed of Oxford could really come true.[26]

Back in June 1915, with all her university dreams on indefinite hold, Vera began work at the Devonshire Hospital. Over the next three traumatic years, war would trash all Vera's patriotism and belief in its moral validity, and all her youthful optimism and exuberance.

Chapter Eleven

'The Day Will Come When We Shall Live Our Roseate Poem Through as We Have Dreamt It'

Vera and Roland

'He interests me so deeply & so strangely.'

From October to December 1914 Roland waited to be sent to the Front with his battalion, the 7th Worcesters. He and Vera corresponded often, about life at Somerville and in the trenches, the progress of the war and its moral justification. The Christmas holidays were a turning point in their feelings for each other:

Monday December 14th
I am longing for [a photo] of Roland, about whom I think every time I see soldiers – which is nearly all the time as they are stationed at the Empire [Hotel], & I cannot go out without meeting some of them. In the evenings The Park is crowded with the Tommies walking out with girls. This evening we had a variety entertainment at the theatre, the proceeds of which are going to provide comforts for the soldiers…it was all very good & went down extremely well…in the choruses of which all the Tommies, who were crowded about different parts of the building, joined in.

After sending her photograph to Roland, Vera went shopping in Manchester with Edith:

Wednesday December 16th
I …bought a little black moire & velvet hat with red roses…I quite enjoyed myself, especially when we entered a 3d. bazaar to buy toys for Mrs Kay's grandchildren, & found a surging crowd of poor people, & an atmosphere cuttable with a knife. We departed thence armed with a red rubber-ball, a scarlet & blue soldier who was also a money-box, a tin side-car & an engine.

Soldiers garrisoned in Buxton practising bridge building in Buxton Gardens.

….[A letter from Roland] seemed partly to insist that he has not come to regard the contemplative side of life as a waste of time, which I suggested last week that he probably had – & partly to ask what I want for my 21st birthday. He says he never considers me as 15 months older…It is so strange – not that I should be 21, for I often feel like that, & sometimes, especially since June, I feel more like 100 – but that he should be barely 20….He interests me so deeply & so strangely, this serious-minded, brilliant, unusual young man.

For Vera's 21st birthday, Roland gave her five expensive books: Kipling's *Seven Seas*; Hardy's *Tess of the D'Urbervilles*; Maeterlinck's [illegible – possibly *Monna Varana*?]; Turgenev's *On the Eve*; and Pierre Lote's *'Pecheur d'Islande'*. She 'loved every single thing he sent me… his choice is excellent & decidedly cosmopolitan'. Four days later, Vera's twenty-first birthday mad her end of year reflections even more melancholy than usual:

Wednesday 29th December 1914
There is nothing whatever to say about it. To be of age according to the law & to be one's own mistress does not impress me at all, nor does it fill with grave & sober reflections. It is having nothing definite to do that makes another year seem a burden; when one is on the way towards achieving

Vera and Roland's studio portraits. (*McM*)

one's object, & things are happening, one's life is made up by events & not increasing years.

Pessimism soon dissipated. In a 'day of surprising realisations and developments', Vera and Edward travelled by train see Roland in London. Her favourite aunt, Edith's sister Belle, chaperoned the couple, ensuring they had as much time alone as possible. Roland accompanied the women on a shopping trip:

> So, I said 'well you can come to the dressmakers if you like, & you can even help me choose stockings if you associate me with anything so prosaic as stockings, but I do bar you coming with me while I try on blouses'. He promised that he would wait outside very patiently & nothing would persuade him to change his mind…So we went to D.H.Evans & I took a thoroughly long time over choosing blouses & stockings. I told Roland it was not at all proper for him to wander about the ladies department but he said he often did such things…[at the dressmakers] I asked him what colour I should choose for the sash of my coat & skirt… when he said he didn't like the one I wanted I told him I did not require his directions![1]

After helping Vera choose a hat, Roland took her and Belle to meet his mother for lunch at the Criterion in Piccadilly. Vera and Marie Leighton got on well immediately and Vera's ardent diary entry about her is in true 'grand passion' style. The group discussed children:

Aunt Belle by various questionings discovered that I possessed the incongruous quality of loving children. She asked Roland if he did & he replied 'I am afraid I don't very much'. I chuckled to myself & determined to remember that remark, although Aunt Belle was telling us how Daddy had always hated children until his experience with us and he [Roland] did say he would love a child of his own.

During 'the most precious evening of my life thus far', Vera, Roland and Aunt Belle went to supper before going to see *David Copperfield* at the theatre. They had a 'melancholy but unsentimental' discussion about how they wanted to die: Roland said he would like a burial like that of the Vikings of old, put in a boat, set on fire, and drifting out to sea. Vera asked if he would like to be killed in action:

He answered quite quietly 'Yes I should; I don't want to die but if I must, I should like to die that way'. I sat looking at him with his dark expressive eyes & broad strong figure & suddenly was conscious of my deep sense of tragedy in my heart both for my sake & his; for mine because I love him & for his because it seems the greatest crime in the world that so brilliant an intellect & so promising a character should soon be exposed to danger & death.

That evening, Vera realised that her 'old dreams & aspirations grew pale', diminishing her once-fierce ambition and desire for independence. She noted in her diary 'the feelings which, ever since I had known him might quite possibly arise between us, were no longer a dream but a reality …in this time of tragedy there can be no postponement'.[2]

The following day, Roland saw her and Aunt Belle off at St Pancras:

I leaned out of the carriage window & waved to him once & then I could not look anymore, but sat silent & motionless, capable of neither words or tears or anything else, & yet extraordinarily conscious of that very feeling of immobility. I wondered if in days to come I should look back on that evening as the beginning of the great story of my life, or as an occasion which in silent remembrance I should forever mourn. [I would give] all I lived & hoped for…not to astonish the world by some brilliant & glittering achievement, but some day be the mother of Roland Leighton's child … And the New Year, with all its giant possibility of grief & joy came in while I sat motionless in the train, watching the dim railways lights in a blurred mist go swiftly by.[3]

Vera's retreat into these more traditional feminine responses was very different from her pre-war coolness about passion and emotion and her valorisation of cool rationality. After visiting Louise Heath-Jones and Florence Bervon in Reigate, she returned to Buxton on 2 January. Roland wrote thanking her, 'so very much. It has been such a delight to be with you these two days. I think I shall always remember them in their wonderful incompleteness and unreality.... you are a dear, you know'. Vera was now very unsettled:

> Sunday January 3rd, 1915
> I went with Mother through the thick snow to St John's this morning, though not feeling much like church, for to-day there is a universal intercession service for peace... Probably I was in an easily moveable state, but church did move me to-day... I felt inconveniently like crying. I could not help thinking of Roland, & praying for him despite my small belief in that kind of prayer...I could not, dared not, leave anything undone while there was the remotest possibility might be of some help to him.

> Monday January 4th
> I tried to work & failed disgracefully. Miss Fry is certainly right in saying that to care for anyone at all is a serious interference to work. It is almost a pity I could not have remained unmoved until college is over. But let my work suffer if it must! After all it is the creative artist, rather than the scholar, that I want to be.

On 16 January, 'by means of various judicious turnings of the conversation & by assertions that I probably should not have time to send the telegram [home] saying I had arrived until after tea', she and Roland engineered an unchaperoned lunch at the Grand Hotel in Leicester. He insisted on travelling with her to Oxford before returning to his garrison in Peterborough. She realised 'this mad dream must come to an end', writing to Roland next day 'how I am going to get through this eight weeks? I told you I should feel unsettled'.

While college soon had its 'usual capacity...for making everything else seem very remote', war began to preoccupy Vera more often. On 26 January, news that one of Roland and Edward's school friends had been killed led her to lament that the war was taking them all, 'the eloquent, the young, the beautiful & brave' and there could be no justification for that. In a debate at the Oxford Women's Debating Society that day, she voted for the motion 'this house deplores the use of Indian native troops'.

While Roland waited impatiently to be sent to the Front, Vera still enjoyed university life but was, as she told him, finding it harder to justify:

> I think it is harder now the spring days are beginning to come to keep the thought of war before one's mind – especially here where there is always a kind of dreamy spell which makes one feel that nothing poignant and terrible can ever come near.[4]

'I hope heaven will be kind and bring you back.'

Three days before Vera returned to Buxton for Easter 1915, Roland heard he was finally to go to France. Although she had been expecting the news, it was 'none the less a terrible shock to me. I can hardly realise that the moment has come at last which ends my peace of mind…He says he can't possibly go… without seeing me'.[5] Edith and Arthur invited Roland to stay at Melrose, and Vera and her mother had one of their heart-to-heart conversations:

> Tuesday March 16th
> I talked a great deal about Roland to Mother who was quite sympathetic & seemed anxious to find out just how much he had 'made love to me' & seemed surprised to find how little he had done so obviously. I told her about the Leicester episode on my way to Oxford last time. She did not seem at all annoyed but very amused.[6]

Vera met Roland at the station. At Melrose, Edith left them alone in the morning room, where they discussed why he wanted to go, and their belief in the moral reasons for war:

> Friday March 19th
> Roland had a settled conviction he was coming back – not quite whole perhaps but he hoped I should not like him less if he was, say, minus an arm…A clairvoyant had told him he would be in danger many times but would always just escape.

After tea they walked around Buxton in a blizzard, and with light coming through the black sky and a lull in the snow, they walked a little way up the Manchester Road:

> We remembered as we stood there gazing on the general dismalness how this time last year we had walked up that same road, he & I, Edward & Maurice, on a sunshiny Sunday evening, when the first indications of mutual interest were beginning to dawn on our minds….the recollection was a sad one.

'The Day Will Come When We Shall Live Our Roseate Poem Through'

At Melrose, Vera changed into her 'pretty blue & grey dress which everyone says I look so nice in, hoping he would think so too and I believe he did'. After dinner, they sat together on the sofa in the upstairs drawing room:

> ....in the dim lamplight with the fire flickering cheerfully in the grate. We remained there very close together until 12.0 with his arm along the back of the sofa nearly round my shoulders...Never before have I experienced such a feeling as seemed to fill that quiet room with such an intensity of emotion that everything grew quite dim.

After breakfast alone together, Vera accompanied Roland to the train station:

> On the ground the snow was lying very thick & the air was icy cold, but the sun was shining brightly overhead and everything all round looked dazzling and white. All the way to the station we scarcely spoke a word...I shall never forget the look of the station so early on that cold bright March morning...In the distance the railway bridge & the snow-covered signal boxes gleamed in the brilliant light...As the train was almost due to start I got up into the railway carriage to say goodbye to him. He held my hand a long time & looked at me in complete silence so sorrowfully that I wished I could have cried to ease the pain in my heart...I did not wish him glory or honour or triumph; in comparison with seeing him again, I cared about none of those things. So all I could say was just 'I hope Heaven will be kind to me & bring you back'... I got down from the carriage.... There was a light bustling on the platform and the train began to move... He... remained learning out of the window looking sadly at me as I stood motionless watching the train until it disappeared altogether and where it had been there was nothing but the merciless sunlight shining on the rails... I felt so stunned & cold as I turned & walked slowly out of the station.... Whatever the future may bring – whether it be the sorrow I fear more than anything on earth, or the joy which now I scarce dare dream of, much less name – as long as I have memory & thought, I shall not forget today & yesterday. My beloved one has been here and departed again, & now indeed I may see his dear face never any more.

As soon as he returned to his garrison, Roland wrote:

> And so, it is over now – the parting – 'Only a turn of the head' – And all that is left to wait and work and hope. But I *am* coming back, dear. Let

it always be 'when' and not 'if'. The day will come when we shall live our roseate poem through – as we have dreamt it'.⁷

The next day Vera was overcome with sadness but, with characteristic fortitude, found hope:

> I had another violent fit of desperation this morning. I suppose I must get used to them, but they alarm me a little & make me wonder what I may do if Roland dies…I think of how little there is of any tendency for the war to end, of how he is in the trenches day in & day out…of the long weary months ahead, & wonder how I shall ever bear them… [but] hope springs anew in the human heart – I suppose physical existence would be impossible without it…I felt a weak and cowardly person after all to shrink from my share in the Universal Sorrow, when after all it was only right that I should have to suffer too, that I had no longer an impersonal indifference to set me apart from the thousands of breaking hearts in England to-day …And I went to bed, I prayed, as I had promised, that God might bring him back.⁸

Roland sent her an amethyst brooch with a card inscribed 'In Memoriam':

> Like a good omen, the amethyst was full of light. I held it up in front of the fire for a moment & the red glow reflected in it made it look like a great drop of blood.⁹

Vera went into town to buy him a fountain pen, and realised she was not the only person in Buxton to be acutely anxious:

> Our housemaid is very troubled about her young man who is at the front in the 1st Sherwood Foresters. She has not heard anything of him for three weeks, & to-day a parcel she sent him was returned – without however any intimation of his death. They may of course merely have lost sight of him for the time being but it does look rather bad.¹⁰

Over the next few days, Vera found great comfort in Buxton's beautiful surroundings:

> Wednesday March 25th
> After tea a sort of restlessness came over me which urged me to go into Corbar Woods & stand by the tree beneath which Roland & I sat nearly a year ago, & where we first began to feel that interest in each other which

has led to so much…the place was hallowed by the memory of his presence, so that even the bareness of the tree-trunks & the greyness of the distance which showed between them could not prevent my soul from making itself felt in a vague aspiring, and an intense spiritual consciousness of love & vital inner life striving for self-expression… as I gazed at the lonely hills behind me & the faint gleam of the sunset sky in the greyness above …I knelt on the damp ground beneath the tree and prayed to that omnipotent Being that Roland might return. Then I walked slowly away, intending on April 20th to revisit the place.

Vera's diary became increasingly an outlet for long heart-wrenching accounts of 'weary thoughts, anguish & weakness…more thinking, more wrestling with ideas, till my mind whirls with the force of thoughts that crowd in upon it … the first real trouble I have ever known dawned on me.'[11] In the face of torment, Vera hoped 'the best future one can build for oneself either in terms of sorrow or of joy is founded not on events & circumstances but on the growth of the Soul itself.'[12]

On 31 March, Roland's battalion made the crossing from Folkestone to Boulougne before going to Ploegsteert Wood a few miles from the French-Belgian border where they would remain before being sent to the Somme

Early twentieth century Ashwood Dale towards Topley Pike, one of Vera's many bicycle routes around Buxton. (*PtP*)

in June. On the day of Roland's crossing, Vera went for another of her many bicycle rides:

> I rode slowly along the sunlit patches, bathing myself in the light and warmth. I … whispered to myself 'He and I will one day walk along that path…Often I got down from my bicycle to lean over the wall or gate, inspired to dreamy meditation…by the beauty of all that lay before my eyes…his path now will be from one danger to another, with the Shadow of Death beside him every hour.

Now sure that university was no longer worthwhile, Vera did not want to return to Oxford. On the anniversary of his first visit to Melrose, Roland wrote from Ploegsteert Wood near the Belgian border, which the men nicknamed 'Plug Street Wood':

> I read [your letter] by candlelight sitting on a little wooden bench outside my dug-out. I am sitting there now writing this, while the sun shines on the paper and a bee is humming round the bed of primroses in front of me. War and primroses! At the moment it does not feel as if there could be such a thing as war…At times I can quite forget danger and war and death and think only of the beauty of life and love – and you.

He went on to describe finding a dead British soldier hidden in the undergrowth and arranged for him to be covered over with earth, adding another to the graves in the wood.[13] He sent Vera some violets, which she pressed and kept in her diary.[14] After reading his letter, Vera wrote:

> Saturday April 17th
> my courage gave way a little when he ended 'Do not worry on my account. Goodnight & much love. I have just been kissing your photograph'. My eyes filled with the most stinging tears…Sometimes I think it is less the thought of his danger than the ardent desire for his presence…and when he writes such things as this – & he has never admitted so much before – I want him terribly badly, & the thought of what it may be if he returns, but is so likely never to be, is almost more than I can bear…I never thought I should ever say to anyone such things as I write to R. I suppose the nearness of death breaks down the reserves & conventions…the longing for his presence drives me nearly desperate; I can scarcely keep it in check, much less face the thought I may have to do without it for ever more. Thinking about that makes me feel utterly heart-sick & almost physically faint…

'The Day Will Come When We Shall Live Our Roseate Poem Through'

Two of Roland's fellow officers at Ploegsteert Wood, photograph taken by RL. (*McM*)

when just a few words at the end of such a letter tell me how much he cares himself – it is even more unbearable than feeling how much *I* do.

Vera berated herself for weakness and lack of endurance, wondering what 'would he think if <u>he</u> saw how weak and incapable I am?'. Reading love scenes in Turgenev's *On The Eve*, one of his birthday presents, made her think of 'Roland and me – not what we have ever risen to in each other's presence, but what I believe we are both capable of rising to. All the rest of the day I felt wild with desire for him [and] a need to feel him near me & be able to touch him before this pain at my heart will cease to torment me & drive me desperate'.[15]

Tuesday April 20th, 1915
I went to the place in Corbar Woods where he & I sat & talked the whole morning…just a year ago to-day. Then, there were leaves on the trees, the sun beat down through the branches, & we sat on the dry ground…To-day everything was grey & damp; scarcely a sign of spring had yet appeared. Above my head the tree-tops tossed & moaned; water dripped from the leafless boughs with dismal sound…I stood there thinking & thinking, wondering how I was going to bear it all.

A week later, Vera went to stay with Cora in Surrey, staying up all night talking about 'the horrors of war & the problems of truth raised by them'. The next day they 'discussed sex questions':

I propounding my theory, which dawned on me when first I knew I loved, that sex attraction has a threefold nature of spirit, mind & body, just like our whole being & that we ought not to despise the physical attraction, so long as it is the symbol of a spiritual union also just because we have it in common with all creation.[16]

News of Neuve Chappelle, in which English men were killed by our own guns, sparked Vera's horror and renewed her anxiety:

It is too terrible, this reckless waste of life, the only thing worth having in the universe. Naturally this horrible truth does not come out in the dispatch – it would undoubtedly stop recruiting if men thought they were to be shot down by their own guns. Roland is dreadfully near Lille.[17]

Vera copied long extracts from Roland's letters into her diary. She had asked him to 'tell me of the horrors he sees because women are no longer the sheltered darlings of men's playtime, fit only for the nursery or the drawing room, certainly no woman *he* was interested in would ever be just that'.[18] Vera noted in her diary that he was becoming disillusioned with trench warfare:

'it is nothing glorious …it is all a waiting & a waiting & a taking of petty advances…And it is all for nothing – for an empty name, for an ideal perhaps'. He had just received the letter I wrote after he told me he had been kissing my photograph [and says] 'When all is finished & I am with her again, the original shall not envy the photograph … But may it not be better that such sweet sacrilege should be an anticipation rather than a memory?'

Reluctantly Vera returned to Oxford. Recalling Roland's criticism of a 'life of scholastic vegetation', Vera told him if war showed no sign of ending, she would continue nursing after her summer volunteering because it demanded the greatest degree of self-sacrifice. As casualties increased, Vera became more distracted from her studies, her and Roland's letters longer and their discussions about war more heartfelt. She talked to Miss Penrose about taking a leave of absence to become a trainee Voluntary Aid Detachment nurse.

With news of many more casualties, May 1915 was, as Vera noted, a 'dreadful month'. Roland wrote to tell her about the first death of one of his men, describing how he took things out of his pockets to send back to 'someone somewhere who will see more than a torn letter, & pencil & a knife & a piece of shell …I cannot help thinking how ridiculous it is that such a small thing should make such a change… it is a glorious warm summer day which helps one to forget many things'. Vera observed in her diary 'all through these letters of his I can see so plainly the artist & soldier alternating'.[19] She longed for the end of term so that she could begin nursing.

On 6 June Vera noted 'his third month out there'. Roland had written to remember:

> Speech Day & all that I had hoped of Oxford…And I couldn't keep the tears out of my eyes afterwards when Sterndale Bennett played Karg-Elert's 'Clair de Lune' in the Chapel…You were sitting at the back near the door & I couldn't see you without looking round…It all seems very far away now. I sometimes think I must have exchanged my life for someone else's.

Just a few weeks earlier Vera had asked him whether it 'is an ideal for which you are personally fighting, and is it one which justifies all the blood that has been and is to be shed?'[20] Over the following nine months, her question would be answered.

Chapter Twelve

'I Found a Lot of Old Dance Programmes Which I Tied Up And Put Away'

The End of Provincial Young Ladyhood

'We were childishly and ardently conscientious.'

On Sunday 27 June 1915, dressed in the unfamiliarly plain grey dress of a voluntary nursing assistant, Vera reported for duty to Miss Hyland, Matron of Buxton's Devonshire Hospital. After years of enjoying her beautiful clothes, Vera was not looking forward to dressing every day in the same unbecoming uniform, but was glad her Buxton dressmaker, Mrs Fowler, had managed to alter it so skilfully to fit her. Just three weeks earlier, she had recorded gaily in her diary:

> Roland wrote it would be nice if he could get wounded & get sent to Somerville & lie in a deck-chair & talk to me. He wonders what I will look like in a nurse's uniform – supposes it can't be very becoming to anybody – thinks it a pity to wear a horrid stiff collar when you have such a nice neck to cover up in it. This & the suggestion I must look very charming in a green overall are about the first compliments he has ever paid me. I wonder if he really thinks I am pretty.... It would be just like him to say so the less he thought so.[1]

Fashion-conscious middle-class women like Vera took for granted all the coded signals of social status and individual taste conveyed by their elegant clothes. A nurse uniform, with

Vera at Melrose, July 1915. (*SC*)

its extremely strict specifications, including precise dimensions of a belt and amount of starch in an apron, symbolised the subjugation of individuality.² While Vera would later note her 'deep fear of merging [my] own individuality in the impersonal routine of the organisation', at the start of her nursing career, the uniform was, as it was for many volunteers, a potent symbol of a heroic yet feminine sacrifice for wartime service. And, in any case, Vera's days of sartorial extravagance would soon be a target for a poster campaign by the National Organising Committee for War Savings, admonishing women to curb their extravagance:

> Many women have already recognised that elaboration and variety in dress are bad form...but there is still a large section of the community...who appear to make little or no difference to their habits. New clothes should only be bought when absolutely necessary....Luxurious forms of hats, boots, shoes, stockings, gloves and veils should be avoided. It is essential, not only that money should be saved, but that labour employed in the clothing trades should be set free.³

It was just over two months since the Devonshire had become a fully-fledged military hospital; for the first nine months of war, it was mainly a convalescent facility for those with rheumatism and shell shock, or 'low moral fibre' as it was then known. By summer 1915, it was dealing with a hundred soldiers. When Vera postponed her university studies, thousands of women were taking up war work. In 1914, nearly six million women over the age of ten worked in industry, domestic service, and commerce; by the time conscription was introduced in 1916, over a million had replaced men in many occupations. From 1916 to the end of the war, another half a million women would become bus drivers, farm workers and munitions factory operatives, nurses and office workers.

Vera became an assistant nurse for the Voluntary Aid Detachment (VAD), set up in 1909 to fill gaps in territorial medical services. Female detachments staffed VAD hospitals and auxiliary units but as the number of medical units at home and abroad escalated, it became increasingly difficult to keep ordinary hospitals fully staffed. By March 1915, the War Office agreed that VADs could augment trained nursing staff and a few months later, allowed a year's experience and a good hospital reference to enable them to work in hospitals overseas. Between 1914 and 1918, more than 90,000 women served as VADs; 10,000 in hospitals under the direction of the War Office. Of those, 8,000 served overseas, in France, Malta, Serbia, Salonika, Egypt and Mesopotamia.

Government recruitment campaigns used maternal and religious imagery to encourage women to volunteer as nurses, proclaiming parity of status between the public school educated men who enlisted as officers and the socially privileged women who became VADs. Diverse in age, they were the daughters of local gentry, landowners, army officers, clergy, and professional men. Some were from an aristocratic background. By and large, while they brought a range of life skills to their unfamiliar new role, the majority had never had, nor expected to have, any paid employment, or seen male bodies.[4] According to Vera, most were:

Red Cross recruitment poster. (*IWM*)

> …like myself, very young and quite unsophisticated. When we first joined up our chief preoccupation was the fear of being turned down for incompetence after the month trial with which every voluntary nurse's army career began. Disturbed… by the unfamiliarity of our duties…we were childishly and ardently conscientious; inspired by a pathetically high patriotic idealism, we had a touching faith in the righteousness of our cause and the disinterested Olympian virtue of war-time leaders …[5]

VADs had to adapt immediately and without complaint to tasks familiar only from having servants: mopping floors, making beds, washing up, preparing and serving food, counting laundry, and running messages. There was no scope to exercise judgement and the work involved the tyranny of routine and remorseless drudgery, but some found an almost religious satisfaction in it.[6] As more hospitals became military facilities, VADs increasingly took on medical roles which, predictably, created tensions with professional nurses. Although Vera would later record her great admiration for her trained colleagues, she was not the only VAD to experience resentment from nurses antagonistic to women with a handful of first aid certificates and a few months training. For their part, many VADs were unused to taking orders of any sort and especially not from those they regarded as their social inferiors.[7]

'I can honestly say I love nursing'

Vera threw herself wholeheartedly into an arduous schedule, working from 7.45 until lunch at home, and again from 5 to 9.15 pm. The hospital building made nursing duties even more difficult. Built in 1779 as stables for the Devonshires, the Estate donated it in 1857 to the trustees of the Bath Charity and Cotton Districts Convalescent Fund for a hospital to treat Lancashire mill workers and others. Nurses were not allowed to cross its diameter, which contained an inner circle for convalescent patients, so that everything forgotten or newly required meant a run round the circumference. Vera noted how 'the continuous walking around the unresistant stone floors must have amounted, apart from the work itself, to several miles a day'.[8]

Vera and Roland continued their long, frequent letters.[9] For a long time she was oblivious to the true horrors of war and optimistic about her contribution to the war effort. In one letter to Roland:

> June 28th
> I can honestly say I love nursing ...Another nurse & I have three wards to look after between us... I have to take the men their breakfasts ...prepare the tables for the doctor, with hot water etc, tidy up & dust the wards & make the beds. These latter are not made in the ordinary way but in a particular method you have to learn how to do, & are called medical beds.

Interior of Devonshire Hospital. Designed by the Estate's architect, Robert Ripon Duke, the dome is a stunning architectural achievement and the largest unsupported dome in Europe.

Not every sick person has medical beds, but cases of rheumatism always do. Then I have various other jobs…such as going round with the doctor to see the patients, bandaging limbs, helping semi-helpless patients to get up & put their clothes on (I had extreme difficulty this morning in putting on a man's sock for him!), waiting on the nurses while they do massage etc, taking round milk at lunch time, preparing dinner & in general being at the beck & call of the nurse who is over me… very few come from the trenches, it is too far, but go to another hospital first. One man …had six operations before coming to my ward & is still almost helpless.'

Part of another letter:

July 3rd
I am very disappointed about your leave & could be more so, only I won't let myself think too much about it. I had hoped that before you went into the actual thick of the fighting, I should see you once again, & learn to realise you tangibly …Perhaps after all it is a compliment paid to us by Fate – for I always think that people who are given the most strain on their endurance are usually those who are capable of enduring most…..

Nursing is going on well – I like it more & more. The chief things it spoils are my shoes and hands!... I like all my patients immensely – particularly a sandy-haired lance-corporal from the Devon Regiment. He is quite helpless; I have to get him up every day & bandage his leg. He was wounded in four places, each bad; he has been on his back for many months & is likely to be on it many more, but he is always cheerful, & everything is always right for him. It is really a pleasure to look after him. I would rather look after Tommies than officers – except one officer. Sometimes I try to imagine he is you – only he is very thin, which does not aid the fancy! They are all most amusing about the tea in the morning, they call it 'khaki-water' (with some justification) and have a different exhibition of wit over it every day. I have to be very solemn & dignified & act as if I were at least 10 years older than those boys of my own age (fortunately the nurse's dress helps the illusion) but it is usually very difficult to keep my face straight.

To Vera's relentlessly frenetic brain which had been 'consistently … thinking & pondering for the last 5 or 6 years', the exhausting work was a 'great rest', helping her to be less anxious. She realised just how much her privileged upbringing had made her totally unprepared for basic tasks such as preparing meals for her patients:

To me, for whom meals had hitherto appeared as though by clockwork and the routine of a house had seemed to be worked by some invisible mechanism, the complications of sheer existence were nothing short of a revelation.[10]

Vera noted in her diary 'I have never worked so hard in my life; it gives me a little insight into the lives of those who always have to work like this'. She told Roland she was unfazed by washing and dressing men:

July 10th
Mother quite expected I might feel uncomfortable & embarrassed about having to go about strange men in bed, & dust the wards with them getting up all around me, for I have scarcely seen any men in bed (not even Edward and Daddy)…I think I must have been a nurse in a previous existence – or else had seven husbands or something of that sort.

As for Roland, he was beginning to lose his belief in what he once thought of as 'the beauty of war', regarding it as little more than a depressing, demeaning trade. Vera did not recognise how cynical he was becoming, and continued to believe that the horrors of war could be justified if they put an end to war for ever. She was anxious when he did not write:

July 18th
Whence this long silence, dear? I know of course that there is some good reason for it – I am almost afraid to know what. I am so sorry I have not written for so long. I have been extremely busy, but that is not the reason as I am never too busy to write to you. But I have been waiting to get a letter before writing again – expecting to get one every day, every post in fact. I have such a dread of writing a letter & getting it returned unread by the person for whom it was intended – I think that is the most horrible way of learning about casualties that there is. But I cannot wait any longer now, as if you have not written just because you have too much to do, you must be wondering what has become if me & my correspondence… If there is nothing wrong, you'll forgive this selfish anxiety, won't you? As a day or two ago I picked up the 'Times' & saw 'Heavy fighting between Arras and Armentieres'… Goodbye, dear. A Field Service postcard is all I ask.

July 21st
…Dear pedantic soul, I was so relieved to hear from you. When you are marching about I expect the time goes quickly without your realising it,

and when I am at the Hospital I have not much time to think about being anxious, only in the times between when I have leisure to be selfish, I do begin to wonder & surmise...

A few days later Vera received a 'long & intimate' letter from Roland, with details of life in the trenches and telling her affectionately 'your letters to me are like an interrupted conversation'. But Vera's delight at hearing from him was short-lived when she heard that one of her favourite soldiers at the Devonshire was never going to walk again ('although he does not know this yet'). A week later she wrote to Roland:

July 28th
...I heard a day or two ago that there is a faint chance of my getting into a large London Hospital as a V.A.D...at Camberwell (No 1. London General)...it has recently been greatly extended & contains over a thousand beds...I should love to go there as they get all the wounded straight from the trenches...Fully trained nurses are rather scarce just now, and it is counted that two V.A.Ds take the place of one trained nurse (though I don't think they do really, I had no idea what a capable person a trained nurse was till I went up to the Hospital).... you have to sign on for six months & get paid at the immense rate of £20 a year, but you get your board and lodging free as well.

On 29 July, Vera was greatly upset by a report in *The Times* of the Battle of Neuve Chapelle. She wrote to Roland:

I can hardly bear to read about it, for the thought that you or Edward might get mixed up in a similar barbarous and sanguinary business. It all seems so wicked too – just a pure orgy of slaughter, of terrible and impersonal death, with nothing in the purpose and certainly nothing in the result to justify the perpetration of anything so horrible. War does bring to light the fundamental contradictions of human nature in a state of semi-civilization such as ours. It is quite impossible to understand how we can be such strong individualists, so insistent on the rights and claims of every human soul, and yet at the same time countenance (& if we are English even take quite calmly) this wholesale murder...I suppose it makes matters worse to have such thoughts, but when you think how easily that pile of disfigured dead is heaped up in a few minutes by a sharp Artillery fire, and yet what an immense and permanent difference each single unit thus shamefully cut off makes to a whole circle of individuals, you feel that if you are not mad already, the sooner you become so and lose the power to realise, the better. It is no wonder that so many women laugh with such bitterness at the criminal folly of men.

As the recruitment drive stepped up again, Edward heard he was being sent to the Front. Vera confided her fears in a letter to Roland but lauded her brother's cool courage:

29th July
We have heard definitely from Edward that he is coming here tomorrow, for I suppose, the last time…I almost wish he could go without my seeing him again. Every time I see him I feel he is more indispensable, & it doesn't do to feel that people are indispensable now-a-days, though I am guilty of it with regard to more than one person.… There are some things I feel about his going that I feel about no one else's, and which indeed no one could understand unless they had all their life been very fond of one particular brother or sister. But it is like flinging a large piece of one's Past into Limbo, not knowing if one will ever get it back.

One conclusion at any rate is that I think he realises what he is in for as well as anyone *can* know who has not been out there. You can picture…how coolly he has studied the question of the worst horrors of war, in stories, newspaper articles, and official reports …He has also talked to several wounded back from the Front, all of whom seem to have been of a rather depressing nature with a great horror of going back. When I spoke to him at Oxford I realised he had fully taken in all that they had told him and was ready to face what might be.

The Brittains outside Melrose, July 1915. (*SC*)

Mounting casualties and a slowing of the rate at which men were enlisting led Lord Kitchener to appeal for another 300,000 volunteers, and the government increased munitions production. In Buxton, the duke of Devonshire urged those still at home to prepare for a new National Registration Act on 15 August 1915. It was the first census to collect information about all citizens aged 15 to 65,

Lorries on the Crescent. (*PtP*)

revealing how many men of military age were still civilians, how many could be spared for war work and, more pressingly, how many could join the armed forces. The *Advertiser* instructed readers how to fill in the Registration form and asked them to support the Chancellor of the Exchequer in his plea for the nation to invest in The War Loan and receive interest of five per cent per annum: 'The man be rich or poor, is little to be envied who, at this supreme moment, fails to bring forward his savings for the security of his country.'

The General Superintendent of the Devonshire Hospital appealed for motor drivers 'to give our soldier patients (numbering about 100), a motor ride on Bank Holiday, 2 August.' As the first anniversary of the outbreak of war loomed, the duke of Devonshire, in his role as President of the Derbyshire Committee of The Central Committee for National Patriotic Organisations, organised meetings in every community to 'strengthen public opinion to prosecute the war with unabated vigour, and so hasten the day when an honourable peace can be attained'. Buxton was fast losing its air of genteel elegance.

Assuming he was about to go to France, Edward came home for a couple of days:

Friday July 30th
I went with the motor to meet Edward. He appeared looking very big and extraordinarily healthy...I almost wish he had not come. I can regard his going almost with equanimity except when he is here & then I feel how

indispensable he is. Daddy insisted on asking him his opinion about …the general situation… and treating his answers as words of wisdom. Edward however did just say that soldiers did not bother themselves much about the general situation, their chief object was to get trained and be ready to do their part, whatever it was; they did not trouble their heads to carp and criticise; only civilians had time for such things.

On a long evening walk, he and Vera talked about war very seriously, with Edward repeating his half-haunting instinct he would not return. Before he left Buxton, they made their last cycle road over the moors between the Leek and Macclesfield roads and 'had a splendid tea in an isolated cottage'. The next day Florence Bevon and Louise Heath-Jones came to stay. Learning that 'Miss H-J is mad to do some war-work – munitions, nursing or motor-driving', Vera observed wryly 'none of which she would be any use at'.

'So much I had meant to say to him was unsaid'

After almost five months at the Front, Roland was increasingly disillusioned and cynical. Responsible for thirty men in atrocious conditions, his patriotism and high ideals about the glory of war were giving way to a sense of its utter futility. He came home on a week's leave and on 20 August met Vera in the first-class ladies' waiting room at St Pancras station. Without the intimate connection of letters, and with Roland tired and distant, they both felt awkward with each other. Covering many pages in her diary, Vera recorded their short time together in vivid, heartfelt detail. Feeling dislocated and confused, they travelled by train to Buxton, and then via London to the Leighton family home at Lowestoft in Suffolk. Vera responded to Roland's proposal of marriage by asserting she would not wear a ring, or have their engagement announced in *The Times*.

Two days with Roland's family was, Vera wrote in her diary, a time that 'will shine out in my memory like a beacon long after nearly all else has passed into oblivion'. Vera was moved when Roland showed her the poem he had written in April after finding a dead soldier in Ploegsteert Wood and sending her violets from the wood:

> Violets from Plug Street Wood,
> Sweet, I send you oversea.
> (It is strange they should be blue,
> Blue, when his soaked blood was red,
> For they grew around his head;
> It is strange they should be blue.)

> Violets from Plug Street Wood,
> Think what they have meant to me –
> Life and Hope and Love and You –
> (And you did not see them grow
> Where his mangled body lay,
> Hiding horror from the day;
> Sweetest, it was better so.)

Vera had to return to nursing duties. They said goodbye at St Pancras station:

I felt as if I wanted to cry. So much I had meant to say to him was unsaid, and yet it seemed, as he agreed, to be no good saying any more. He said very bitterly he didn't *want* to go back to the front, and this glimpse of England and real life had made him hate France more than ever. I couldn't believe I was really going to part from him; it was so queer to look at him that I tried to commit to vivid memory his features, and to think that in a little more than a few minutes they would only be an image in my mind.

At St Pancras he wanted to pay for my ticket, but I wouldn't let him, saying I must assert my independence more than ever now. Again I wished desperately it was over, and yet felt at the same time that for him to go away from me was quite impossible. Conversation was difficult & in jerks...

It was difficult to realise that what I had thought about so much – the possibility of finding a man whom I could love, which seemed so impossible – had really happened. 'Roland, am I really engaged to you?'

He looked down at me, his face very pale and a kind of quiet blaze to his dark eyes. 'Yes' he said, in the low and rather musical tone of his deepest emotion...But when the time for getting into the train came near, the crowd of people around my carriage was very depressing...I reminded him sadly of a sentence in the first letter he wrote me after we parted before. 'Someday we shall live our roseate poem through – as we have dreamt it.' A little wistfully I said that it seemed further away now than ever. He only said 'We must – we *shall*.'

A stir in the crowd indicated the train's imminent departure....He was in a sort of despair, quite oblivious of the crowd. He stopped & kissed me passionately almost before I realised he had done it...I hadn't realised until then that this quiet & self-contained person was suffering so much.

The whistle sounded & the crowd moved a little away from the door. But he still stood close to me and as the train began to move he pressed my hand almost violently, and drawing my face down to his, kissed me again, more passionately than ever. And I kissed him, which I had never done before, and just managed to make myself whisper 'Goodbye'. He said nothing at all, but …began to walk rapidly down the platform…I… watched him walking away through the crowd. But he never turned again… It was over.[11]

Vera was desolate. Waiting at Millers' Dale for the connecting train to Buxton underneath the towering rockface of Chee Gorge, 'I looked up at the white moon shining above the deep blue mountain & it seemed to pierce into my heart and say to me 'Changed. Changed. Changed.' Returning to Melrose, Vera learned that Arthur and Edith had rushed to the south to see Edward off to the Front:

The unsympathetic servants… could not even remember to unpack my case for me…with a weariness gone into oblivion, I sat up till about 1.30 thinking of the hateful, depressing house [and]my farewell to Roland. There seemed to be nothing left for I felt that Roland was taking all my future & Edward all my past…At last I got into bed & ended the saddest day I had ever known.

Edward's posting was another false alarm. On returning to Buxton, and hearing the news of Vera and Roland's engagement, Arthur told her, with customary tactlessness, 'it seemed very ridiculous because of course Roland wouldn't come back'. I felt inwardly very angry indeed but merely said I thought that all the more reason for being engaged to him while he *did* exist'.

Roland wrote that everything felt unreal except for the 'memory and the pain and the insatiable longing for Something which one has loved. I feel as if someone had uprooted my heart to see how it was growing'.[12] Vera's diary is again full of heart-wrenching anxiety:

And yet every letter I get causes me a great deal of pain as well as of joy. Oh Roland! Why did you ever come & make me love you? I could have done so well without love – before it came – I with my ambition & life work & occupation. I shall never again be able to work towards worldly triumphs with the same disinterested concentration

The dances, amateur dramatics, sport, and music that once filled Vera's days were a distant memory, while, in place of women displaying the latest fashions, horses garrisoned in Buxton paraded through the Gardens.

There were occasional reminders of Vera's old life; in September, she, Edith, Edward and a friend went to see 'Tannhauser' at the Opera House. The following week, Vera invited someone from the hospital to dinner at Melrose and then

Soldiers parading through Buxton Gardens (*PtP*)

to see 'Carmen' performed by a provincial opera company. But there were also sporadic tensions over 'enemy aliens':

> Thursday September 16th, 1915
> Three soldiers smashed up the shop belonging to the son of Wenzel, the hairdressers today because he was foolish enough to say he was German and proud of it. I and everyone else sympathised very much with the soldiers, who are spending the night in the lock-up. The Wenzels father and son are enemy aliens, and as such should have been interned long ago. They would have been but for the slackness of the authorities here.

While Vera remained patriotic, Roland condemned the empty rhetoric of chivalry, patriotism, honour and sacrifice, and the way in which poets like Rupert Brooke romanticised war. There was a growing gap between Roland's day to day experience and Vera's rather sentimentalised, unshakeable belief in heroism. His letters became less spontaneous and sometimes he did not reply at all.

Vera confided her intense anxiety in her diary but found consolation from corresponding with Marie Leighton, recording happily in her diary Mrs Leighton's reassurances that ' if love could guard him he would be well guarded, for in all the thousands of men around him there cannot be another more adored & cherished in two women's hearts than he is in yours & mine'. She told Vera she was glad they were both 'waiting & hoping & suffering together, for it *is* suffering, this helpless waiting, however brave one may try to be', continuing with more light hearted news about sending Roland 'his weekly cake and a collar for the new dog he and his fellow officers had picked up'. Vera noted that, 'independent as I would be, I could not do it without her loving strength. She cannot know how much she means to me'.[13]

'Back once more in the dreams of those days'.

More casualties required more VADs. On 24 September Vera took the early train from Buxton for an interview at the No 1 London General Hospital in Camberwell, spending a 'joyous morning wandering about London by myself more freely than I ever had before'. On her return, Vera realised that troubled Maurice Ellinger had carried a torch for her all along:

> Mother informed me that for Maurice's sake she had told Mrs Ellinger about Roland & me. She said Mrs Ellinger seemed very taken aback & looked quite crestfallen. But she said she would tell him, and I am glad I have not had to do so.

A few days later, Maurice wrote her a 'bitter' letter:

> I attempted to answer ...but it was difficult, as I did not know quite where I stood with regard to him. Roland does not believe in platonic friendship & it is quite possible that Maurice does not either.[14]

The Battle of Loos at the end of September resulted in over 50,000 casualties. Vera's anxiety grew, noting 'long, long casualty lists' in the papers, adding that they 'dare not print stories of horror on their principal pages'. She noted that the wounded 'have already begun to come into London. I may be sent for any moment'. Vera was not the only one who feared the worst:

> Mother met several people in town who are anxious about relatives or friends. Feelings on hearing news of victory are terribly mixed – no-one knows what it may have cost them indirectly. Class distinctions slip away & are lost in this great community of anxiety.

With the call to London imminent, Vera sat in the huge loft space at Melrose going through old letters, school reports and Buxton ephemera:

Wednesday September 29th
I was back once more in the dreams of those days – ardent, impersonal dreams & ideals in which no man ever had part... love of a man never entered my dreams & the part I played in *Eager Heart* put the vision of a child there but never a man... For now it has come nothing will ever be the same again & there will be terrible readjustment of all my life if he is dead...But now – if I could give all else up to keep him, I would give it glad...

I found a lot of old dance-programmes which I tied up & put away with a sort of half-sorrowful indulgence a middle-aged woman might show when coming upon traces of her youthful folly. Some of the men I once danced with are dead – almost all are out where Death & Danger surround them every hour, or soon will be there. I wonder if I shall ever go to another dance. Very unlikely. Then I finished my papers & awoke to the present world of pain & suspense & Roland. Dreams – ideals – bow down today before this terrible human love & in this hour, my heart knows only one prayer.

The Times reported the death of a Buxton school friend and cricket team mate of Edward:

Friday October 1st
Judging by the obituary notices already in The Times, the list of officer casualties is going to be terrible. There were nearly 50 this morning. Among them, to the great grief of us all, is that of 2nd Lieut. Maurice Greenhalgh, who used to go to Holm Leigh with Edward, was a great friend of his, & always competing with him for the top of the form...Greenhalgh was a small, frail-looking boy whom we used to nickname Hackershmidt – very fair, & delicate in complexion. Father was more upset about it than I have ever seen him so far over anyone, as he was very fond of Greenhalgh when he was a little lad. Edward will be very sad indeed.

After several false alarms, Edward announced that his posting to the Front might really be imminent. Beside himself with anxiety, Arthur vented his anger:

Saturday October 9th
Father has been perfectly awful since he heard Edward really is going to the Front. He talks of giving up the house, the business, the motor, his railway contract, & of doing things which vary from having nothing to do with us to shooting himself!...It really is quite indescribable.

When Vera asked indignantly whether her career was not important too, he said decidedly 'No, Edward was the one who must be given an occupation & the means to provide for himself'. Vera resolved, yet again, to prove Arthur wrong:

> The secondary sex again!…But I will show them…Hitherto, although he has after difficulty permitted such what he calls whims as going to Oxford, he has never regarded me as anything more than a plaything. Someday the plaything's intense reality & achievement will astonish him.

In the event, Edward's hopes were dashed once more. While his army friend Geoffrey Thurlow departed for the Front in October, Edward would have to wait another four months before Vera and Edith finally saw him off on 'a grey, unutterably dismal afternoon' at Charing Cross station for the crossing to France.

Meanwhile, Vera longed for Roland's physical presence, worrying that she was able to 'visualise [his] features even less than I could before':

> He is such a brilliant, incomprehensible & elusive person that unless he sends letters to emphasise his humanity, he tends to become quite an abstraction…Though I cannot even in imagination see his face, the mere remembrance of his touch is enough to thrill me.[15]

Three days later, the government used the killing of Nurse Edith Cavell to encourage more people to enlist and more women to serve as nurses. On Saturday 16 October, Vera heard she must report immediately to the No 1. London General, and would receive board, lodging, and £20 a year, the same renumeration as a parlourmaid. She told her parents 'it was a huge incentive to prove I could earn more or less keep myself by working'.

> Sunday October 17th, 1915
> I mostly packed all day the things I have to take, & arranged for the disposal since Mother & Father are leaving Buxton, of what I did not want to take….I visited the spot where Roland & I sat [Corbar Woods] & talked the first time he came here, & bade it farewell, for even if he & I remain after the War is over, it is not very likely we shall come to Buxton again. This evening the leaves are falling fast, & the dusk enveloped all the glorious tints of autumn in a sad neutral shade.

Within eighteen months, the Devonshire would no longer be Buxton's main war hospital and the heyday of the Hydro, Palace and Empire was to end for good after being requisitioned by the government for thousands of disabled and convalescing Canadian soldiers, cared for by hundreds of medical and rehabilitation personnel. Almost overnight, Buxton's resident population of 12,000 grew to 27,000, about 5,000 more than today's number.

'I feel the end is not destined to be here & now.'

Vera enrolled at the London hospital with Stella Sharp.[16] After the good-humoured atmosphere of the Devonshire, and being able to return to a comfortable home, Vera now experienced the discipline of a highly regimented hospital, more strenuous work, 12-hour days, and spartan accommodation. Working on a ward of sixty acute surgical cases, Vera told Roland she had to deal with gruesome war wounds ('holes in various parts of the body you could put your foot into') amputations, and shell shock. Interleaved in the December 1915 pages of Vera's diary is a clipping from *The Spectator* magazine:

> Thousands of girls who have led easy and cloistered lives, remote from everything that is not pretty and agreeable and smooth have been pitchforked, after only a few weeks training, into hospitals full of men maimed and disfigured by terrible and repulsive wounds. They have not quailed.

From her first sight of wounded soldiers at Somerville College to the end of the war, Vera would never 'cease to be moved by pity for the shattered bodies and minds of those she nursed', nor did she ever really develop the ability to conceal her feelings.[17]

She continued writing often to Roland, but his replies were sometimes stilted and intermittent. He had become, as he eventually told her, absorbed in his own world. This detachment was common amongst First World War soldiers at the Front as a way of coping with the distress of remembering home and everyone there who mattered and, for Roland, the complete collapse of the values of honour and glory he took with him to war. As for so many soldiers and those at home, there was a yawning gap between Roland's experiences of war and the idealised images held by Vera and his family.[18] Coming across the 'fleshless, blackened bones' of German bodies, Roland tried to convey to Vera his jaded feelings about the waste and horror of war. He converted to Catholicism but did not tell his family or Vera. She failed to see, or could not see, the huge change in him. In *Testament of Youth*, she was to construct Roland as a 'poet hero …whose whole nature fitted him for the spectacular drama of a great battle'.[19]

His letters were sometimes distant, writing that 'you seem to me rather like a character in a book or someone whom one has dreamt of & never seen. I suppose there exists such a place called Lowestoft and that there once was a person called Vera Brittain who came down there with me'.[20] She worried that his personality might be damaged beyond repair, writing to him 'war kills other things beside physical life, and I sometimes feel that little by little the Individuality of You is being as surely buried as bodies are of those who lie beneath the trenches'. Roland was contrite and for a while his letters became warm again:

> I am writing in the dugout that I share with the doctor. It is very comfortable (possessing ... an easy chair, stove, an oil lamp, a table complete with tablecloth) & I am feeling pleasantly tired but not actually sleepy. Through the door I can see little mounds of snow that are the parapets of trenches, a short stretch of railway line, & a very brilliant full moon. I wonder what you are doing? Asleep I hope – or sitting in front of the fire in blue & white pyjamas? I should so like to see you in blue & white pyjamas. You are always very correctly dressed when I find you, and usually somewhere near a railway station, n'cest-ce-pas? [sic] I once saw you in a dressing gown with your hair down your back, playing an accompaniment for Edward in the Buxton drawing room. Do you remember?[21]

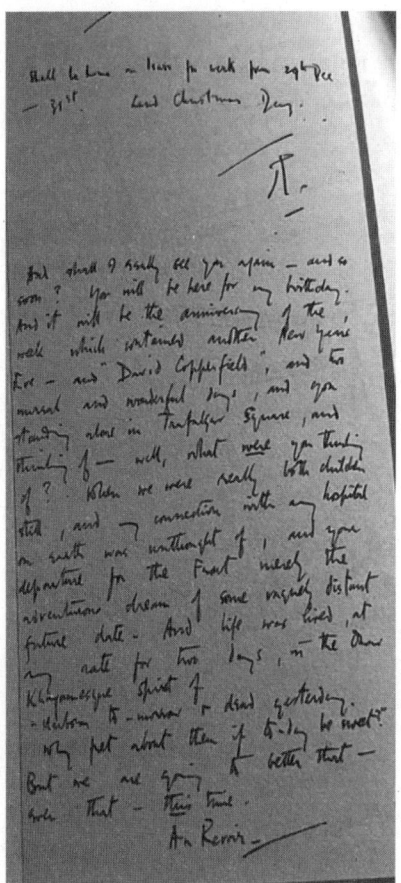

Roland's final note to Vera, and her reply, December 1915.

News that he might get leave in December filled Vera with joy. Roland was more circumspect, wondering if it might have been better if she had never met him and observing that 'anticipation is very sweet, and better often, one thinks, than the realisation. It was so last time, I remember'.

A couple of weeks later, a letter written in trenches deluged by heavy rain and surrounded by ever-deepening mud, confirmed Roland would be in England from 24 – 31 December. Vera replied 'life seems quite irradiated now when I think of the sweet hours that may be ahead'. The hospital matron agreed to grant Vera leave over Christmas so that she could join her parents at the Grand Hotel in Brighton where they had taken up residence after leaving Buxton earlier that month. After disembarking on Christmas Eve and spending Christmas Day with his family nearby in Kelmer, Roland planned to join Vera in Brighton on Boxing Day. On 15 December, she wrote to him:

> I would like to write you a specially nice letter tonight, because I expect this will be the one I promised you should have for Christmas…The rain is pouring down on the hut roof – and I wonder if it is pouring down on you, amid your cold & mud…I am just longing to see you, with a chance of being clean & dry at last, sitting with me in a comfortable room before a nice warm home fire….Well then, a Merry Christmas! Perhaps soon after you get this you will be here again to answer it in person…But somehow I feel the end is not destined to be here & now. We have not fulfilled ourselves – and 'Some day we shall live our roseate poem through'. Au Revoir, dearest.

Full of joy but trying not to allow herself to feel too thrilled, just in case something happened, Vera helped decorate the hospital wards. At Christmas communion in the hospital chapel, she thanked 'whatever God there be for Roland and for all my love and joy…the sweet sound of the organ & the sight of the wounded men who knelt & stood with difficulty made tears come into my eyes – tears of gratitude and joy & a still further intense unnameable emotion… And I thanked God for the Beloved and prayed for his safety and our happiness'.[22]

Chapter Thirteen

'I Say Goodbye to All I Care For'

Lost Youth

'The sweet anticipation of the morning'

Arriving in Brighton in the afternoon of Christmas Day, Vera walked along the promenade to the Grand Hotel. Gazing at the grey tossing sea, she worried what sort of crossing Roland might have had. Still, she thought, 'at any rate he should be safely in England by this time' and probably had not been able to send any messages because of Sunday and Christmas delays to telephones and telegrams. Reluctantly she decided to go to bed and think of 'the sweet anticipation of the morning'.[1]

Her much longed for reunion with Roland was not to be. Dressing with her usual care in the new pale blue Crepe de Chine blouse and navy-blue skirt she had bought two days earlier, Vera received a message there was a telephone call. She leapt up joyfully, rushing to hear the 'dear dreamed-of tones of the beloved voice'. Instead, Roland's sister Clare told her he had died at the Casualty Clearing Station at Louvencourt on 23 December.

Shot through the stomach by a German sniper while mending the barbed wire, Roland's wounds were so serious the surgeon could not save him. Heavily dosed with morphia, he received Last Rites and was recorded in the official death list as a 'trench wastage' because he was wounded during routine duties when things were quiet. Roland's end was devoid of all the heroic limelight he once imagined.

He and Vera had met just seven times, for a total of seventeen hours, with hardly any time alone and the most chaste physical contact. On a page in her notebook about Uppingham Speech Day in 1914, Vera had noted briefly that 'Leighton, one of the cleverest boys in Uppingham, came to lunch …'. Over the page, she later sellotaped a poem by Alice Meynell.

> And we met. You knew not me,
> Mistress of your joys & fears;
> Held my hand that held the key
> Of the treasure of your years,
> Of the formation of your tears.

For you knew not it was I,
And I knew not it was you.
We have learnt, as days went by.
But a flower struck root & grew
Underground, and no one knew.

Days of days! Unmasked it rose
In whose hours we were to meet;
And forgotten passed. Who knows,
Was earth cold or sunny, Sweet,
At the coming of your feet?"
              Alice Meynell (from *The Unmasked Festival*)[2]

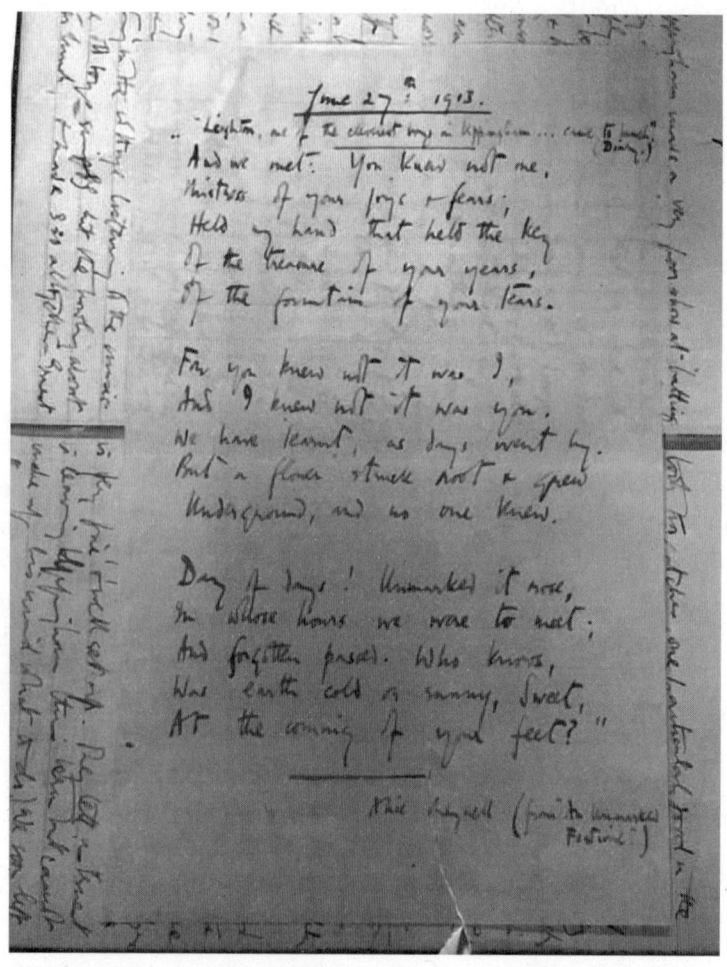

Alice Meynell poem in Vera's diary.

In the final pages of her 1915 notebook, Vera copied out letters to Marie Leighton from Roland's commanding officer, the surgeon who tried to save him, and his priest.

'I remembered all those dear afternoons.'

Stricken by grief, Vera purchased a mourning engagement ring. Barely able to get through the next few weeks, she considered giving up nursing for clerical work at the War Office and found a room to rent in Bayswater. But she changed her mind and decided to apply to nurse in Malta. In September 1916, she and Stella went there together.

Roland's death was just the beginning of more tragedy. Victor Richardson, Roland and Edward's Uppingham friend, had become a great source of comfort to Vera after Roland died. He was blinded in April 1917 and a few days later, Vera heard Geoffrey Thurlow had been killed, shot through the lungs, at Arras. It was another devasting blow; Vera had become close to him too, writing 'I loved Geoffrey.... after Roland he was the straightest, soundest, most upright person I have ever known'. After seeing newspaper advertisements in which women who lost husbands or fiancés offered to marry and care for a wounded

From left to right, Edward, Roland and Victor in Uppingham OTC, 1913. (*McM*)

soldier, Vera sat on rocks looking out to sea, holding the telegram of Geoffrey's death. She decided to go home and offer to marry Victor, sailing for England on 22 May. She did not arrive in time; Victor died on 9 June. Edward wrote:

> I suppose it is better to have had such splendid friends as those three were… but yet, now that all are gone it seems that whatever was of value in life has all tumbled down like a house of cards…We started alone, dear child, and here we are alone again; you find me changed, I expect, more than I find you….But we share a memory which is worth all the rest of the world…. And you know that I love you, that I would do anything in my power if you should ask it, and that I am your servant as well as your brother.[3]

These awful losses destroyed any vestiges of Vera and Edward's patriotism and belief in the war. Vera's next posting to Etaples, very close to the Front, would be the most dangerous and gruesome; 22,000 seriously injured soldiers were cared for by just sixty nurses, in dreadful hospital and living accommodation.

Even worse was to come. In leaking tents and surrounded by the horrendous mud of Passchendaele in 1917, Edward was grief stricken at the loss of his friends and utterly disillusioned. He told Vera how much her letters meant to him ('you have no idea how bitter life is') and longed to see her. His spirits lifted a little when he was sent to the Italian Asiago Plateau in November 1917. Hopeful he would survive the war, he wrote to Vera: 'Some of the country we passed through was very fine; apres la guerre finie there are several places where you and I might like to stay for a while'.[4] Edward's final letter to Vera in May 1918 asked about her plans for a war novel (her initial idea before deciding on a memoir ten years later) and commended her plans to return to Oxford when war was over. He continued:

> …this evening I should like to hear Dr Farner play the same Bach Prelude and Fugue which he played in Magdalen College on the evening of November 15th, 1914. Rations are just coming up on mules and I must

Vera in Red Cross nurse uniform, c.1916. (*SC*)

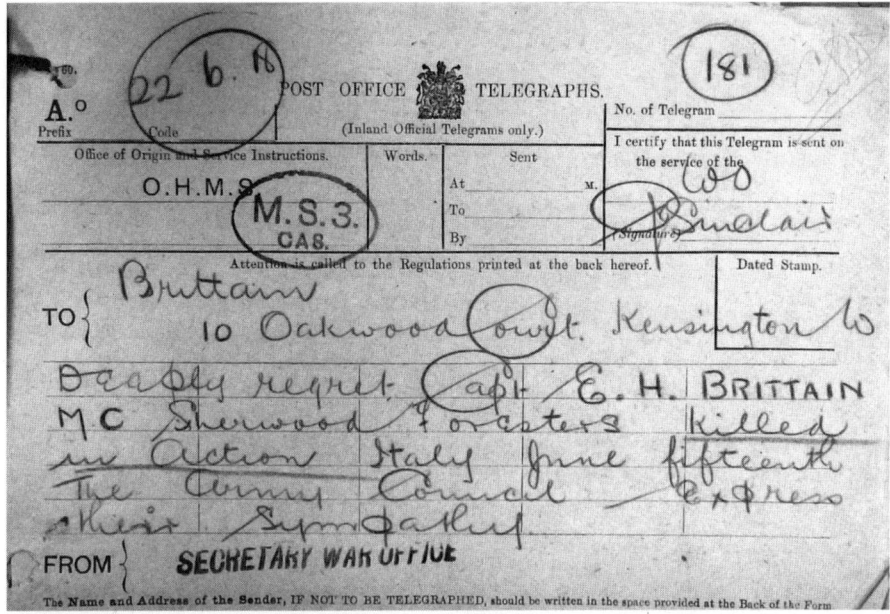

Telegram announcing Edward's death.

stop so as to let this go back on them with the other letters. Sometimes this gets held up in the most extraordinary way. We are waiting for some gramophone records from Selfridges which we sent for a month ago.

Edward was killed in action on the Italian Asagio Plateau on 15 June 1918. Devasted by the deaths of his three friends and traumatised by the barbarity he had witnessed, Edward had, like his sister, lost all the fierce patriotism that drove him to enlist, and was utterly jaded and cynical. As Vera observed in *Testament of Youth*, 'war thrust horror deeper and deeper inward, linking the dread of spiritual death to the apprehension of physical disaster'.[5]

Of all the losses Vera suffered, Edward's death was the worst blow. Noting in her diary 'I say goodbye to the last of all I care for', years later she said 'his loss I can reconcile least of any'.

Arthur never overcame his grief and Vera lost her best, most forgiving ally and closest friend. As children, they had been each other's sole companion. Growing up with a very bright, ambitious older sister, Edward seemed to take women's equality for granted. Although sometimes critical of Vera's feistiness, he was always her champion: when her essay won her a place at the 1913 Oxford summer meeting, Edward was the first person she told; when she was unsure whether to try for Somerville's more rigorous entrance examination, he told Vera she had more brains than anyone he knew and must go for it; when

Vera aged 4, Edward aged 2, 1897. (*McM*)

Vera and Edward at Melrose, 1913. (*McM*)

she won a Somerville scholarship, Edward said his sister had 'saved the family reputation for brains'; when their father threatened not to let Vera go to Oxford, Edward's response was to remark 'placidly but firmly, that if I could not be sent to Oxford he wouldn't go either'. Throughout the war, they maintained a regular, affectionate correspondence.

After learning of her brother's death, Vera looked at his portrait, painted after being awarded the Military Cross for bravery in the Battle of the Somme:

> Fate might have allowed him the little, sorry compensation of the chance to make his lovely music in honour of [the memory of his friends killed earlier in the war]....And as I remembered all the dear afternoons and evenings when I followed him on the piano as he played his violin, the sad, searching eyes of the portrait were more than I could bear....I began to cry "Edward!

Edward portrait by C.H. Rimanoczy, 1917. (*SC*)

'I Say Goodbye to All I Care For'

Peace day celebrations in Buxton, 1919. (*PtP*)

Oh Edward! " in dazed repetition as though my persistent calling and crying would somehow bring him back.[6]

War had, as Vera put it, 'smashed up' her youth, as it had for hundreds of thousands of others. While Buxton celebrated returning soldiers, the Brittains and their Buxton friends, including Lady Vaudray, the Scott-Moncrieffs, Garnetts, Greenhalghs, Coxes and Lawsons mourned sons and husbands. As junior officers, the young middle-class men so eager to enlist were part of a demographic group which experienced significantly higher mortality rates than other officers, and the army as a whole.[7] Uppingham lost about one in 5 of every boy that served, Edward's Buxton school lost 25 boys: of those leaving Holm Leigh in the six or seven years before 1913, at least a third of each year's intake, in some years half, never returned.

'Only ambition held me to life'

Amongst many fearful diary entries about Roland in 1915, Vera had confided 'if [war] takes him from me, the shadow of it will be over all my life.'[8] At the end of the war, she was utterly broken, existing in a state of numb disillusionment and on the brink of a nervous breakdown; 'no one, least of all myself, realised how near I had drifted to the borderland of craziness'.[9] Over four years, Vera had gone from a gilded life in which she was able to fulfil her intellectual ambition and felt fervently patriotic when war broke out to a bitter realisation of just how politically naïve and easily duped she and her generation had been.

In 1924, she explained to Gordon Catlin that the losses she endured were the 'wholesale sweeping away of every dear anchor that held me to life, added to the relentless buffeting for so long, by the waves of uncharted seas'.[10] After 'falling more deeply and ardently in love than I had ever been or was likely ever to be', Roland's death led Vera to feel she had sublimated her emotions 'with repressions, controls, abstentions, and inhibitions'.[11] In *Testament of Youth* she said 'love no longer meant the invading passion that for me had burnt itself out, once and for all, in 1915.'[12] In the late 1930s she would recall:

> I ended the First World War with my deepest emotions paralysed if not dead… Roland had taken with him all my future & Edward all my past…. It was Edward's death, rather than Roland's which turned me into an automaton… It left nothing. Only ambition held me to life.[13]

The youthful exuberance and optimism we saw in Vera's Buxton diary and letters had given way to anxiety and introspection, feelings of deep insecurity and lack of confidence. Hyper-sensitive, angry, full of survivor guilt, Vera had lost her religious belief and was convinced she would never marry or feel desire again. Her shredded nerves could lead to unpredictable emotional outbursts, especially when ill or overwrought. She came to believe she had inherited the melancholy, pessimistic strain in the Brittain side of the family.

Yet Vera's character, always volatile, retained a strong instinct for self-preservation and moral purpose. Resuming her studies at Somerville in 1919 and feeling completely alienated from her much younger fellow students, Vera met the vivacious, supportive, always empathetic Winifred Holtby.[14] After graduating in 1921, they decided to live together in London.

It was the start of what Vera was to describe as 'the second life Winifred has given me'. Despite her remorseless criticism of her Edwardian provincial upbringing, its emotional stability, social attributes and middle-class values would be a crucial foundation for Vera's life in post-war London.

Chapter Fourteen

'A Provincial of the Provincials, In Heart Though Not In Mind'

Buxton's Daughter

'Intellectual and anxious to benefit the world.'

A school essay in 1911 asked 17-year-old Vera Brittain to imagine 'A Sitting Room furnished on £25' (about £3,000 today). Enthusing about a second-floor London apartment, Vera envisaged a sitting room adorned with stylish Waring and Gillow oak furniture, a glass-fronted bookcase for her beloved books and a window seat, lit by a standard light, overlooking the street below. Using sale fabric, Vera would make plain blue curtains and cushions.[1]

A decade later, 28-year-old Vera and 23-year-old Winifred Holtby moved into a tiny studio flat at the top of a Georgian townhouse in Doughty Street, Bloomsbury, a lively part of London near the British Library. There was no street view or space for Waring and Gillow furniture, but Vera's youthful dream was not far off the mark. Their 'penurious independence' was a joyful new experience. A few months later, a larger apartment on the same street enabled Vera and Winifred to indulge their shared liking for blue and fuchsia fabrics, blue Spode plates and antique blue pots and their fascination for Bloomsbury's bohemian, slightly edgy atmosphere.[2]

As Vera's novels, memoir and journalism show, the cluttered décor and stuffy middle-class Edwardian grandeur of Melrose were not the only features of her provincial upbringing she was glad to leave behind. In the light of all her criticisms of her early life, what part did it play in Vera's post-war success?

In 1921, Oxford awarded degrees to women for the first time and Vera and Winifred graduated with 130 fellow students. Despite being a little disappointed with their second-class degrees, they set out enthusiastically to build careers as writers and campaigners for feminism and international peace. In the heady atmosphere of post-war London, Vera and Winifred shared literary ambition, social and political values. They were each other's mentors, critics, and cheerleaders, discussing ideas for articles and lectures, plots and characters for novels, proof-reading and editing each other's work, introducing agents and publishers, and developing their social and political networks. Supporting themselves with part-time teaching at St Monica's, and tutoring daughters of wealthy families, Vera and Winifred made their mark as writers in a new, burgeoning market for middle-class feminist fiction, and in newspapers, new progressive journals and magazines such as *Everyman, New Statesman* and the feminist *Time and Tide*. Their new life was, as Vera described in her second memoir, *Testament of Friendship*, 'strenuous, independent, enthralling'.

As prolific journalists and adept speakers, she and Winifred believed in the power of persuasion through writing and public speaking. During the 1920s they gave extension lectures

Winifred and Vera, 1920s. (*SC*)

for Oxford university and talks on international security for the League of Nations. Promoted first by the London Lecture Agency and after the success of *Testament of Youth* by the book's publishers in England and America, Vera gained a great deal of satisfaction from 'my well-developed speaking voice' and was, as always, simultaneously immodest and very self-critical of her performances.

After war ended in 1918, many working-class women were pushed out of the labour market and back into the home or domestic service, and both sexes suffered mass unemployment in the late 1920s. In contrast, the lives of many talented, educated, highly ambitious women had been transformed by university and the war: Ruth Allendyne, Vera's autobiographical character in her 1936 novel *Honourable Estate*, observed 'at least this century, if [war] did smash the world for thousands of women, it has given them the compensation of work'.[3] By 1921, there were women doctors, scientists, members of parliament, magistrates and lawyers, including Carrie Morrison from Buxton, who became England's first woman barrister in 1922. Writing to Winifred, Vera celebrated their new options:

> it does make one feel somehow guilty that one avoids [teaching] ... through no merits of one's own – yet I think we should not only be absurd, but wrong, if we joined the great army ... People like you and me – intellectual,

anxious to benefit the world, and yet possessed of sufficient means to choose the form of expression their intellectuality shall take, are very few & far between & yet very much needed ... I think it would be wrong not to take advantage of the fact that Fate has made one such a person.[4]

Vera's second life did dispel some of war's shadows, but they never quite left her. In 1924, she said 'I have known intensity, but not intense happiness, if happiness at all ... all happiness is to me incredible.'[5] Nor did Vera lose her self-awareness and honesty, knowing she was prone to 'too serious intensity', 'the old apprehension-bogie of unquiet nerves', and that some of her and Winifred's friends found her ego-centric and emotionally demanding.[6] Winifred described Vera as:

> [Someone who] life has battered, and who has been given by circumstance and heredity such a temperament that every blow and every snub, even every casual coldness makes a wound ... the War has left a real sickness of apprehension ... but never for a moment does she give way, nor lose her sweetness, nor her tenderness for suffering, nor imagination which is constantly trying to devise ways for protecting other people from the sorrow she has known.[7]

But, as Winifred told Vera, there was also an impressively enduring side to her character, 'burning fiery furnace or whatever you please to call it – stronger than any circumstances that ever arose yet'.[8] Winifred's warmth and fulsome praise, her almost maternal concern for Vera's health, her indulgence of her friend's wayward character and self-absorption, enabled Vera to regain some of her former confidence and vitality. She depended on Winifred more than anyone else, writing to her in 1933, 'I would have been suicidal without you.'

'Women who are persons, and women who are merely related to persons'

If the frivolity Vera 'held so dear' in her youth was much diminished, her idealism and strong sense of moral purpose came to the fore. Campaigning with Winifred for the Liberal parliamentary candidate in the 1923 general election, Vera overlooked the fleeting insights Buxton had given her of how the poor lived:

> for the first time ... I came into contact with the homes of the poor and learnt, as my provincial middle-class upbringing had never permitted me to learn, the semi-barbarous conditions – intensified beyond calculation by the War and its consequences – in which the poor lived.[9]

Vera joined the Labour Party in 1925 and campaigned for Gordon in 1931 when he stood (unsuccessfully) as its parliamentary candidate in Brentford and Chiswick and (again unsuccessfully) for Sunderland in 1935. Vera became a member of the executive committee of the Fabian Society and toyed briefly with the idea of standing for Parliament in 1927, telling Winifred she did not care whether it was for the Labour or Liberal party; it was social reform that was paramount.

Vera became a major feminist figure, working for the Six Point Group to campaign for widows' pensions, equal rights of guardianship for married parents, reform of laws dealing with child assault and the position of unmarried mothers, equal pay for teachers, equal pay and opportunities in the civil service.[10]

Publicity for Vera's American tour to publicise *Testament of Youth*. (*SC*)

Pointing to the 'terrible inert mass of womanhood' and the ignorance that had led naïve women like her to support the First World War, Vera used her journalism to argue that women had a moral obligation to be well-informed about current affairs, and to resist the temptation to 'hug their domestic chains'. Women needed to embrace technological and collective methods to reduce housework and take on the social responsibilities of work rather than hiding at home. For Vera, work was the only route to independence and respect, enabling women to test themselves in a public arena, notably through public service.

Vera regarded provincial life as a particular barrier to these goals. During 1926, she spent six months in Ithaca, New York so that Gordon could continue his academic career at Cornell, observing scathingly to Winifred 'the trouble is that in every provincial community – like Buxton – there are too many women with nothing to do but kill time', and criticising how the wives of professors were just 'as preoccupied with their houses, children and local scandals as provincial Buxton.'[11] She told Gordon: 'well nothing in etiquette or custom ever regulates satisfactorily the relations between women who are busy and women who have nothing to do, between women who are persons, and women who are merely related to persons.'[12] Dependence on men made women idle and frustrated, encouraged them to cling to the false security of outmoded notions of femininity and wasted their talent for public service.

A crucial part of Vera's feminist reputation was her advocacy of 'semi-detached marriage', in which Gordon pursued his career in the United States for six months and joined her, Winifred and the children in London for the rest of the year. In her journalism and to Gordon and Winifred, Vera proclaimed that her 'great object is to prove that work & maternity are not mutually exclusive ... this is a matter of principle I care about more than motherhood itself'. Vera also wanted to show that friendship between women was as important as marriage, motherhood and a career.

Vera in the 1920s. (*SC*)

Like many middle-class feminists of the post-war era, Vera's politics were rooted in the class superiority her upbringing had instilled. She believed that an educated female elite devoted to public service should replace the 'best' of the men lost in the war, that vigorous, intelligent women should have children, bring them up to make a positive contribution to society and maintain standards of literature, art and music. To these ends, Vera co-founded the Babies' Club in Chelsea, the first welfare centre for middle-class mothers. In 1926 she was a member of the organising committee for the Marie Stopes Organisation which campaigned for birth control and sexual reform.

Also typical of middle-class feminists in the 1920s were Vera's beliefs in the social importance of small families, with enough money to support children:

> Are we really working for eugenic birth control if we persuade our few thoroughly civilised individuals to descend even to the standard of the slum-dweller? ... How else, save by children brought up in decency and order, and nourished on the beauty and affection which complete control of circumstances alone makes possible, are we to leaven the national lump of mediocrity and inefficiency?[13]

'Forced to make one's way out of a wrong environment.'

Ambition, the kudos of an Oxford education and literary acclaim never ameliorated Vera's belief that her obscure, 'low-brow' provincial background was a hindrance. She was haunted by feelings of inferiority, especially with women from more cultured backgrounds, such as Emily Penrose, who was related to Aldous Huxley. When Virginia Woolf invited Winifred to write her biography in 1932, Vera recorded in her diary a lively discussion between Winifred, Vera and Gordon about whether:

> ...it was better to be born a member of the cultural aristocracy (like Virginia and Naomi [Mitchison]) or be like W. & myself forced to make one's way out of a wrong environment into a right one & become a little vulgar in the process. Personally I cannot think it anything but an incomparable advantage to have been absorbing platonic philosophy & acquiring a respect for scientific truth at an age at which I was wasting my time & ruining my taste by reading Longfellow & Mrs. Henry Wood while W. endeavoured to find scope for the activity of her mind in lavatory copies of the Ladies Realm.[14]

Vera feared that she would be seen as a 'social pusher' rather than just intellectually ambitious, and desperately wanted the approval of successful literary women like Cicely Hamilton, a suffragette playwright who had founded the women writers' suffrage league in 1908, and others such as E.M. Delafield, Rebecca West and Rose Macaulay. She was very insecure, describing herself to Winifred as an 'egotistical little poseuse' who 'feels petty and parochial and conventional ... bragging impotently about unimportant things'. The youthful propensity for fleeting 'grand passions' we saw in earlier chapters also emerged occasionally, such as her brief and rather torturous obsession with the successful author Phyllis Bentley in 1932.

Despite Vera's merciless criticism of her provincial upbringing and her youthful desire to overcome what Joseph Ward in Buxton had called the demoralising effect of conventionality, 'the things we do because others do them', she confessed 'I am always dominated by a Bourgeois Monarchy of habit and tradition.... I rebel but can never quite throw it off'.[15] Her domestic set-up in 1930s London might have been unconventional but was founded on the solid middle-class values she was brought up with. Like her parents, Vera wanted material and emotional security and a well-run, comfortable home. She valued moderation, order and self-control, believed in establishing a good reputation and bringing up children well, and encouraging people to improve themselves by using their talents and energies effectively. While Edith Brittain in Edwardian Buxton had directed her sense of duty towards family and charity, Vera's daughter Shirley Williams observed that Vera also placed duty before her own happiness, directing her energies to progressive philanthropic and political causes: 'my mother believed our obligations to society should balance our gifts; that from those to whom much is given, much is expected. Words that mean little in our generation I associate with her – old-fashioned words like honour and duty. She gave them meaning.'[16]

Other markers of Vera's provincial upbringing endured. Again, like her parents, she and Gordon wanted the social and cultural privileges 'the right school' could confer. Neither wanted a 'secondary public school' for John and put his name down for Eton, only to be daunted by the difficulty of getting him in without having a relative who had gone there. In any case, Vera worried that top-ranking establishments fostered sexist attitudes and, in the end, John went to Harrow. As for Shirley, Vera wanted a progressive education that would qualify women to earn their own living in industry, business or a profession; give them a sense of moral values; help them contribute to the struggle for a peaceful, constructive civilisation; show them how to use their leisure profitably; make them aware of the world and take an interest in it.[17] Shirley eventually went to St Paul's and both children would follow Gordon and Vera to Oxford, Shirley to Somerville, John to Hertford College.

'You have by inheritance a position to maintain'

The tension between idealism and materialism that fuelled many of Vera's fervent diary entries in Buxton was always present. She recognised that being head girl at St Monica's and going to Oxford were advantages but in always seeking to castigate and satirise her privileged upbringing, she never acknowledged how it laid the foundations for her later success. This oversight was typical of the vibrant group Robert Skidelsky termed "Professional World Improvers' – the middle-class army of progressives as it regrouped after the First World War. In his review of the 1987 memoir by Vera's son John Catlin, Skidelsky noted that, like other members of that group, Vera, Winifred and Gordon depended on 'two survivals from the Victorian age still considered indispensable: servants and unearned income'.[18]

Vera's youthful desire to eschew material comforts gave way in London to her reliance on the Victorian 'survivals' Skidelsky identified. In the 1920s and 1930s, neither she or Winifred admitted publicly that establishing their careers required unearned income of about £200 a year (about £10,000 today) donated by affluent fathers.[19] Vera also had shares in Brittains Ltd, which gave her a private income of about £225 a year, and Arthur continued his habit of giving her occasional gifts of money, including £500 to invest in 1931 (about £25,000 today), 'a very agreeable arrangement as it will enable my banking in general to be more elastic ... I can lecture, finish [*Testament of Youth*] and not have to write articles.' A further financial boost came when Arthur put up half the cost of 19 Glebe Place, a semi-detached house with a long sunny walled garden in a quiet cul-de-sac off the King's Road in Chelsea, in those days an interesting bohemian area of artists, actors and writers. Winifred put up the other half and the two women joined the 30 per cent of the population who owned their own home at that time.

When Vera worried about the cost of servants, Gordon suggested she economise by lowering her standards of domestic order and comfort, either by becoming 'slovenlier' or doing more housework herself. Arthur stepped in to pay the servants' wages, telling Vera to inform her husband 'you have by inheritance a position to maintain and I am not going to have you do domestic servants' work.'[20]

As the major breadwinner from the start of her marriage, *Testament of Youth* gave Vera some very affluent years: the first royalties enabled her to give Gordon £500, followed by an annual allowance of £200. Until the 1940s they enjoyed an annual income of about £2,000–£3,000 (about £100 – £150,000 today) plus unearned income. After Arthur's death in 1935, around £1,600 a year from his estate helped pay for Vera and Gordon to move to a more prestigious home (2 Cheyne Walk) in 1937 and for the £500 annual cost of servants. Vera worried that their affluent lifestyle was 'bordering on ostentatious'.

'We don't want a lady ... only someone younger and less opinionated'

Just as live-in servants had been indispensable for middle-class life in Edwardian Buxton, they were also essential for post-war women like Vera and Winifred to create and maintain their literary and political careers. When the friends first lived together, they tried to stay on top of the cleaning and cooking but neither had learned to cook, and they both loathed housework. Vera wrote to Winifred:

> I am rapidly being converted to Bolshevism – 'the abolition of female domestic slavery by the establishment of communal kitchens, laundries & mending houses run by professional domestic workers' sounds so nice, especially when one returns from a day's work ... to the momentarily alien and overwhelming domesticity of one's home!'[21]

In the absence of radical collective solutions, they abolished their own domestic slavery by employing help. Vera advised Winifred: 'we do not want a lady, only someone younger & less opinionated ... a clergyman's daughter would suit us very well. Still, one can't be too particular.'[22] Their second apartment was supported by a woman who did two hours' housework each day and their third had room for a live-in maid. Following a couple of unsuccessful attempts to recruit someone suitable, Winifred reported happily that her 50-something nanny would move down from Yorkshire: 'Nursie is over the moon at the idea of London and Life. She says she has never really been on her own. Now she's going to live! ... She says you will have breakfast in bed whenever you like!'[23] 'Nursie' stayed for five years, until John Brittain-Catlin was born in 1927.

At Glebe Place, the Brittain-Catlin-Holtby household relied on a cook/housekeeper, butler/handyman, two maids, a nurse for the children when they were small, and a part-time secretary. This level of support was indispensable for Vera and Gordon's semi-detached marriage, Vera's determination to combine motherhood with a career and the intensive social schedule all three needed for professional networking. Vera told both Gordon and Winifred that a 'certain £1,000 a year' was essential for motherhood; without that secure income, she said, the wife becomes tied to the house, and this is detrimental to her welfare and that of the children. Servants were also essential for motherhood: 'America – where nurse-maids and servants are prohibitive to all but the very rich – gives me a dreadful idea of having children.'[24]

After a dramatic drop in the number of servants during the war, by the 1920s, domestic service was, once again, the only realistic occupation for working-class women and the biggest area of female employment. In 1930 Vera employed 18-year-old Amy Francis as a maid. From a nine-sibling family, she had won one of a small number of grammar school scholarships but was unable to go because her father, a coalman, could not afford the uniform.[25] Amy married Charles Burnett, the butler/handyman at Glebe Place, and the couple worked for the Brittain-Catlins until Vera died in 1970.

Vera's much-vaunted criticism of domesticity belied how she was often overwhelmed by her own appreciation of the elaborate routines and comfort she took for granted in Buxton. Vera valued 'beauty, cleanliness and order' as much as Edith had in Buxton, instituting the same rituals of menu planning, formal meals, and the annual upheaval of spring cleaning the entire house. Shirley Williams recalled:

> My mother ran, presided over, not a home but a household ... [with] something called a staff ... at least three people whose relationships to one another were formal ... This world of order my mother ran [was] the slowly disintegrating remnant of the Victorian age ... that lost pre-war world of class and order where everyone knew their place.[26]

If 'managing the servants' was a problem for the provincial 'matrons' Vera caricatured in her writing, she and other progressively minded career women had their own difficulties. In her highly successful *Diary of a Provincial Lady*, fellow feminist writer E.M. Delafield served up humorous anecdotes about her own fraught relationship with servants for an appreciative middle-class readership. Vera did appreciate her servants, telling Gordon, 'when I hear about how other people's domestic "helps" behave, I realise they are worth everything.' Nonetheless, she confided to Winifred she was 'terrified' of 'managing the maids' and of 'persuading Amy to clean the steps without a massive row', or arguing with both maids 'on account of the time off they still expected, however much I was left in the lurch'.[27]

Publicity photograph, 1934. (*McM*)

By the 1930s, a maid's wages had risen to £1 a week but discipline and terms of service in Vera's London homes were identical to those in pre-war Buxton. She required her servants to be in by 10 p.m. and work a twelve-hour day from 7 in the morning, with Sunday and half a day off in the week. According to one of Vera's maids, 'Miss Brittain' was a rather remote, formal employer, although Amy Burnett remembered her as always kind and concerned about the welfare of Amy's family.

Vera did understand that her domestic burdens could not begin to compare to those of working-class women, but she never examined the inherently exploitative nature of the servant–employer relationship. And just as in Edwardian Buxton, Vera, like many wealthy middle-class women, only really knew about working-class women's lives through her servants. A London acquaintance remembered her as having a 'touch of the lady bountiful', never really at ease with working class people.[28]

'We invited crowds of a hundred or more'

Pre-war provincial dinner parties and 'At Home' entertainments were good foundations for the soirees and parties to which the Brittain-Holtby-Catlin household 'invited crowds of a hundred or more'. These gatherings brought together established and aspiring writers, publishers, literary agents, potential reviewers of books, journalists, the editors of *Vogue* magazine, *Time and Tide* and various left-leaning and feminist publications. Some were old acquaintances from Oxford days. Writers mingled with Labour Party activists, politicians, actors and social reformers.

In 1932, Vera introduced the successful author Phyllis Bentley to her London circle, noting in her diary that she was keen to point out to her provincial guest the contrast between cosmopolitan parties and the 'snobbishness, exhibitionism, conventionality or mere propinquity [like attracts like] … that provokes the giving of parties in the provinces'.

It is hardly surprising Vera found her London acquaintances far more interesting than Edwardian Buxton's businessmen, financiers, merchants and their wives. Nonetheless, she seems disingenuous, or perhaps just naïve, about the 'utterly different basis' of her provincial and metropolitan milieus. Fragmented between feminist, left-leaning middlebrow Chelsea, highbrow, modernist Bloomsbury, and more traditional Hampstead (which included H.G. Wells), London's literary elite was rife with skirmishes over literary status and function, gossip and perceived slights of each other's work. Snobbery, exhibitionism and 'mere propinquity' abounded. Just as Vera's Buxton diary revealed tedious provincial gossip, including her own indulgence in it, so do her London diaries and correspondence with Winifred, and the diaries of writers such as E.M. Delafield and Virginia Woolf. Praising *Testament of Youth*, Virginia Woolf assessed its author: 'not that I much like her. A stringy, metallic mind with, I suppose, the sort of taste I should dislike in real life'.[29] Both publicly and in her diary, Woolf was equally snobbish about 'provincial' Winifred Holtby.[30]

'A pretty face … [and] an agreeable new frock'

Enjoyments from Vera's provincial life lasted all her life. She loved dancing at parties and the Café Royal, on the luxury cruise ships that took her to the United States for publicity tours, and at parties feting her when she got there. Vera's great love of elegant clothes and a striking appearance, honed on Buxton promenades and at society dances, were, she said, 'an obstinate remnant of my Buxton upbringing'.

Being a provincial debutante and an Oxford student had enabled Vera to establish her own distinctive style and shape an ideal image of middle-class womanhood. As a young woman, she rejected prejudices that serious women could not enjoy male attention and fashionable, feminine clothes, lamenting how many clever women, such as her tutors at Oxford, became 'grim-looking, desiccated spinsters in appalling tweeds' who lost 'their womanliness and feminine attractiveness'. Winifred and Vera disagreed with feminist icon Olive Schreiner's criticism that 'an intense love of dress and meretricious external adornment is almost invariably the concomitant and outcome of parasitism'.[31] Instead, these two feminists delighted in fashionable, eye-catching outfits, discussing style, accessories and fabric, and criticising colleagues who wore drab, out-of-date garments. In 1921, Vera enthused to Winifred in her usual vivid way about an outfit for an interview to become a League of Nations lecturer: 'I am going in my dark blue frock... a soft tulle & straw black hat of Mother's with a hanging lace veil & my best buckles on black suede shoes!'[32] She and Winifred admired clever, inspiring women who were glamorous and clothes conscious, such as Rebecca West, who gave a lecture at the London School of Economics on 'the modern novel' that was 'exquisitely funny, brilliant and often wise' while 'wearing a stunning smoke-grey silk dress, sable coat and huge hat with a drooping plume'.[33]

Appearance was essential for the authoritative persona Vera wanted to project to British and American literary societies, political groups, lunch events and women's groups. In the post-war era of the best-selling book club and fierce competition for a growing market of serious, educated women readers, publishers expected their leading authors to promote their work. Already a popular public speaker, Vera was in huge demand after the publication of *Testament of Youth*. Provincial newspapers gave her glowing reviews: the *Leeds Mercury*, for example, told readers that the audience appreciated 'Miss Brittain's platform presence' and the keen intelligence 'behind those lovely eyes of hers'. In 1933, Vera undertook a gruelling tour of thirty-four lectures in twenty-five American towns, reporting that audiences were especially appreciative of how she looked. So too were pupils she taught at St Monica's during the 1920s: years later, some recalled her striking looks, remote, slightly intimidating manner and beautiful clothes. Nonetheless, Vera was keen to avoid any impression she lacked intellectual seriousness:

> Wednesday July 6th, 1932
> I asked Phyllis if she thought the accidental possession of a pretty face impaired the values of an intellectual person ... while having a pretty face gives almost as much satisfaction as possessing an agreeable new frock ... it is in no way to be compared to the ability to write a great book.

'Provincial by their breeding!'

Of all the 'obstinate remnants' of Vera's much-criticised provincial upbringing, the most productive was her fierce anti-provincialism:

> Buxton left me deeply imbued with a form of snobbishness which I do not suppose I will ever outgrow ... The universal middle-class snobberies

of birth, wealth and Anglicanism I soon repudiated ... But from the snobbery of metropolitanism, the superiority of the Londoner towards the small-town dweller, I do not think I am likely to recover, even though the calm voice of reason ... tells me that the wireless and cinema and the long-distance motor 'bus have probably transformed the provinces out of all recognition since 1915.[34]

Promoting the publication of *Testament of Youth* in an article titled 'Provincialism' for the *Manchester Evening Chronicle* on 1 September 1933, Vera asserted that 'nothing short of an earthquake will ever transport me back to the provinces'. She rehearsed familiar themes from her earlier writing: 'the large numbers of silly women who fill their lives otherwise empty with the futile playing of bridge', provincial pettiness, 'the wicked marriage market' and the 'obsession with keeping up appearances'. All these, she wrote, were still a big part of provincial life.[35]

Writers who compared the superiority of London with the shortcomings of their own provincial upbringing struck a raw nerve with writers who remained in the provinces. Phyllis Bentley used her popular weekly column for the *Manchester Evening Chronicle* to issue a lively rebuttal. 'Yes,' she wrote, 'all these futilities, these narrow and petty limitations are *indeed* present' in the provinces, but they are also 'prevalent in the section of London society which Miss Brittain frequents not because they are Londoners but because they are people of high intellectual distinction'. Bentley observed sharply that the pettiness and snobbishness Vera disliked did not arise because people were provincial; rather, they were 'the universal mark of the vulgar and ignoble mind wherever the body housing it chooses to reside'.

Phyllis acknowledged from her own experience 'the desperation of the active and intelligent girl, returning from school or university to be the daughter at home before the war'.[36] Yet, she observed, these women were not confined to the provinces; they were also in the London suburbs. Listing many of the 'luminaries' she knew in Vera's social circle, Phyllis added, 'The most brilliant artists, politicians, journalists, drama critics, are likely to be found in London because their work takes them there ... but all these brilliant Londoners are provincial by their breeding!'

Although Vera's Oxford degree, refined accent and elegant cosmopolitan lifestyle made Phyllis Bentley feel 'thoroughly provincial', she deeply resented metropolitan snobbishness, especially when it was directed towards northern towns by those who had been brought up in them, and she disliked the 'fashion and impetuosity' of London literary circles.[37] The *Manchester Evening Chronicle* paid Phyllis well for her columns, syndicating them to other northern newspapers and proclaiming her 'northern commonsense' in the face of London faddishness.[38]

Being 'provincial by their breeding' was essential for the success of a flourishing feminist literary circle which included Vera, Winifred, Storm Jameson, E.M. Delafield, Rebecca West and Phyllis Bentley. These women shared ideas for plots and characters, recommended agents and publishers, and reviewed each other's books in magazines and journals. Capitalising on an increased sense of freedom for middle-class women brought about by war, education and suffrage, more women became professional writers in the 1920s and 1930s than at any time in British history. There was a booming new market for middlebrow, socially aware fiction. 'Circulating libraries' fuelled a huge readership, especially in the provinces; Boots, for example, had 400 libraries, with over half a million subscribers eager for the latest titles. In 1925, 25 million books were exchanged; by 1939, it was 35 million.[39]

Eschewing the modernist experimentation and interest in characters' inner lives favoured by the Bloomsbury circle, Vera and her literary circle engaged with social and political issues.[40] Their female protagonists were often overtly autobiographical, or based on people the authors knew; young, middle-class, spirited, clever, ambitious, frustrated or ground down by provincial expectations and mores.[41] Popular plotlines saw women escape from an oppressive provincial life to university or London or, if escape was not possible, coping, like Muriel Hammond in Winifred's 1923 novel *The Crowded Street*, by subverting expectations of marriage and domesticity. Sometimes a protagonist returned to the provinces as an emancipated social reformer, such as Sarah Burton in Winifred's posthumous best-seller, *South Riding*. A recurring plot line was women's struggle towards empowerment and self-definition, the goal to 'take your life in your own hands and live it'.[42]

These themes evolved from a strand in late Victorian fiction in which 'new women' struggled to throw off middle-class expectations in order to become free spirits.[43] In Vera's first three novels, a moral decision is a turning point for female protagonists to gain autonomy. The feminist narrative in *The Crowded Street* is, as Vera noted, not only about the part played by the marriage market in the lives of provincial women, but also 'the search of the burdened, frustrated soul for some magic experience lying just beyond the confines of daily life'.[44]

Testament of Youth brought the feminist anti-provincialism of Vera's novels and journalism to a worldwide audience. After attempting first to write a fictional account of her experiences of the war and the fate of the men she loved, Vera settled on an 'autobiographical study' of her first twenty-five years. When it came to her 'provincial young ladyhood', Vera chose to portray it as stifling and philistine, her parents as obdurate and unsupportive, and her escape to university, against great opposition, as a single-handed feminist triumph.

There is absolutely no doubt that Vera disliked aspects of her early life and gaining a scholarship to Oxford was a significant and inspiring achievement. But in exaggerating this powerful story and highlighting the oppressive dullness of her middle-class provincial life, Vera erased all her youthful enjoyment and exuberance and all the advantages her upbringing had given her.

'Obstinate remnants of my Buxton upbringing'

In what ways, then, should we regard Vera Brittain as 'Buxton's daughter'? It is fairly certain she would have loathed that epithet. Nevertheless, as we have seen in this book, while Vera railed against provincial young ladyhood, she could never shake off its 'obstinate remnants'. Assumptions of class superiority, material security, domestic comfort, the indispensable support of servants, even the ability to throw a good party, were essential for Vera's career. Others, like a love of a distinctive sartorial elegance, were crucial for the authoritative image she wanted to present, and for sheer enjoyment too.

Vera shared some remnants of her upbringing with her parents, such as a deep love of music, belief in a good education, the values of hard work and aspiration. Even less palatable influences, such as deep feelings of social and cultural inferiority, of being a philistine provincial, bolstered Vera's characteristic determination to succeed.

While these enduring influences would have come from a middle-class upbringing in any Edwardian provincial town, others undoubtedly came from Buxton's unusual atmosphere as a fashionable, lively 'estate' resort. For upwardly mobile, aspirational families like Vera's, Buxton offered more social segregation and exclusivity than other provincial towns, enabling them to enjoy a more privileged, comfortable life than they would have had elsewhere. This, and Buxton's isolation made unrest elsewhere seem remote and irrelevant. Buxton gave Vera a foundation of emotional stability and social tranquillity from which to work out what future she wanted, and the sort of woman she wanted to be. She had time to develop a deep love of reading, write an extensive diary, plan novels and indulge her love of music, sport, dancing, clothes and amateur dramatics. Buxton's cossetted atmosphere also made the controversial ideas of charismatic Reverend Ward more prominent than they might have been elsewhere. For his restless young admirer, Ward's support for her ambitions, his own idealism and religious courage, reinforced Vera's determination to create a meaningful life.

And, for all her derision of 'unintellectual Buxton', it was Mrs Harrison, another local figure Vera admired greatly, who arranged for John Marriott, one of Oxford University's most experienced senior academics, to teach in Buxton. Mrs Harrison encouraged Vera to go to university, obtained all the necessary paperwork to enable her to enter the essay competition for the 1913 Summer Meeting and was not the only Buxton 'matron' to support Vera's intellectual ambition.

In myriad ways, then, and despite not having a good word to say for her provincial upbringing, this period shaped Vera's extraordinary character, her ideas and beliefs. Most of all, Edwardian Buxton provided an especially colourful backdrop for the compelling feminist, anti-provincial narrative that made her famous.

Chapter Fifteen

'Where the Tawny Crested Plover Cries'

Remembering the Past

'I felt indeed a revenant'

Vera looked up from her book as the train slowed over the viaduct for its approach into Buxton's London-Midland station. It had been 32 years since she travelled in the opposite direction to become a VAD nurse in London. Today, 18 March 1947, 54-year-old Vera Brittain was tired. With Britain still suffering severe post-war restrictions, her latest lecture tour around northern and midland towns, travelling in cold and dirty trains, had been more gruelling than usual. Two weeks earlier severe nationwide floods had created long detours; for once, Vera felt quite relieved to be in Buxton.[1]

After receiving an unexpected invitation from 'the forgiving Public Library …to lecture at the Winter Gardens Pavilion', Vera offered a talk on 'America from Within'. As she gathered her belongings, she wondered how she would be received in her former hometown, writing later 'I felt indeed a *revenant* and was surprised by the warm ovation from the crowded hall'.[2] Her lecture was at 7pm but she does not record whether she stayed overnight or travelled back to London.

When Vera made her first return visit to Buxton in 1935, she noted dismissively in her diary that 'the complacent little health resort had changed less than any other place I have visited in recent years'. Her fleeting visit did not allow Vera to see just how much Buxton had already changed. By the early 1920s, most of Vera's social circle had left Buxton and many grand villas, including Melrose,

Vera in her forties. (*SC*)

had been converted into apartments, a process that continues today. The Pavilion and Buxton's largest hotels turned to the burgeoning post-war conference market for custom, including St Ann's which the Harrisons ran until 1927.

Buxton would never recover its prosperity or social cachet. By the time of Vera's final visit in 1947, the National Health Service was running the Baths and the Ministry of Labour had converted a hotel and one of Buxton's grandest architectural gems into convalescent homes for industrial workers. The Hydro (which became the Spa Hotel in 1924) and Empire were sinking into terminal decline. They would eventually be demolished, and their vast sites used for social housing (the Empire in 1964 and the Spa Hotel in 1973). In the 1960s and 70s, Vera and Edward's schools were demolished. St Ann's struggled on as a hotel until the 1980s when it finally closed.

Vera's own circumstances were also much changed in 1947. Three weeks after her 1935 visit to Buxton, her troubled and depressed father drowned himself in the Thames at Richmond. When war ended the import of cigarette papers in 1915, Arthur had objected to the decision by his co-directors that Brittains Ltd should manufacture them and was ousted. Retirement at the age of 51 left a man of his vitality totally unprepared for a life without work, and Edward's death three years later led to worsening bouts of depression. In 1934, Arthur attempted suicide, telling Vera his neurologist's diagnosis that having a 'highly skilled technical brain, and not having been able to use it for so long, it has turned upon me'. After 1918, Vera attributed her own tendency towards melancholy to Arthur's side of the family which had a history of mental illness, including his sister Edith (the aunt advising Vera to be kinder to Bertram Spafford in 1914) who killed herself in 1926.

On 29 September, five weeks after Arthur's death, Winifred Holtby died of kidney disease at the age of 37. This devasting loss led Vera to doubt whether she could make a third life after the 'second life' Winifred had created, confiding in her publisher 'I don't know how I will go on living without her'.

Winifred Holtby, portrait painted from a photograph, by Frederick Howard Lewis, 1936. Vera said it was an extraordinary likeness: 'it had all her personality – vitality, intentness and humour'. (*SC*)

Edward (on left) and fellow junior officers. (*Mark Bostridge*)

These tragedies compounded the pain of the previous year when Vera learned that, for all her closeness to Edward, there were aspects of his complicated life she had been completely unaware of. In 1934, Charles Hudson, his commanding officer, asked to meet Vera to correct the account of Edward's death in *Testament of Youth*. Unfortunately, her diary between November 1933 and September 1934 and many of Edward's war letters are missing, and there is no record of what Hudson told her. However, his unpublished memoir recounts his warning to Edward that letters opened by the Army Base Censor had revealed Edward and a fellow officer's sexual activity with men in their company. Forbidden by the Military Police to tell Edward he was under investigation and would certainly face a court martial and public disgrace, as well as probable imprisonment, Hudson was reluctant to deceive an officer he liked and respected. A day later, during a counterattack on enemy lines, Edward was shot in the head by an Austrian sniper. He was the only officer killed, a tragedy compounded by the possibility that he engineered it to avoid the humiliation of being court martialled and sent to prison.[3] Hudson later found out it was likely Edward had died when going forward to find out what was happening to his platoon on an outpost in no-man's land. It would not be until 1939 when Edith told Vera she had destroyed the diary in which Edward reported his involvement in what her mother called 'homosexual doings at Uppingham'.[4]

His death remains shrouded in mystery.

'A belief in the transcendence of love over power'

In the face of these new waves of suffering, Vera's deep sense of moral duty and public service enabled her to carry on. She continued campaigning for feminism and pacificism, writing articles, novels and, in 1940, *Testament of Friendship*, a biography of Winifred and their relationship. Nonetheless, after her friend's death, Vera's writing voice was never as confident, nor her work as well-received.

By 1947, the international acclaim of the 1930s was a distant memory. Reminiscent of Joseph Ward's spiritual influence in 1914, Vera was inspired by Canon Dick Shepherd to become a pacifist in 1937. Her campaigns against the Second World War, and especially the mass bombing of German cities in 1944, led friends to ostracise her, and writers like George Orwell, and politicians such as Franklin D. Roosevelt, to criticise her publicly. Interest in Vera's work declined, especially in the United States, and sales of *Testament of Youth* fell from ten to twenty thousand a year to between two and five thousand.

In *Humiliation with Honour*, published in 1943, Vera explained that her pacifism was a Christian commitment to 'nothing other than a belief in the transcendence of love over power'. Her own experience of humiliation led her to see it as enabling man to master his own soul. Nonetheless, Vera found it hard to come to terms with the deepening of 'my own sense of inferiority and consequent inertia due to long unpopularity', and with her 'worn, haggard and

Vera speaking at the Dorchester Peace Rally, 1936. (*SC*)

anxious appearance'.[5] The lure of London life had palled, and Vera yearned for genuine friendship, describing herself in 1947 as 'a Staffordshire born provincial who has never learned to feel quite at home in cosmopolitan highbrow circles' and who 'finds a chat over a cup of tea a far more enjoyable experience than a literary party at Claridges or a ceremonial dinner at the Waldorf Astoria'.[6] And she felt burdened, sometimes unbearably, by the pressure of earning enough money to maintain a lifestyle she increasingly regarded as too ostentatious.[7]

Despite Vera's jaded sensibilities, she continued to campaign tirelessly for pacifism and other political causes until the end of her life. Vera died in 1970 at the age of 76. Her will asked for her ashes to be scattered on Edward's grave in Granezza, telling Shirley Williams in 1967 'for nearly 50 years, much of my heart has been in that Italian cemetery'.[8]

By then, Vera believed she had been forgotten. Eight years later, Carmen Calil, head of the feminist publishing house Virago, decided to re-issue *Testament of Youth* in its Classic Non-Fiction series, which rediscovers forgotten women writers. It catapulted Vera back to the top of the best-seller lists where she stayed the following year following the BBC's award-winning dramatization of *Testament of Youth*. Broadcast to great acclaim in Britain, the United States and Canada, it was repeated in 1980 and 1992.

Today Buxton's erstwhile resident is more famous than in her lifetime. *Testament of Youth* has been dramatised for television, ballet and cinema, continuously in print through nineteen editions and translated into Swedish, Norweigan, Italian, German, Spanish, Dutch and French. It is studied in schools and on university courses in First World War history and women's studies, while Vera's life and work continue to be the subject of biographies, blogs, and academic research. Edited selections of her diaries, journalism and letters have been published. The BBC broadcast the war letters for radio in 1998, and made Vera's experiences of the First World War the subject of a 2008 television dramatisation. The 'life and testaments of Vera Brittain' have been a specialist subject on *Mastermind*. There are public commemorations in her birthplace, Hamburg and Berlin, and an English Heritage plaque on the London house where she and Winifred shared their first apartment in 1921.

Things are rather different in Buxton which has just two plaques, both paid for by individual admirers. Installed in the 1980s, one is on an obscure wall in the Pavilion and the other on the gatepost at Melrose. There seems to be an immoveable civic indifference in Buxton to a proper commemoration of Vera Brittain.

'Today I feel only a remote relationship to the girl who lived in Buxton'

Perhaps Buxton's long-running lack of enthusiasm is understandable. When Vera anticipated an unenthusiastic reception in 1947, perhaps she was thinking of her unpopular pacifist views. Or perhaps she knew some of her Buxton audience might resent her twenty-year derision of their town and its residents; as the introduction to this book observed, over a hundred years after Vera lived in Buxton, some still do!

Why, given the more nuanced account in this biography of Vera's Edwardian upbringing, was she so critical of this period in her life? The reasons are as complicated as she was.

The preface to Vera's 1930s diary notes 'today I feel only a remote family relationship with the girl who lived in Buxton and went to Oxford. I feel closer to my ten-year old daughter'. In *Testament of Youth*, she felt a deeper affinity with her contemporaries than with her younger self and pointed to the impossibility of seeing 'ourselves and our friends and lovers as we really were' because people resemble 'strange ghosts made in their image, with whom they have no communication'.[9]

Vera is far from alone in those feelings. Called on to narrate our own past, we all, to a greater or lesser extent, subconsciously and consciously, reinterpret events, people, and our younger selves. Sometimes we want to complement or justify an image of ourselves as we are now, and we forget the details of events, or what we were truly like. Sometimes we want to erase unpleasant experiences or unappealing aspects of our youthful character. We imagine and misremember things. Memory is full of imperfections as we, again consciously and unconsciously, construct a sense of self and try to make sense of it. Even the prompts of a diary, letters and photographs might be only partially useful in creating an authentic autobiography: as Virginia Woolf once observed, 'people are all over the place'! And Julian Barnes reflects that age makes one realise

Ready for a Buxton winter, Melrose, 1913. (*SC*)

'memory resembles an act of imagination rather than a matter of simple mental recuperation'.[10] Vera's feelings about her stifling provincial life are also commonplace; since time immemorial, young people have yearned for escape and adventure, a more meaningful life, to meet more interesting people than the friends of one's parents.

Yet beyond these universal feelings and barriers to remembering the past, Vera had endured a brutal war that created an unbridgeable chasm between a lively, exuberant young woman full of hope and energy, and the psychologically and physically exhausted woman who had to rebuild her life.

Vera was 36 when she embarked on *Testament of Youth* in 1929. Fourteen years had passed since she left Buxton, she had been married for four years, had one child, and was expecting a second. Vera was a renowned feminist campaigner, member of the Labour party, a League of Nations lecturer, and a prolific journalist. When it came to representing her early life, Vera had already published two autobiographical novels challenging traditional roles for middle-class young women, one of which excoriated pre-war provincial society, and was planning a third.

In portraying this period, Vera created three compelling contrasts. One was between an idealistic, 'mentally voracious' young woman escaping from

Vera leaning out of the dining room window at Melrose, c.1912. (*McM*)

oppressive 'provincial young ladyhood' to university and achieving feminist womanhood in 1920s London. The second was between a bored provincial 'debutante' and a progressive, cosmopolitan woman who had risen above her philistine, provincial background. The final contrast was between an Edwardian life of 'rich materialism and tranquil comfort' untouched by events in the outside world, and a calamitous war which 'smashed up' her youth and that of her gullible generation.

As we saw in Chapter Fourteen, Vera's skilful telling of her Edwardian provincial upbringing chimed perfectly with the popular feminist fiction and journalism for which she was already known. She also knew she was writing the 'sort of book no one has written before'. A question in Vera's 1914 Somerville entrance examination had required her to explicate Thomas Carlyle's view that 'history is the biography of great men'. When a male acquaintance at a London literary party heard Vera was writing her autobiography, he responded scathingly 'I wouldn't have thought anything in your life was worth reading!' *Testament of Youth* turned such notions upside down and redefined the genre of autobiography.

There are many reasons, then, why Vera chose not to highlight sides of her pre-war persona that felt psychologically remote after everything she had been through. The outcome in *Testament of Youth* was a tidied-up version of her younger self which showcases the morally serious, idealistic, ambitious feminist and omits the diary's endearingly exuberant and romantic, emotionally volatile and prickly girl. In this version, Vera's escape from provincial boredom and bigotry, and her spirited resistance to obdurate, conservative parents and acquaintances, make a much more compelling story than the unfashionable reality of enjoying life as a Buxton debutante, being supported by loving parents and inspired by locals such as Joseph Ward and Mrs Harrison.

'My tendency to withdraw from experience.'

Seven handwritten notebooks for the years 1911, 1913–1917 and Vera's correspondence highlight poignantly just how much youthful vitality she lost in the war. After March 1915, when Roland went to the Front, Vera's diary was increasingly full of foreboding and anxiety, and a sense of her youth slipping away:

> O glorious time of youth indeed! This is the part of my life when I ought to be living every moment to the full, tasting the sweetness of every joy, full of love & life & aspiration & hope, exulting in my own existence. Instead I can only think how weary the hours, wonder how I will get through their aching suspense...Ah! those who are old & think war is so terrible do not know what it means to us who are young. They at least

have had their joy, have it now to think & look back on; for us the chief part of our lives, the part that makes all the rest seem worthwhile, has either never dawned, or else we have for a moment seen what is possible only to have it snatched from our eyes.[11]

In the 1920s and early 1930s, Vera did recover some of her earlier vibrancy, writing 'I basked in the sunshine of Winifred Holtby's affection & became a less inhibited character & shed much of my tendency to withdraw from experience. I came to recognise & fight that tendency'.[12] When Phyllis Bentley met Vera in 1932, she described her as having 'such a gift for life', while publisher Harold Latham remembered 'a tiny woman with shining eyes and an intense amount of vitality'.[13]

Vera aged 48, portrait by William Rothenstein, 1941 (*SC*)

After Winifred's death, and her own fall from grace, Vera in later life became, as her children and great friend Paul Berry remember, rather humourless, overwhelmingly anxious, and socially awkward, a woman almost permanently in a state of worry.[14] After Edith died in 1948 at the age of 79, Vera lamented there was no one left to talk about 'the small things that made up a picture of my childhood – the pugdog called Koko with whom Edward and I played, the bicycle rides over the Buxton moors, the journey to Uppingham. Except in the recesses of my mind, these things were gone, scattered like my mother's ashes on the wind.[15] In 1968, just two years before her death, and very unwell, Vera wrote 'Roland had always represented to me a kind of vision of our joint future; when that vision died, much of the life we had shared together died with it'.[16] According to Paul Berry, it seemed in Vera's later years as if '*Testament of Youth* belonged to an earlier self she didn't want to confront'.[17]

'A vanished world'

Testament of Youth uses an enduring trope of First World War literature, a lost Arcadia of Edwardian innocence and tranquillity. In elegiac prose, Vera paints a picture of 'three radiant days' at Uppingham School for its annual speech day in July 1914, 'the one perfect idyll I have ever experienced…a lovely legacy of a vanished world before the world crashed into chaos'. She contrasts a retrospective sense of foreboding with romantic optimism:

> I do not believe that any of the gaily clad visitors who watched the [Officers' Training Corps] carrying out its manoeuvres …in the least realised how close at hand was the fate for which it had prepared itself or how many of those deep and strangely thrilling boys' voices were to be silent in death before another Speech Day… The afternoon was so hot, and our desire for conversation so great, that Roland and I were relieved when … we could lose ourselves in the crowd at the Headmaster's garden party. I remember today how perfectly my dress – a frilled pink ninon with a tiny pattern, worn beneath a rose-trimmed lace hat – seemed to have been made for our chosen corner of the garden, where roses with velvet petals softly shading from orange through pink to crimson foamed exuberantly over the lattice-work of an old wooden trellis…I… still have Roland's verses, *In the Rose-Garden* to renew the fading colours of a far-away dream.[18]

A year later, she told Roland ruefully, 'for me I think the days are over of sheltered peaceful comfort & unruffled peace of mind. I don't think they will ever come again'.

In that vanished world, one unremittingly positive aspect of Vera's youth in Buxton was the emotional and spiritual solace she gained from its dramatic moors and wooded dales. When Vera felt the euphoria of a 'grand passion', the triumph of being successful, spiritual inspiration, or was lonely, melancholy, and bored, the beauty of a sunrise, a lovely evening sky, a wild wind on the moors, brought out her romantic, idealistic side, and soothed the feelings that sometimes overwhelmed her:

> … the hills & the great wide spaces will always be with me as long as life shall last & perhaps even beyond that…I think one needs to grow into a mood which is not acquired all at once…in order to understand this wild country, something that is great enough to appreciate all that is grand & noble & sublime, though awe-inspiring & austere in this majestic scenery.[19]

Sometimes 'the mystery of a dim light …wandering about at twilight… or going out into the stillness of a summer night' could make Vera feel 'it was a most wonderful world'.[20] Shirley Williams recalled that her mother's 'most enduring pleasures were birds, trees and flowers; relics of a Buxton childhood'.[21]

Just three months before war upended everything, Buxton's 'majestic scenery' was the setting for Vera and Roland's first feelings of attraction to each other.

On the second day of his 1914 Easter visit to Melrose, Roland, Vera, Edward, and Maurice went for a ten mile walk in the Goyt valley, 'in all its lovely spring freshness', returning home down 'the wide road which leads over lonely undulating moors through Whaley Bridge to Manchester'.

In her happy diary entry, Vera reports she and Roland discussed 'many things' while Maurice and Edward talked about dreams. She gave Roland a hard time about his conceit and pretensions and 'he didn't resent what I said or how I said it'. Her youthful feminist confidence leaps off the page.

When they got home, Roland went up to her bedroom and she showed him all the books she had rearranged, 'which he greatly admired' and 'preferred my books to his classical possessions'. Vera noted 'he must like & be interested in me to some extent'. After supper, Roland entertained his friends with an account of going with his mother to have his palms read by Cheiro, the celebrated clairvoyant, and repeated the famous man's predictions. The three 'sat & discussed psychic research & premonitions etc and never noticed the oddness of our number'.

It was not until years later that Vera came across *Nachklang*, the poem Roland wrote the day after their walk. The German word translates as 'resonance', 'reverberation', 'reminiscence', 'recollection', 'after effect', 'repercussion':

> Down the long white road we walked together,
> Down between the grey hills and the heather,
> Where the tawny crested
> Plover cries.
>
> You seemed all brown and soft, just like a linnet,
> Your errant hair had shadowed sunbeams in it,
> And there shone all April
> In your eyes.
>
> With your golden voice of tears and laughter
> Softened into song: 'Does aught come after
> Life,' you asked. 'When life is
> Laboured through?
>
> What is God, and for all which we're striving?'
> Sweetest sceptic, we were born for living.
> Life is Love, and Love is –
> You, dear, you.

Long White Road towards Buxton, early 1900s. (*PtP*)

Testament of Youth describes Vera and Roland's final Buxton walk in March 1915, the last part of which was 'down the long white road'. A heavy blizzard accompanied their discussion about Death:

> As we walked down the hill towards Buxton the snow ceased and the evening light began faintly to shine in the sky, but somehow it only showed us the more clearly how grey and sorrowful the world had become.[22]

Today the 'long white road' is the A5004, known as Long Hill. Its rough white limestone is long gone, of course, and so too is the silence of an era with very few motorcars. Now the tarmac surface thrums with lorries and the noisy whine of motorbikes tearing past earnest cyclists training on its steep twisting inclines.

Vera on the drive at Melrose, 1914. (*SC*)

The plover is still there, on the moors of Axe Edge and the Goyt Valley, although he is harder to hear these days. But on a sunny April evening, when the traffic subsides, the 'lovely spring freshness' and his occasional distant cry evoke, fleetingly, a truly happy moment in the lost youth of Buxton's restless, exceptional, resident over a hundred years ago.

Vera Brittain's Life – A Brief Chronology

1864
(Thomas) Arthur Brittain, Vera's father, was born.

1868
Edith Mary Bervon, Vera's mother, was born in Aberystwyth, North Wales.

1893
Vera Mary Brittain was born in Newcastle-Under-Lyme, Staffordshire.

1895
Edward Harold Brittain was born in Macclesfield, 30 November.

1905
The Brittains moved to a new house in Buxton, Derbyshire and Vera started school at the Grange.

1907
The Brittains moved to a new home, and Vera went to St Monica's boarding school near Reigate in Surrey.

1908
Edward went to Uppingham, a boys' public school in Rutland.

1911
At the end of December, Vera returned to live in Buxton.

1912
18-year-old Vera came out as a 'provincial debutante'.

1913
Vera and Edith attended University of Oxford's 'extension' lectures in social history. Vera decided to apply to Somerville College, Oxford. After passing the entrance examinations, Somerville awarded Vera a small annual scholarship.

1914
In April, Roland Aubrey Leighton, a school friend of Edward, visited Buxton. Over the next 12 months, he and Vera fell in love. When war was declared, Roland and Edward abandoned plans to go to Oxford and enlisted as junior officers. Vera went to Somerville College.

1915
Roland was sent to France. In June, Vera postponed university to serve as a voluntary nursing auxiliary at Buxton's Devonshire Hospital. She and Roland became engaged. Vera left Buxton in October to work as a Voluntary Aid Detachment nurse at the No. 1 General Hospital in Camberwell, London. Roland died of wounds in France on 23rd December.

1916
Edward departed for the Western Front in February. At the end of September, Vera went to St George's Hospital in Malta.

1917
After Roland died, Vera became close to Victor Richardson, an Uppingham friend, and Geoffrey Thurlow, Edward's army friend. Victor died of injuries and Geoffrey was killed in action. Vera went to the 24 General hospital at Etaples in France, and Edward was posted to the Italian Front.

1918
Edward was killed in action on the Asiago plateau in Italy on 15th June. Vera's first book, *Verses of a V.A.D.*, was published in November.

1919
Vera returned to university and met Winifred Holtby.

1921
After graduating from Oxford, Vera and Winifred lived together in London and began their careers as feminist journalists, novelists, and campaigners for feminism and peace.

1923
Vera's first novel, *The Dark Tide*, was published.

1924
Vera's second novel, *Not Without Honour* was published. She began a short courtship with George Edward Gordon Catlin, a political scientist working at Cornell University in Ithaca, New York.

1925
Vera joined the Labour Party, and she and Gordon married in London.

1926
Vera accompanied Gordon to Cornell as a 'faculty wife' but decided her career came first. They decided on a 'semi-detached' marriage, living apart for six months each year. Over the next few years, Winifred often lived with them, a period Vera said was 'the nearest thing to complete happiness that I have ever known or hope to know'.

1927
John Brittain-Catlin was born. Vera and Winifred were well-known campaigners for feminism and peace, producing an impressive output of journalism, book reviews and campaigning literature, and speaking at public events.

1929
In November, Vera began writing *Testament of Youth: an autobiographical study of the years 1900 to 1925*.

1930
Shirley Brittain-Catlin was born. As Shirley Williams, she later became a successful Labour politician before co-founding the Social Democratic Party in 1981.

1933
Testament of Youth was published in August, by Gollancz in Britain and Macmillan in the United States. It was an immediate success on both sides of the Atlantic. Gordon sought selection as parliamentary candidate for the Labour Party, and Winifred campaigned for racial equality in South Africa.

1935
In July, Vera visited Buxton's war memorial. Three weeks later Arthur Brittain committed suicide by drowning in the Thames at Richmond and in September Winifred died of Bright's disease (renal sclerosis), aged 37.

1936
Vera's third novel, *Honourable Estate*, was published, to mixed reviews.

1937
Vera and Gordon moved to 2 Cheyne Walk, a fine Georgian house overlooking the river Thames. Vera Brittain became a sponsor of the Peace Pledge Union, campaigning against war through speeches at public rallies, pamphlets and a fortnightly newsletter. As an absolute pacifist, she rejected military or violent intervention under any circumstances.

1940
Testament of Friendship, Vera's biography of Winifred Holtby was published to mixed reviews.

1942
Vera's high-profile pacifism made her increasingly unpopular with friends, acquaintances, British and American politicians.

1943
Humiliation with Honour was published.

1944
Vera wrote an appeal against the Allies' saturation bombing of German cities: *Seed of Chaos: What Mass Bombing Really Means* in Britain, and *Massacre by Bombing* in the United States. This attracted widespread public and political hostility and sales of her work dropped dramatically in the United States.

1945–1957
Vera campaigned against apartheid, colonialism and nuclear proliferation, and for Indian Independence. Her third memoir *Testament of Experience* was published to unfavourable reviews.

1957–1970
Vera wrote and campaigned for peace, hoping a new generation might discover her work. She died in 1970 after a long decline brought on by a fall on the way to a speaking engagement. She was 76.

Notes

Introduction
1. 26 July 1935
2. Other Buxton men killed in the war are listed on memorials elsewhere.
3. The MC was not added to Edward's listing until the 1980s.
4. Letter to W.H., Showalter and Showalter 2022 p359
5. Bostridge 2014 pxvii
6. Quoted in Shaw 1999 p220
7. Brittain 1933 p53
8. Brittain, 1933 p55
9. Vera to H. Swanick 20 July 1933, PBC
10. Brittain 1947 p150
11. Bailey 1989 p6
12. Kennard 1989 p25
13. Berry and Bostridge 1995 p261

Chapter One
1. The house is now hidden amongst housing estates.
2. There is no record of the date for the move, but a letter from Vera to Edith (away visiting her mother) enthusing about painting lessons at The Grange is dated 30 March 1905. PBC.
3. Brittain 1924 p22. From 1905, tar and crushed stone began to replace limestone on Britain's main roads. Buxton centre and surrounding villages still had limestone roads in the 1930s.
4. Letter to EB 'Sunday 1904', PBC.
5. *Buxton the Mountain Spa*, official handbook, Bureau of Information, 1912.
6. *Buxton Advertiser* 7 January 1905.
7. 'Buxton as an educational centre', *Buxton Advertiser*, 18 February 1905.
8. Hyde quoted in Langham 2001 p231.
9. Milner 2000 p105
10. Berry and Bostridge p529,
11. By 1900, the French manufacturer was the largest in the world. Arthur's car was 'robust, versatile and capable of conveying passengers over considerable distances' with a top speed of 30 miles an hour.
12. Milner 2000
13. Berry and Bostridge 1995
14. Brittain 1933 p20
15. Brittain 1933 p19
16. Langham 2001
17. Langham 2001 pp207–8.

18. Brittain 1933 p50. Technically, the Edwardian era was just a decade from 1901 to 1910 but many historians mark its ending as 1914.
19. Neither of the Brittains' Buxton homes had a garage but Saunders on Spring Gardens advertised heated lock-up garages and a delivery service.

Chapter Two
1. Brittain 1947 p147
2. Brittain 1947. Vera's juvenile fiction had qualities that presaged her future novels: idealistic and moralistic, infused with references to religion and death, with noble, independent, self-sacrificing heroines (see Kennard, 1989). Copies of Vera's pencil illustrations are in the PBC.
3. Berry and Bostridge 1995 p29
4. Founded in 1853, Cheltenham Ladies' College was England's first public school for girls. See Waller 2022. Being able to follow a University of London degree leading to a portable qualification for teaching was unusual for a head mistress in 1906, not only in Buxton.
5. Buxton Trade Directory 1912
6. The Grange prospectus 1912
7. Lena was born in 1858, third of four children to a vicar. She left Buxton in 1929 for Middlesex and died in 1943. I am grateful to John Kingsland for information on Lena Dodd and The Grange School.
8. Charles Prestwich Scott and his wife were committed to the 'love of truth, duty and the exercise of reason', and believed pupils should acquire 'knowledge through difficulty rather than success through ease'. Commemoration of Founders – Withington Girls' School (wgs.org)
9. St Monica's newsletter, PBC
10. After various uses, the site was developed for assisted living apartments in 2023.
11. Brittain 1924 p37
12. Brittain 1924 p11
13. Brittain 1933 p33–34
14. Brittain 1947 p148
15. Vera maintained a close relationship with both women. Soon after she left St Monica's in 1911, Heath-Jones had a nervous breakdown. She resumed teaching but experienced a long period of severe mental illness in the 1920s and died in 1931. Bervon continued to run the school until 1931 and died in 1936. Vera wrote moving obituaries for both women in *The Times*.
16. Copy of 1911 Reflective Record, PBC
17. Brittain 1933 p39
18. Brittain 1933 p40
19. Brittain 1933 p44
20. Some upper middle-class women who would be Vera's literary contemporaries in the 1920s and 1930s, such as Virginia Woolf, could not expect a coherent, useful education, let alone an emancipating one. Many had a governess but no formal schooling. Encouraged by her academic father, Woolf's high level of culture came from her own voracious determination to learn and her passion for literature.
21. Douglass, S.
22. Brittain 1933 p41
23. Copy of 1911 Reflective Record, PBC
24. This requirement lasted until 1944.

25. 2 April 1914
26. Berry and Bostridge 1995 p29–30
27. 11 July 1914
28. 2 July 1914
29. Brittain 1933 p43
30. Brittain 1933 p40
31. Brittain 1933 p29
32. MHSG and WHSG records list pupils from Buxton in the early 1900s whose parents worked in shipping, carriage building and the wine trade. Carrie Morrison's father was a wealthy copper broker on the London Metal Exchange.
33. Brittain 1933a p31

Chapter Three
1. Built in 1863, the Hydro was owned by one of Buxton's richest businessmen.
2. Correspondence for St Ann's 1912 – 1946, CA
3. Vera recorded Mrs H's account of this event in her diary for 19 November 1913.
4. 1 January 1913
5. Delafield 1932 p5
6. Beaumann 1983/1995 p14
7. Brittain 1924 p66
8. Brittain 1933 p51
9. Brittain 1933 p57
10. Designed by the Devonshire Estate's architect, Henry Currey, the Palace was built in 1864 adjacent to the two railway stations (opened in 1963) for services between Buxton, London and Manchester.
11. Henry Currey designed Corbar Hall in 1852 for Blackburn brewer Henry Shaw.
12. Brittain 1924 p50
13. 6 April 1913
14. 12 April 1913
15. 18 December 1913
16. 17 January 1914

Chapter Four
1. Goldman 1995
2. Marriott's eminent position was a forerunner to the current director of the Department for Continuing Education (DCE). By the end of his life, Marriott had done over 10,000 lectures and taught into his eighties.
3. 13 March 1913.
4. University Extension Bulletin 1912–1913, DCE
5. Cambridge and London also offered extension lectures but Oxford had the widest reach.
6. Robinson 2009
7. University Extension Committee Report 1912–1913, DCE
8. Oxford's DCE has a large display of these old boxes.
9. The *Derby Telegraph* reported Buxton's Society meetings.
10. University Extension Bulletin Summer 1912, DCE
11. 20 January 1913
12. In 1890, winners of successful essays included two carpenters, two clerks, a fustian weaver, an artisan in a government dockyard and three teachers.
13. 19 March 1914

14. University Extension Bulletin 1912 -1913, p2 DCE
15. Marriott 1946 p106
16. Brittain 1933 p66
17. 18 December 1913
18. Brittain 1933 p74
19. Brittain, 1933 p73
20. 28 January 1914
21. 2 February 1914
22. 25 May 1914
23. Brittain 1933 p92
24. Gorham, 1996

Chapter Five
1. Melrose did not have coal-fired central heating until 1925.
2. 1911 census
3. See Lethbridge 2013, Powell 1968
4. Powell 1968 p91
5. Powell 1968
6. Lethbridge 2013
7. The 1905–1915 letter book for Sarah Meggitt-Smith shows the extensive domestic correspondence and administration of a middle-class Buxton woman. MLA.
8. It seems Buxton rents were sometimes negotiable – Park House, advertised for a 'small quiet family of the better class', started at £150 a year before Sarah Meggitt-Smith agreed to £90.
9. Brittain 1924 p29
10. Bailey 1989
11. Osband 1991
12. Birkenhead was Britain's first public park, created by Paxton in 1847.
13. Much of Paxton's parkland is now covered with housing, although his trees still remain.
14. Heape 1948
15. Brittain 1933a p30
16. Roberts, 1992
17. His most well-known film was the 1964 version of *Mary Poppins*.
18. *Buxton Herald*, 6 January 1911
19. 7 January 1914
20. Brittain, 1924 p37
21. 24 February 1913
22. 31 January 1913
23. 24 January 1914
24. Letter to GC, April 1924, PBC
25. Chapman became an adviser to the Board of Trade during the First World War, then British economic representative to the League of Nations, advising on economic sanctions and tariffs.
26. 8 December 1913

Chapter Six
1. 17 April 1914
2. It is now owned by the National Trust.
3. All extracts from Roland and Vera's letters are either from Berry and Bostridge 1995, or Bishop and Bostridge 1998. The edited letters in Bishop and Bostridge, between EdB, VR and GT, broadcast by the BBC in 1998 and on CD in 2014, are profoundly moving.

4. Stoop revolutionised tactics and standards of fitness and discipline at club and national level. During the First World War, he won the Military Cross for bravery in Baghdad. His obituary on Harlequins' website states he should not have been dropped from the English team in 1913. See Cooper 2014.
5. Bertram, Vera and Edward's letters quoted in Berry and Bostridge 1995.
6. 9 June 1914
7. 1 July 1914
8. People who have become rich with 'new' money or ascended the social ladder from humble origins.

Chapter Seven

1. 4 January 1914.
2. Letter from Joseph Ward's son to Mark Bostridge, PBC
3. *Buxton Advertiser*, Saturday 8 January 1913
4. 2 December 1913, when Mrs Fowler (Vera's dressmaker) told her about Ward's problems. She and her quarryman husband were the basis for two main characters in *Not Without Honour*.
5. 5 December 1913, reported by Mrs Fowler, whose husband was in Ward's class.
6. 23 November 1913
7. It is likely Ward had a Nottingham accent. As Arthur Clark in *Not Without Honour*, he 'had a musical voice, in spite of the roughness of an unrecognisable accent'.
8. Ward, A. 1888
9. Buxton's expansion created demand for a richer choice of denomination. Eleven churches were built between 1849 and 1900. St Peter's dates from the twelfth century, extended in the late 1880s to accommodate Fairfield's growing population.
10. Filmed in Egypt and Palestine, the first cinema depiction of *Christ* in 1912 was controversial. In 1998, the United States Library of Congress deemed it 'culturally, historically or aesthetically significant' and selected it for the National Film Registry.
11. 2 February 1914
12. 31 May 1914
13. 22 March 1914
14. Brittain 1924 p247.
15. After Buxton, Ward worked for Dr Barnardo's until 1916, then Chaplain for the YMCA, administering to troops and factory workers around Britain. After his wife died in 1926, Ward remarried and became a popular vicar in Preston, then Southport. He joined the Labour Party but disillusioned in the 1930s, he ceased to be involved in politics. He was a prolific writer of plays, poems and hymns, published several collections of sermons and was one of the first presenters of what is now the BBC's 'Thought for the Day'. Ward died in Essex in 1958.
16. Brittain 1933 p54.
17. Email to the author from Nicolas Sagovsky, Visiting Professor, King's College London, 1 July 2021.

Chapter Eight

1. 1 August 1914
2. Bostridge 2014 p199
3. Lomas 2008 p88
4. 3 August 1914
5. 10 August 1914

6. 11 August 1914
7. 14 August 1914
8. The Lady, 13 August 1914
9. 20 August 1914
10. 26 August 1914
11. 6 August 1914
12. 27 August 1914
13. 5 September 1914
14. 1 September 1914
15. 30 September 1914
16. 1 October 1914
17. 8 October 1914
18. George Eliot quoted by Brittain 1933 p98

Chapter Nine
1. 13 June 1913
2. Copy of 1911 Reflective Record, VBA, PBC
3. 1 April 1913
4. Brittain 1928
5. Brittain 1933 p58
6. Brittain 1939 p7
7. 5 February 1914
8. 15 February 1914
9. 5 November 1913
10. 11 December 1913
11. Parable in St Luke, 14, 23. 'Highways and hedges' points to a lower class of the population of an Eastern country – tramps and squatters content to sleep under the shelter of a hedge or fence.
12. 29 June 1914
13. 13 November 1913
14. 19 November 1913
15. 9 January 1913
16. Matthews 1984 p131
17. Nevinson 1938
18. Matthews op cit.
19. Quoted in Berry and Bostridge 1995 p237
20. Emrys James played Arthur with an authentic Staffordshire accent in the 1979 BBC dramatization of *Testament of Youth*. Dominic West played Arthur in the 2014 film with his own muted Eton accent. In a 1937 clip from a BBC radio programme, Vera's 'received pronunciation' sounds very like a young Queen Elizabeth II, captured by Cheryl Campbell (1979) and more approximately by Alice Vikander (2014).
21. Brittain 1957 p442
22. 5 February 1913

Chapter Ten
1. Robinson 2009
2. 24 October 1914
3. 20 November 1914
4. Reynolds 1996

5. 28 November 1914
6. Berry and Bostridge 1995 p530
7. Armitage 1965
8. 2 December 1913
9. Letter to EB 29 November 1914, PBC
10. Letter to EB 18 November 1914, PBC
11. Letter to RL 16 November 1914
12. BS did enlist in 1917 and survived the war. He married a Buxton woman in the 1920s.
13. Letter to EB 14 February 1914, PBC
14. 'Goodnight, Babette', poems and songs, by Henry Austin Dobson (1840–1921) and 'The Dear Departed', a satire of the degradation of moral values in the British middle class by William Stanley Houghton.
15. Letter to RL 28 February 1915
16. Lady Ottoline Morrell (1873 – 1938) was an English aristocrat and society hostess, with a circle of friends including artists, writers, sculptors and poets. She and the philosopher Bertrand Russell had a long affair.
17. 24 April 1915.
18. Letter to RL 15 April 1915
19. Letter to RL 21 May 1915
20. Letter to RL 26 May 915
21. Letter to RL 20 May 1915. From the late eighteenth century, rank and file British soldiers were known as 'Tommies'. The term was widely used during the First World War.
22. Letter to EB 19 May 1915, PBC
23. 5 May 1915
24. Letter to EB 17 April 1915, PBC
25. 10 June 1915
26. Brittain 1957 p450

Chapter Eleven
1. 31 December 1914. D.H. Evans was one of London's popular department stores.
2. 30 December 1914
3. 1 January 1915
4. Letter to RL 28 February 1915
5. 15 March 1915
6. In 1915, the phrase 'making love' referred to expressions of romantic intent.
7. Letter to RL 19 March 1915. The poem he refers to is *In the Rose Garden* which he wrote about sitting with Vera in the rose garden at Uppingham Speech Day July 1914; see Chapter Fifteen.
8. 19 March 1915
9. 20 November 1915
10. 22 March 1915
11. 26 March 1915
12. 29 March 1915
13. Letter to VB 20 April 1915
14. Today, over a hundred years later, they are still in the notebook, faded but intact.
15. 18 April 1915
16. 9 April 1915
17. 15 April 1915
18. 25 April 1915
19. 31 May 1915
20. Letter to RL 25 April 1915

Chapter Twelve
1. 6 June 1915
2. Ouditt 1994
3. From Imperial War Museum poster.
4. Little 2012
5. Brittain 1930
6. See Bagnold 1918
7. See Ouditt 1994
8. Brittain 1933 p164
9. See Bishop and Bostridge 1998 for an edited selection of the war letters between Vera, Roland, Edward, Victor Richardson and Geoffrey Thurlow
10. Brittain 1933 p165
11. 20–24 August. The unpublished diary for these few days covers many pages, even longer than the extract in *Chronicle of Youth*. Both versions are unbearably moving. Only a tiny extract is reproduced in this chapter.
12. Letter quoted in diary 29 August
13. 28 September 1915
14. 3 October 1915
15. 9 October 1915
16. They nursed together until 1917
17. Berry and Bostridge 1995 p87
18. See Hynes 1990
19. Brittain 1933 p242
20. Letter quoted in Berry and Bostridge p90
21. 26 November 1915 op cit.
22. 23–25 December 1915

Chapter Thirteeen
1. 25–26 December 1915
2. Alice Meynell, a well-known suffragette, writer and poet.
3. Letter to EB 11 June 1917, Bishop and Bostridge 1998
4. Letter to VB 15 November 1917, Bishop and Bostridge 1998
5. Brittain 1933 p143. PBC, SC
6. Brittain 1933 p439. Created in 2021, the Brittain-Williams room at Somerville College, displays the 1917 portrait of Edward above the Melrose piano on which he and Vera played duets.
7. Bostridge 2014
8. 29 September 1915
9. Brittain 1933 p496
10. Letter to GC 2 July 1924, PBC
11. Berry and Bostridge 1995 p194
12. Brittain 1933 p579
13. Brittain 1939 p8–9
14. Vera used her experience of Somerville after the war for her first autobiographical novel, *The Dark Tide*, published in 1923.

Chapter Fourteen
1. 'A Sitting room furnished for £25', McM
2. Holtby and McWilliam 1937

3. Brittain 1936 p546
4. Letter to WH 23 November 1921, quoted Gorham, p160. The requirement for women teachers to be unmarried was lifted in 1944.
5. Letter to GC 27 July 1924, PBC, SC.
6. Letter to WH 16 July 1926, Showalter and Showalter, 2022.
7. Letter 1923 in Holtby and McWilliam 1937.
8. Letter to VB 27 March 1921, Showalter and Showalter, 2022.
9. Brittain 1933 p575
10. For analysis of Vera's feminism, see Gorham 1995
11. Letter to WH 24 January 1926 in Showalter and Showalter, 2022
12. Letter to GC 17 December 1926 PBC
13. 'Our Malthusian Middle Classes', *Nation and Athenaeum*, 1927, quoted by Gorham 1996 p200
14. 15 October 1932. Virginia Woolf came from an upper-middle class, literary dynasty and Naomi Mitchison, the Scottish writer, from the upper-class Haldanes.
15. Letter to GC 9 March 1924, PBC
16. Williams 1993
17. Aims outlined in a speech Vera gave to Annual Speech Day at Newcastle-Under-Lyme High School for Girls in 1935. Thanks to Cath Pearce (whose mother Kathleen Rhodes heard Vera's speech) for providing the 1935 school magazine.
18. Skidelsky 1987
19. Shaw 1995 p110; see also Gorham, 1995
20. Letter GC to VB 11 January 1932; letter AB to VB 21 March 1932, quoted Berry and Bostridge, p544
21. Letter to WH 22 November 1921, quoted Gorham 1996 p162
22. Letter to WH quoted Gorham, p162
23. Letter WH to VB 16 April 1922 quoted Shaw, p114
24. Letter to WH 30 April 1926, Showalter and Showalter, 2022
25. Williams 2010
26. Williams 1993
27. Letter to WH 28 December 1932, quoted Gorham, p226
28. Letter to PB, PBC
29. Berry and Bostridge 1995 p264
30. See Shaw 1995, Showalter and Showalter 2022
31. Berry and Bostridge, p177
32. Letter to WH quoted Gorham, p186
33. WH quoted Berry and Bostridge, p177
34. Brittain 1933, p55
35. Brittain 1933
36. Phyllis Bentley came from a similar background to Vera: her father was a junior partner in a woollen mill, the family had a comfortable but not lavish lifestyle in Halifax and education at Cheltenham Ladies College had led Phyllis to regard her hometown as philistine, and its residents to see her as somewhat stuck up. There were also differences. Surmounting huge opposition from her parents, and confined as a carer for her mother, Phyllis became a successful writer. In 1932 her fourth book, *Inheritance*, made her a best-selling author. When she was commissioned to do a weekly column for the *Manchester Chronicle*, Vera noted that 'huge posters of her were splurged all over Manchester'.
37. Bentley 1962
38. Russell 2008
39. See Beaumann 1983

40. See Jean Kennard 1989. Vera and Winifred's exceptionally close working and personal relationship enabled them to borrow from each other's lives and to pick up themes and characters from each other's novels in subsequent work.
41. For example, Virginia Dennison (*The Dark Tide*), Christine Merrivale (*Not Without Honour*, Ruth Allendyne (*Honourable Estate*) were based on Vera, Joanna Burton (*Land of Green Ginger*) and aspects of Muriel Hammond (*The Crowded Street*) on Winifred. Authors also used women they knew: Winifred for Daphne (*The Dark Tide*), Edith Brittain, Mrs Harrison and Mrs Fowler (*Not Without Honour*), Phyllis Bentley (*Honourable Estate*). In *The Crowded Street*, Vera inspired the brilliant, idealistic, and mercurial Delia Andrews who leads Muriel Hammond to reject a destiny as provincial wallflower in favour of public service.
42. Holtby 1923 p232
43. See Beauman 1983
44. Brittain 1940 p162

Chapter Fifteen
1. Britain 1957 p417. One of Vera's many British lecture tours involved a week of travelling by train between Chester, Bradford, Blackpool and Huddersfield. She said she sometimes felt 'jaded by the continuous racket'.
2. Brittain op cit.
3. Edward's homosexuality and the mysterious circumstances of his death were uncovered by Mark Bostridge in 1989; see Berry and Bostridge 1995, Bostridge 2014; also Hudson 2007.
4. There have been fictional versions of Edward's death: in *Honourable Estate*, Vera portrayed the brother of the main character engineering his First World War death because his love for another man had been discovered. See also Barker 2012, Winn 2023.
5. Letter to GC July 1945 PBC
6. Brittain 1947 p67
7. Letters to GC 1949 PBC
8. Berry and Bostridge 1995 p523
9. Brittain 1933 p13
10. Barnes 2021
11. 19 April 1915
12. Brittain 1940
13. Berry and Bostridge 1995 p254; see also Catlin 1987
14. Vera's 1930s diary, and letters to Gordon and Winifred have none of the exuberance in her pre-war writing, apart from a brief glimpse in 1934 when Vera enthused to Winifred about falling in love with George Brett, her married American publisher (her feelings were not reciprocated).
15. Brittain 1957 p448
16. Berry and Bostridge p521
17. PB to CL 18 August 1979 PBC
18. Brittain 1933 p90
19. 5 November 1913
20. 19 October 1913
21. Williams 2010
22. Brittain 1933 p230

Selected Bibliography

Archive Material

1. 'Juvenilia', photographs, complete copy of 1913–1917 diary notebooks, McM
2. Notes, cuttings, letters VB to GC, copy of 1911 'Reflective Record', for *Vera Brittain. A Life* PBC, SC
3. Letters between PB and CL, 1978–1980 PBC, SC
4. Photographs and memorabilia, SWC, SC
5. Devonshire Estate correspondence/plans/drawings for houses on The Park, 1900 -1935, Correspondence John Milligan Harrison and the Devonshire Estate 1912 -1935, DE
6. Letters, cuttings, photographs, MLA
7. *Buxton Advertiser* 1905–1915, Buxton Library
8. First World War posters, IWM
9. University Extension Bulletins 1905–1915, DCE, University of Oxford
10. Records 1905–1915 Manchester High School for Girls, Withington High School for Girls
11. Lena Dodd information, Cheltenham Ladies College
12. Buxton memorabilia 1905 -1915, Buxton Museum
13. Edwardian Buxton/WW1 Buxton photographs, PtP

Vera Brittain Works

Verses of a V.A.D., London, Erskine MacDonald, 1918
The Dark Tide, Grant Richards, 1923
Not Without Honour, Grant Richards, 1924
'Mrs Pankhurst and the older feminists', *Manchester Guardian*, 20 June 1928.
'The real V.A.D. – from fancy back to fact', *Manchester Guardian*, 22 May 1930
'Provincialism', *Manchester Evening Chronicle*, 2 September 1933
Testament of Youth – an Autobiographical Study of the Years 1900–1925. Gollancz, 1933, Virago 1978
Honourable Estate: A Novel of Transition, Gollancz, 1936
Testament of Friendship, Macmillan, 1940, Virago, 1980
Humiliation with Honour, Andrew Dakers, 1942
Seeds of Chaos. What Mass Bombing Really Means, The Bombing Restriction Committee, 1944
Account Rendered, Macmillan, 1945, Virago, 1982
On Becoming an Author, Hutchinson, 1947
Born 1925. A Novel of Youth, Macmillan, 1948, Virago, 1982
Testament of Experience. An autobiographical study of the years 1925–1950, Gollancz, 1957, Virago, 1979
Chronicle of Youth. Vera Brittain's War Diary 1913 -1917, Bishop, A. ed. With Terry Smart, Gollancz, 1981, Phoenix Press, 2000

Chronicle of Friendship: Vera Brittain's diary of the Thirties, 1932–1939, Bishop, A. ed., Gollancz, 1986

Letters from a Lost Generation – First World War Letters of Vera Brittain and Four Friends, Bishop, A. and Bostridge, M. eds. Abacus Books, 1998

Testament of a Generation: the journalism of Vera Brittain and Winifred Holtby, Berry, P. and Bishop, A. eds. Virago, 1998

Because you died. Poetry and Prose of the First World War and After, by Vera Brittain. Edited and Introduced by Mark Bostridge. Virago, 2008

Between Friends: the letters of Vera Brittain and Winifred Holtby, Showalter, E. and Showalter, E. eds Virago, 2022

Film/TV/Radio

Vera Brittain introducing Dame Ethel Smyth and the 'March of Women' from BBC's 'Scrapbook for 1912', recorded 9 March 1937, BBC Sound Archives

BBC TV *Testament of Youth*, 1979

BBC Films *Testament of Youth*, 2014

BBC Radio *Letters from a Lost Generation*, broadcast 1998; released on CD 2014

BBC Radio *Vera Brittain: A Woman in Love and War*, 2008

BBC Radio *Edward Brittain and the Forgotten Front* 2018

Books and Articles

Vera Brittain and her contemporaries

Bailey, H. *Vera Brittain. The Story of The Woman Who Wrote Testament of Youth*, Penguin, 1987

Bentley, P. Response to Vera Brittain, *Manchester Evening Chronicle*, 9 September 1933.

Bentley, P. *O Dreams, O Destinations*, Gollancz, 1962

Berry, P. and Bostridge, M. *Vera Brittain. A Life*, Chatto & Windus, 1995

Catlin, J. *Family Quartet*, Hamish Hamilton, 1987

Cooper, I. *Immortal Harlequin: the story of Adrian Stoop* CreateSpace, 2014

Glendenning, V. *Rebecca West. A life*, Weidenfeld and Nicholson, 1987

Gorham, D. 'The Friendships of Women: Friendship, Women and Achievement in Vera Brittain's life and work in the interwar decades, *Journal of Women's History*, vol.3, Winter 1992

Gorham, G. *Vera Brittain. Vera Brittain. A Feminist Life*, Oxford, Blackwells, 1996

Groenegan, Peter Sydney John Chapman (1871–1951) labour, economics, public finance, economic principle and economic history – a Marshall student of great academic distinction, in *The Minor Marshallians and Alfred Marshall*, Routledge/Taylor Francis, 2011.

Holtby, A. and McWilliam, J. eds. *Winifred Holtby: letters to a friend*, Collins, 1937.

Holtby, W. *Virginia Woolf*, Wishart, 1932

Lethbridge, L. *Servants: a downstairs view of twentieth-century Britain*, Penguin, 2013

Lonsdale, S. *Rebel Women Between the Wars*, Manchester University Press, 2020

Milner, R. *Brittains of Cheddleton – The Position of Brittains Ltd in the History of Paper Making*, Leek, Churnet Valley Books, 2002.

Nevinson, C.R.W. 1938 *Paint and Prejudice*, New York: Harcourt Brace and Co., 1938.

Reynolds, B. *The Letters of Dorothy. L. Sayers 1899 to 1936*, Hodder & Stoughton, 1995

Roiphe, K. *Uncommon Arrangements: seven portraits of married life in London literary circles 1910 -1939*, Virago Press, 2007

Powell, M. *Below Stairs, Memoir of a Kitchen Maid* St Martin's Press, 1970
Shaw, M. *A Clear Stream: A Life of Winifred Holtby*, Virago Press, 1999
Skidelsky, R. Review of John Catlin's memoir, *Family Quartet*, *Sunday Times*, 27 August 1987
Taylor, A.J.P. *A Personal History*, Coronet Books, 1988
Williams, S. 'Remembering my mother', paper given at 'A Testament to Vera Brittain, Centenary Conference, McMaster University, Ontario, 15 October 1993
Williams, S. *Climbing the Bookshelves: the autobiography of Shirley Williams*, Virago, 2010

History of education
Armitage, W.G.H. *Four hundred years of English Education*, Cambridge, Cambridge University Press, 1965
Douglass, S. unpublished paper *Lena Dodd at Preston High School for Girls*, Preston, date unknown
Goldman, L. *Dons and Workers: Oxford and Adult Education since 1850*, Oxford University Press, 1995
Gorham, D. The education of Vera and Edward Brittain: class and gender in an upper-middle-class family in late Victorian and Edwardian England, *History of Education Review*, Vol. 20, 22–38, 1990
Gorham, D. A woman at Oxford: Vera Brittain's Somerville Experience, *Historical Studies in Education*, Vol. 3, 1–19, 1991
Marriott, J.R. *Memories of Four Score Years: The Autobiography of the Late Sir John Marriott*, Blackie and Son, 1946
Matthews, B. *By God's Grace: A History of Uppingham*, Maidstone, Whitehall Press, 1984
Newcastle High School for Girls, *School magazine*, July 1935, Newcastle-Under-Lyme.
Robinson, J. *Bluestockings. The Remarkable Story of the First Women to Fight for an Education*, Penguin, 2009
Waller, S. *Pioneering Women's Education: Dorothea Beale, An Unlikely Reformer*, Barnsley, Pen & Sword Books, 2022

First World War
Badsey, P.H. *Vera Brittain – The Militant Pacifist: Misconceptions of her Importance in Military History*, Paper presented to University of Birmingham War and Society Seminar, Thursday 6 June 2002
Badsey, P.H. *The Political Thought of Vera Brittain*, PhD Thesis, University of Kingston, 2005
Bagnold, E. *Diary Without Dates*, Heinemann, 1918
Barker, P. *Toby's Room*, Penguin, 2013
Bostridge, M. *Vera Brittain and the First World War, The Story of Testament of Youth* Bloomsbury, 2014
Bostridge, M. *The Fateful Year. England 1914*, Penguin/Viking, 2014
Farr, D. *None That Go Return, Leighton, Brittain and Friends and the Lost Generation 1914 –1918* Warwick, Helion Books, 2010
D'Hoogue, J. (date unknown) *The First World War in High Peak: a look at the effect on family life in Derbyshire's High Peak during the Great War*, Report for the Chapel-en-le-Frith Male Voice Choir
Hudson, M. *The Extraordinary Life of Charles Hudson VC: soldier, poet, rebel*, Stroud: Sutton Publishing, 2007
Hynes, S. *A War Imagined. The First World War and English Culture*, Bodley Head, 1990
Little, S. 'No task too great: VADs and the Great War', Lecture to Thirty-First Annual General Meeting of *Western Front Association*, Manfield College, Oxford, 14 April 2012

Lomax, S. *The Home Front: Derbyshire in the First World War*, Barnsley, Pen & Sword, 2016
Ouditt, S. *Fighting Forces, Writing Women: Identity and Ideology in the First World War*, Routledge, 1994
Roberts, D. Holm Leigh School Buxton and the Great War, www.robertspublications.com/blog
Warwick, A. *Women at War* 1914 -1918, Fontana, 1977
Winn, A. *In Memoriam*, Penguin, 2023

Women's Literature 1890–1940

Beaumann, N. *A very great profession: the woman's novel 1914–1939*, Virago, 1983
Bentley, P. *Inheritance*, Gollancz, 1932
Delafield, E.M *Thank Heaven Fasting*, Howard Baker, 1932
Delafield, E.M *Diary of a Provincial Lady*, Macmillan, 1930
Delafield, E.M, *Diary of a Provincial Lady in America*, Macmillan, 1934
Holby, W. *Anderby Wold*, John Lane, 1923, Virago 1981
Holtby, W. *The Crowded Street*, John Lane, 1923, Virago, 1983
Holtby, W. *The Land of Green Ginger*, Jonathan Cape, 1931, Virago, 1983
Holtby, W. *South Riding*, Collins, 1936, Virago, 1988
Kennard, J. *Vera Brittain and Winifred Holtby: a working* partnership, University of New Hampshire, University Press of New England, 1989
Russell, D. Province, metropolis, and the literary career of Phyllis Bentley in the 1930s, *The Historical Journal*, Vol. 51, 3, 719–740, 2008
Showalter, E. *A Literature of their Own. British Women Novelists from Bronte to Lessing*, Virago, 1984

Buxton history

Bureau of Information, *Buxton as a Mountain Spa. Official Handbook* 1912, Buxton Museum
Heape, R. Grundy B*uxton under the Devonshires,* London 1948
Langham,M. *Buxton – a people's history*, Lancaster, Carnegie Publishing, 2001
Lomas, P. *The Buxton Hydro (Spa Hotel) – the story of the spa town's best known hydropathic between 1866 and 1974*, Bakewell, Ashridge Press, 2008
Roberts, K. *Buxton and its Villas. People and Property*, unpublished study, 1992

Miscellaneous

Barnes, J. On The Sense of an Ending, *The Guardian*, Monday 14 June 2021
Osband, L. *Victorian House Style. An Architectural and Interior Design Source Book*, David & Charles, 1991
Ward, A. M. *Robert Elsmere*, Smith, Elder & Co, 1888

Index

Beale, Dorothea, 19
Bentley, Phyllis, 214, 219–22, 233
Bervon, Florence, 11, 21–2, 27, 56, 58, 173, 191, 242
Brittain, Edith,
   charity work, 16, 60, 141
   education, 27
   homemaking, 1, 17, 59, 69, 217
   marriage, 11–12, 142–3
   relationship with servants, 69
   relationship with Vera, 59, 101–102, 138, 142, 149–52, 142, 174, 233
   social background and aspirations, 11–12
   Vera's portrayal of her mother, 149
Brittain, Edward Harold,
   birth, 12
   character, 151
   death, xiii, 205–207, 227
   education, 27–8
   experience of war, xiii, 197, 204
      Battle of the Somme and Military Cross, xiii
   homosexuality at Uppingham, 147, 227
   musical talent, 28–9, 60, 80–1, 133, 207
   patriotism and desire to enlist, 124–7, 132, 159, 189, 190–1, 196–7
   relationship with Vera, xiii, 91, 126, 159–60, 204–206
      Vera's fears about his fate during First World War, 125–6, 159–60, 166, 189, 190–1
   social expectations for middle-class boys, 27–9
Brittain, Thomas Arthur,
   Brittains' paper mill, 8–9
   depression and suicide, 226
   education, 26–7
   feelings about Edward enlisting, 125–7, 196
   income, 9
   impact of Edward's death, 205
   love of motorcars, 10–11
      commute to work, xii–xiii, 6, 17
   political outlook, 9–10, 50, 148
   relationship with Vera, 57, 59, 63, 148–9, 197

   financial support for Vera 21, 41, 64, 133, 158, 215–16
Brittain, Vera Mary,
   anti-provincialism,
      critical portrayal of Buxton xv-xvii, 31, 34–6, 39, 55–6, 62, 220–1, 230, 231–2
      feelings about provincial background, 22, 30, 139, 147, 213–15, 229, 231
      use in post-war fiction and journalism, 220–4
   appearance, 33–4, 39–40, 43, 52, 58, 135, 139, 182, 219–20, 228–9, 233
   'At Home' entertainments, 77–84, 218–19
   character, 30, 135–6, 137–8, 150–2, 154–6, 193, 208, 211, 231–3
   dependence on servants, 66–8, 154, 161, 215–18
   feminism, 25–6, 29–30, 34, 82–3, 95–6, 139–40, 197, 210–13
   models of womanhood, 26, 154–5, 219–20
First World War,
   early excitement/patriotism, 123–8, 158–9, 164–5
      antagonism to those not enlisting, 127–8, 133, 160
      antagonism to enemy aliens, 131–2, 194
   deaths of Buxton friends, xiiii–iv, 166–7, 196
   suspends university studies, 164–5, 180
   disillusionment with war, 173, 180, 188, 204
   grief and aftermath xiii, 203–208, 211
nursing,
   recruitment of women volunteers, 182–4, 195
   Vera's initial enthusiasm, 182, 185–7
   considers post in London hospital, 188
   harrowing challenges in London, 198
   Malta and Etaples, 203–204
friendship, 18, 22, 137–9, 155

feelings of alienation from peers, 30–1, 120, 137–8
friends,
  Phyllis Bentley, 214, 219–22, 233
  Mrs Harrison, 6, 32–4, 49, 52–4, 56–7, 64, 96–100, 141, 224, 232
  Janet Lawson, 97, 138, 144
  Cora Stoop, 22, 88–9, 137–8, 144, 179
  Stella Sharp, 22, 97, 136–9, 143, 198, 203
  see also 'Holtby, Winifred', and 'Ward, Reverend Joseph Harry'
intellectual curiosity/love of learning, 18–19, 23–4, 30–1, 50, 55, 57, 129, 135
leaves Buxton/ end of 'provincial young ladyhood', 55–6, 195–7
lifelong enjoyments,
  amateur dramatics, 29–30, 43–6, 84, 94, 161
  dancing, 34–9, 193, 219
  clothes and fashion, 34, 38, 39–42, 47, 161, 219–20, 223
  literature, 24, 65, 112, 129
  music, 80–1, 120, 193
  scenery, 3, 97, 234
  sport, 47–8, 88, 99, 193
marriage and motherhood, 91, 96–7, 101–102, 119, 141, 142–4, 171–2, 212–13
political and writing career, 209–10, 211–13, 228–9, 238–40
political ideas (see also 'feminism')
  moral purpose and idealism, 112–13, 120, 130, 158, 211–12
  awareness of social inequality, 115, 140–2, 208, 211, 213, 228
  desire for affluence, 215–16
  Labour party membership, 212
  pacifism, 228–9, 240
  post-death fame, 229
relationship with Roland Leighton,
  attraction and falling in love, 100–101, 169–73, 193, 200
  desire for Roland, 178–9, 180, 197
  first meeting in Buxton, 84–7, 234–6
  fears about his fate in the war, 173–80, 193
  gap between her and Roland's view of war, 187, 194, 198–9
  meeting him on leave, 171–3, 191–3
  joy at news of Christmas leave 1915, 199–20
  Roland's death, 201–203, 233
  see also 'Leighton, Roland Aubrey'
religion, 25, 29, 105–109, 111–17, 120, 228

returning to Buxton, xvii–viv, 225–6
romantic infatuations,
  Adrian Stoop, 88–9
  Bertram Spafford, 89–96, 102, 120, 122, 127–8, 142–3, 150, 226
sense of youth slipping away, 193, 232–3
sex, 119, 144-6, 179–80
university,
  after the war, 64
  decision to apply to Somerville College, 58
  entrance examinations
    preparation, 59–62
    success, 63–4, 129
  first year at Somerville College, 129, 133–4, 152–5, 158, 161
  leaves Oxford, 164–5, 167–8
  'extension' lectures in Buxton/provincial towns, xiii, 19, 55
  Oxford 'summer school', 56–8
  resumes studies after the war, 208–209
writing,
  Honourable Estate, xii, 148, 210, 240
  Humiliation with Honour, 228, 240
  Not Without Honour, xvi, 22, 31, 34, 39, 71, 75, 77, 100, 118–21, 138, 142, 147, 149, 239
  Testament of Friendship, 139, 210, 228, 240
  Testament of Youth, xiv, xv, xvi, xvii, 6–7, 17, 19, 22, 25, 27, 31, 35, 53, 57–60, 71, 75, 77, 100, 121, 123, 134, 138, 142, 147, 156, 210, 220–1, 229–33
  The Dark Tide, 156, 238
Brittain-Catlin, John, xii, 215, 239
Buxton,
  amenities,
    Crescent, 7
    Devonshire Hospital, 15–17, 53, 60, 141, 164, 182–3, 185, 190, 197–8
    Gardens and Pavilion, 5, 12–15, 40, 94, 128–9, 133
    housing, 8, 70–2
    investment by wealthy middle-class, 15
    luxury hotels
      Buxton Hydropathic (the Hydro), 32–3, 35, 45, 123, 162, 197–8, 226
      Empire, 5, 74–5, 160, 169, 197–8, 226
      Lee Wood, 72–3
      Palace, 16–17, 37–8
      St Ann's, 6, 32–3, 226
    Opera House, 13, 45, 128
    The Slopes, xvii
  charity and philanthropy, 16, 49, 141
  church and religion,

Index   257

St John's church, 40, 47, 109, 110, 111, 112, 130,173
St Peter's church, Fairfield 105-7, 108, 114,117, 118, 121
see also 'Ward, Reverend Joseph Harry'
First World War, xiii, 123, 125, 127-8, 131-2, 159-63, 169-70, 189, 193-6, 207, 225-6
heyday as fashionable spa resort, 3, 6, 8, 13-14, 16, 36-7, 71-3, 76-77
leisure and cultural activities,
  amateur dramatics, see Brittain, Vera Mary
  'pictures-in-dumb' shows, 46
  promenades, 12, 39
  society balls, 12, 33-9, 66-70
  sporting facilities, 13, 47-8
middle class life, 70-3, 75-83
newspapers, *Buxton Advertiser*, 5-7, 13-14, 36, 73, 118, 123, 125, 129, 131, 140, 160, 162-4, 190
Paxton, Joseph, 72-4
public lectures and debates, 16, 52-5, 111, 140
scenery, 3
  Corbar Woods, 75, 86, 176-7, 179, 197
  Goyt Valley, 74, 86, 125, 235
schools
  the Grange, 7, 18-20, 25, 31, 226
  Holm Leigh, 7, 22, 27-8, 196, 207
  for working-class children, 29
servants, 8, 65-70, 161
social segregation, 15-16
The Park (now Park Road), 8, 72-5
women's suffrage activity, 140

Catlin, George Edward Gordon, xii, xiii, xv, 212-18, 239-40

Delafield, E.M., 34, 214, 218-19, 222
Devonshires/Devonshire Estate, 4-5, 7, 14-15, 33, 72, 109, 125, 141, 185, 189-90
Dodd, Lena, 19-20, 27, 60, 75, 78, 242

education,
  middle-class girls, 22, 25-7, 31, 156-8
  middle-class boys, 25, 27-9
  working-class children, 29, 158
  Uppingham public school, 28, 125, 127, 145-7, 181, 207
  university, see Brittain, Vera Mary; Penrose, Emily

the Ellingers,
  Maurice, 28, 76, 86, 101, 124, 127, 132, 144-7, 159, 165-6, 195
  Mabel, 33, 38, 43, 45, 76-7, 125, 127-8
  Barnard, 76

Fry, Edith, 24, 26-7, 158, 161, 173

Hamilton, Cicely, 214
Heath-Jones, Louise, 21-3, 26-7, 56, 58, 173, 191
Holtby, Winifred, xv, 157, 208-16, 218-20, 222, 227, 229, 233
Leighton, Roland Aubrey,
  attraction to/falling in love with Vera, 85-7, 100-101, 169-76, 178, 180-1, 191-3
  character, 101
  death 201-203
  desire to enlist, 133
  disillusionment with war, 180-1, 187, 191, 194, 198-9
  leaves for Western Front, 174-5, 177-8
  meets Vera on leave, 171-3, 191-3
  parents
    mother, Marie, 85, 171, 194-5, 203
    father, Robert, 85
  plans to study at Oxford, 85, 128, 130, 133

Morrison, Carrie, 31, 61, 210
Macauley, R., 214
Marriott, John Ransome, 50-3, 55-8, 64, 140
Morrell, Ottoline, 33, 162, 247

Pankhurst, Emmeline, 20, 33, 140
Penrose, Emily, 58, 157, 159, 180

Richardson, Victor, 84, 203
Russell, Bertrand, 162, 247

Sayers, Dorothy L., 154-6

Thurlow, Geoffrey, 197, 203

Ward, Reverend Joseph Harry, Ward, 64, 86, 102-111, 113-21, 130, 143, 150, 214, 223, 228, 232, 245
Wells, H.G., 124, 219
West, Rebecca, 214, 220, 222
Williams, Shirley, xii, 168, 214-15, 217, 229, 234, 239
Woolf, Virginia, 214, 219, 230, 242